Second Language Speech Fluency

Second language (L2) fluency is an exciting and fast-moving field of research, with clear practical applications in language teaching. This book provides a lively overview of the current advances in the field of L2 fluency, and connects the theory to practice, presenting a hands-on approach to using fluency research across a range of different language-related professions. The authors introduce an innovative multidisciplinary perspective, which brings together research into cognitive and social factors, to understand fluency as a dynamic variable in language performance, connecting learner-internal factors such as speech processing and automaticity to external factors such as task demands, language testing and pragmatic interactional demands in communication. Bringing a much-needed multidisciplinary and novel approach to understanding the complex nature of L2 speech fluency, this book provides researchers, students and language professionals with both the theoretical insights and practical tools required to understand and research how fluency in a second language develops.

Parvaneh Tavakoli is Professor of Applied Linguistics at the University of Reading. Her research, which focuses on second language acquisition (SLA), continuously aims to bridge the gap between research and professional practice, and has won awards from the British Council. Recent publications include her co-authored book, *Task-Based Language Teaching* (co-authored with Farahnaz Faez, 2019).

Clare Wright is Lecturer in Linguistics and Language Teaching at the University of Leeds. She is currently President of EuroSLA, and has won awards from the Economic and Social Research Council (ESRC), the British Association for Applied Linguistics (BAAL) and the British Academy for her work in psycholinguistics. Recent publications include *Mind Matters in SLA* (2018) and *Voices and Practices in Applied Linguistics* (2019).

THE CAMBRIDGE APPLIED LINGUISTICS SERIES

The authority on cutting-edge Applied Linguistics research

Series Editors   2007–present: Carol A. Chapelle and Susan Hunston
                      1988–2007: Michael H. Long and Jack C. Richards

For a complete list of titles please visit: www.cambridge.org

Recent titles in this series

Second Language Speech Fluency
From Research to Practice
Parvaneh Tavakoli and Clare Wright

Ontologies of English
Conceptualising the Language for Learning,
Teaching, and Assessment
*Edited by Christopher J. Hall and Rachel
Wicaksono*

Task-Based Language Teaching
Theory and Practice
*Rod Ellis, Peter Skehan, Shaofeng Li,
Natsuko Shintani and Craig Lambert*

Feedback in Second Language Writing
Contexts and Issues
Edited by Ken Hyland and Fiona Hyland

Language and Television Series
A Linguistic Approach to TV Dialogue
Monika Bednarek

**Intelligibility, Oral Communication, and the
Teaching of Pronunciation**
John M. Levis

Multilingual Education
Between Language Learning and Translanguaging
Edited by Jasone Cenoz and Durk Gorter

Learning Vocabulary in Another Language
2nd Edition
I. S. P. Nation

Narrative Research in Applied Linguistics
Edited by Gary Barkhuizen

Teacher Research in Language Teaching
A Critical Analysis
Simon Borg

Figurative Language, Genre and Register
*Alice Deignan, Jeannette Littlemore and
Elena Semino*

Exploring ELF
Academic English Shaped by Non-native Speakers
Anna Mauranen

Genres across the Disciplines
Student Writing in Higher Education
Hilary Nesi and Sheena Gardner

Disciplinary Identities
Individuality and Community in Academic
Discourse
Ken Hyland

Replication Research in Applied Linguistics
Edited by Graeme Porte

The Language of Business Meetings
Michael Handford

Reading in a Second Language
Moving from Theory to Practice
William Grabe

Modelling and Assessing Vocabulary Knowledge
*Edited by Helmut Daller, James Milton and
Jeanine Treffers-Daller*

Practice in a Second Language
Perspectives from Applied Linguistics and
Cognitive Psychology
Edited by Robert M. DeKeyser

Task-Based Language Education
From Theory to Practice
Edited by Kris van den Branden

Second Language Needs Analysis
Edited by Michael H. Long

Insights into Second Language Reading
A Cross-Linguistic Approach
Keiko Koda

Research Genres
Exploration and Applications
John M. Swales

Critical Pedagogies and Language Learning
Edited by Bonny Norton and Kelleen Toohey

**Exploring the Dynamics of Second Language
Writing**
Edited by Barbara Kroll

Understanding Expertise in Teaching
Case Studies of Second Language Teachers
Amy B. M. Tsui

Criterion-Referenced Language Testing
James Dean Brown and Thom Hudson

Corpora in Applied Linguistics
Susan Hunston

Pragmatics in Language Teaching
*Edited by Kenneth R. Rose and Gabriele
Kasper*

Cognition and Second Language Instruction
Edited by Peter Robinson

**Research Perspectives on English for
Academic Purposes**
*Edited by John Flowerdew and Matthew
Peacock*

**Computer Applications in Second Language
Acquisition**
Foundations for Teaching, Testing and
Research
Carol A. Chapelle

Second Language Speech Fluency

From Research to Practice

Parvaneh Tavakoli
University of Reading

Clare Wright
University of Leeds

CAMBRIDGE
UNIVERSITY PRESS

University Printing House, Cambridge CB2 8BS, United Kingdom

One Liberty Plaza, 20th Floor, New York, NY 10006, USA

477 Williamstown Road, Port Melbourne, VIC 3207, Australia

314–321, 3rd Floor, Plot 3, Splendor Forum, Jasola District Centre,
New Delhi – 110025, India

79 Anson Road, #06–04/06, Singapore 079906

Cambridge University Press is part of the University of Cambridge.

It furthers the University's mission by disseminating knowledge in the pursuit of
education, learning, and research at the highest international levels of excellence.

www.cambridge.org
Information on this title: www.cambridge.org/9781108499613
DOI: 10.1017/9781108589109

© Parvaneh Tavakoli and Clare Wright 2020

This publication is in copyright. Subject to statutory exception
and to the provisions of relevant collective licensing agreements,
no reproduction of any part may take place without the written
permission of Cambridge University Press.

First published 2020

A catalogue record for this publication is available from the British Library.

Library of Congress Cataloging-in-Publication Data
Names: Tavakoli, Parvaneh, author. | Wright, Clare, 1966– author.
Title: Second language speech fluency : from research to practice / Parvaneh Tavakoli,
   Clare Wright.
Description: Cambridge ; New York, NY : Cambridge University Press, 2020. |
Series: The Cambridge applied linguistics series | Includes bibliographical references
   and index.
Identifiers: LCCN 2020020656 (print) | LCCN 2020020657 (ebook) |
   ISBN 9781108499613 (hardback) | ISBN 9781108730914 (paperback) |
   ISBN 9781108589109 (epub)
Subjects: LCSH: Second language acquisition. | Fluency (Language learning)
Classification: LCC P118.2 .T356 2020 (print) | LCC P118.2 (ebook) |
   DDC 418.0071–dc23
LC record available at https://lccn.loc.gov/2020020656
LC ebook record available at https://lccn.loc.gov/2020020657

ISBN 978-1-108-49961-3 Hardback
ISBN 978-1-108-73091-4 Paperback

Cambridge University Press has no responsibility for the persistence or accuracy
of URLs for external or third-party internet websites referred to in this publication
and does not guarantee that any content on such websites is, or will remain,
accurate or appropriate.

To our families, for their love, patience and support

Contents

	List of Figures	viii
	List of Tables	ix
1	*Introduction*	1
2	*Fluency from a Psycholinguistic Perspective*	22
3	*Measuring Fluency*	43
4	*Fluency in Second Language Task-Based Research*	64
5	*Fluency in Second Language Pedagogy*	84
6	*Fluency in Second Language Testing*	103
7	*Fluency in Different Contexts*	124
8	*Conclusion*	146
	Appendix: Fluency Descriptors across Time	158
	References	162
	Author Index	187
	Subject Index	188

Figures

1.1	Four approaches to defining fluency (from Tavakoli & Hunter, 2018: 343)	8
1.2	Illustration of Levelt's speech production model (modified from Levelt, 1989: 9, figure 1.1)	10
1.3	Bilingual speech model, following de Bot (1992), Bock and Levelt (1994: 951, figure 2)	12

Tables

5.1	Representations of fluency in second language teaching and learning documents	89
6.1	The College Board's English Competence Examination	105
6.2	Fluency-related rating descriptors in selected standardised tests	108
7.1	Mean (and SD) fluency scores by task at Time 1 (T1) and Time 2 (T2)	143

1 Introduction

Being fluent in a second language, which is often the ultimate personal dream for many second language learners, can be assumed to be the key to being able to communicate effectively and a fundamental aspect of teaching a second language and assessing mastery of it. Governmental language policies, such as China's 'New English Curriculum' introduced in 2003, may include fluency as a goal for foreign language learning. Most internationally recognised language benchmarks, for example, the Council of Europe's Common European Framework of Reference for languages (CEFR), consider fluency as a key aspect of speaking proficiency in a second language, in terms of how far the speaker 'can express themself at length with a natural, effortless, unhesitating flow' (Council of Europe, 2018: 144). Being a fluent and confident speaker can be seen as bringing professional benefits and aiding intercultural communication in an increasingly globalised world (Board & Tinsley, 2017). Language professionals and practitioners, for example, teachers in multilingual classrooms or speech therapists running bilingual clinical assessments, may need to examine fluency in order to identify how best to work with their students and clients (Shohamy, 2011; McLeod & Goldstein, 2012; Tavakoli & Hunter, 2018).

There is thus an increasing need to understand what second language (L2) fluency is and how it can be developed most effectively. Research interest in fluency has expanded since the 1970s (Fillmore, 1979; Riggenbach, 2000; Segalowitz, 2000, 2010, 2016), echoed by increasing interest in its importance for professionals in applied linguistics (Guillot, 1999; Schegloff, 2000; Götz, 2013; Tavakoli & Hunter, 2018), both in first and second language[1] fields. Second

---

[1] Note: by second language (L2), we mean any second, third or other language acquired after a first or mother tongue.

2   *Introduction*

language fluency can be conceptualised in a wide range of ways, from the most general broad sense of global proficiency, to a narrow 'skill' measured as a component of speech production (Koponen & Riggenbach, 2000: 1). Evidence from research and practice suggests that most laypeople/non-expert language users tend to understand fluency in the broadest sense as a demonstration of a speaker's spontaneous language use, often by comparison to a first language (L1) speaker (Brumfit, 1984). Meanwhile, language specialists have a range of much more technical definitions and conceptualisations for fluency, making their research difficult for less specialised readers to access and to make connections between research and practice.

This book therefore has two main aims. First, it aims to offer the readers an advanced introduction to L2 speech fluency, to research conducted in this area, to theoretical frameworks that inform this body of research, and to methodological principles that are used to investigate and measure L2 speech fluency. We will explain the key ways fluency is defined, operationalised and measured, summarising the main empirical studies on L2 fluency and its relation to other key aspects of proficiency and language development, particularly in terms of learner-internal factors such as cognitive processing and automaticity. We will expand the standard temporal assessments of fluency and explore the importance of lexis, grammar and formulaic sequences, as well as personal styles and L1 in the development of L2 speech fluency. Achieving this aim will ensure the book serves as a research manual that provides researchers and postgraduate students with both the theoretical insights and practical tools required to understand and research fluency.

The second aim of the book is to place fluency in a broader perspective, in which it can best be understood by teachers, assessors and language professionals. We will evaluate a range of external factors affecting speech performance across teaching, testing and real-world communication, including task demands, language assessment constraints and pragmatic interactional factors affecting fluent communication. This book therefore aims to provide a unifying account of L2 fluency across different sub-disciplines of applied linguistics, to discuss how these different research disciplines can complement each other and to emphasise the need for a more collaborative approach to researching L2 speech fluency.

1.1 Why Fluency?

In this volume, we will discuss the considerable development that research in second language fluency has made over the past decades and explain the range of definitions and conceptualisations noted above. We will also address some key questions about fluency as a psychological and social concept, fluency as a construct to measure and fluency as a means of some professional practice. Questions we will seek to answer include the following: Is L2 fluency simply an indication of processing ease and speed of production? How does 'spontaneous', 'natural' speech fluency develop? Why should L2 fluency be compared to the fluency of a native speaker? To what extent is fluency affected by context, culture and individual speaker/learner differences? How does it relate to the speaker's own L1 speech? How is fluency used for professional purposes in other language-related disciplines? How can we best operationalise, measure, teach and assess fluency?

Throughout the volume, we consider fluency from two perspectives. First, fluency as speech performance: the 'rapid, smooth, accurate, lucid, and efficient translation of thought or communicative intention into language' (Lennon, 2000: 26). This perspective is based on our understanding of the linguistic and cognitive processes underlying speech production and comprehension, and how fluency develops in terms of automaticity, from slow and effortful to faster and more effective processes in planning and constructing words and sounds into utterances and connected speech. This is what we term the 'cognitive dimension of fluency' and explore in more detail below and in later chapters in this volume.

Second, we also consider the construct of fluency more broadly, as fluency in interaction: the ability to ensure the speaker aims to be comprehensible to the listener; the ability to manage interactions well; and the ability to keep a conversation going appropriately given the context, purpose and audience. Such interactional ease is captured in definitions used, for example by the CEFR, as the ability to 'interact with a degree of fluency and spontaneity that makes regular interaction with speakers of the target language quite possible without imposing strain on either party' (Council of Europe, 2018: 144). We term this the 'social dimension of fluency'.

Our focus on these two perspectives echoes current models of thinking of fluency (Segalowitz, 2010, 2016) as a dynamic multifaceted phenomenon, in which cognitive factors needed for smooth, effortless speech are activated by the social experiences of interaction (Segalowitz, 2016). It seems that these two aspects of fluency, which lead to rather different trajectories for fluency research, are not well connected, whether in domains of research or in the application of research to practice. We see such disconnects as problematic and argue throughout the book for the value of reconnecting insights from

4   *Introduction*

second language interactional and communication research with current assumptions about examining, teaching and testing fluency.

To understand these current assumptions, in this introduction, we set the scene by looking at how fluency has come to be conceptualised and defined. We base this overview on historical investigations of spoken communication and communicative competence and explore their influence on current models of fluency. A brief explanation of the principal speech production models used in cognitive approaches to language use is provided in order to give readers a basic grounding in important terminology and assumptions used in the book, as well as to understand the cognitive dimension that underpins much current research. Although some of the research incorporated here is taken from L1 paradigms, our main focus throughout will be on L2 fluency.

We then discuss how fluency is related to other aspects of linguistic proficiency (complexity, accuracy, lexis) and to the impact of communicative purposes in different tasks, so as to contextualise the challenges of connecting the cognitive and social perspectives on fluency, and to underpin the structure of the rest of the volume.

1.2 What Is Fluency?

1.2.1 Historical Background of Research into Fluency: Definitions and Implications

Interest in fluency has grown throughout the twentieth century, particularly since the 1970s, focusing on fluency as an element within the construct of communicative abilities, which ran parallel to research into the cognitive processes of speech production and skill development (Fillmore, 1979; Dechert, 1980; Anderson, 1983; Levelt, 1989). Charles Fillmore's definition of fluency, although proposed for L1, is seen as one of the seminal views of fluency:

> the ability to talk at length with few pauses; the ability to fill time with talk; the ability to talk in coherent and semantically dense sentences; the ability to have appropriate things to say in a wide range of contexts; and the ability to be creative and imaginative in the language use.
>
> Fillmore (1979: 51)

This view of fluency identifies cognitive, temporal, linguistic and discourse-level elements of fluency: how smoothly or automatically a speaker can produce speech in real time (cognitive), what language resources form the basis for constructing sentences (linguistic) and how to adapt to different listeners and different contexts creatively (in discourse). Disfluency, or lack of fluency, can therefore be demonstrated by speech which is seen as not fully automatic, effortful and slow; is broken up by repeated pauses before or during speech; or contains fillers like 'um' and 'er'.

Such holistic views were used as the foundation of L2 definitions of fluency; for example, Brumfit (1984: 56) referred to fluency as 'natural language use' and defines it in terms of language interaction which is expected to be 'as close as possible to that used by competent performers in the mother tongue in normal life'. This view of fluency remains embedded within a broad sense of fluency as 'spoken language mastery' and remains central to many teachers and speakers' views of fluency as one element contributing to communicative competence or adequacy (Canale & Swain, 1980; Lennon, 1990; Koponen & Riggenbach, 2000; Révész, Ekiert & Torgersen, 2016; Tavakoli & Hunter, 2018). Holistic views of fluency as a mark of developing oral proficiency are also found in assessment criteria such as the English speaking exam of 'fluency and coherence' conducted by the world-wide International English Language Testing System (IELTS) (IELTS, 2018) or the CEFR assessment of the ability to 'interact with a degree of fluency and spontaneity' with native speakers 'without strain' (Council of Europe, 2018). However, as will be discussed in Chapter 6, such definitions of fluency as a component of proficiency tend to be rather vague and circular.

1.2.2 Relationship of Fluency to Communicative Competence

The broad sense of fluency can be found in early conceptualisations of communicative competence for L2 language learning and teaching (see, e.g., Savignon, 1972; Canale & Swain, 1980; Widdowson, 1983; Brumfit, 1984). However, at this stage, there was little interest in the mechanisms assumed to underpin fluency or how it develops during the acquisition process. Within some research domains such as generative second language acquisition (SLA), the L2 speaker's ability to perform based on inherent acquired competence was typically seen as developing naturally over time and as a result of sufficient interaction, if it was considered at all (Brumfit, 1984; Gregg, 1996; White, 2003). However, as evidence emerged that fluent communicative competence was not easy to achieve, especially for instructed learners (Savignon, 2007), researchers turned towards examining more systematically might not either foster or hinder fluent communication.

From the start, there was an acknowledgement of the need for training for learners to overcome problems with repairs, silences and hesitations (Savignon, 1972), though the goal of L1-level temporal

6   *Introduction*

rapidity or pragmatic appropriateness and creativity was not seen as particularly relevant. Faerch, Haastrup and Phillipson (1984) added fluency as a specific component of communicative competence, combining linguistic and pragmatic abilities for communicating effectively. Considering Fillmore's definition, they similarly distinguished three components of fluency, requiring efficient cognitive and linguistic processes. These components were semantic fluency (coherence or appropriate planning of meaning), lexical-syntactic fluency (ability to put form on the meaning) and articulatory fluency (speed and smoothness of putting speech segments together). Others around this time similarly pointed out the complex nature of fluency, which must be seen not only as more than simply 'uninterrupted flow' (Lehtonen, 1978: 67) but also as 'normal, acceptable and relaxed linguistic behaviour' (ibid). Leeson (1975) and Pawley and Syder (1983) also noted that pausing and repair were features of native-speaker speech, so should not be definitive indicators of learner disfluency. These studies highlighted the multiple components of fluency as part of the concept of communicative ability (competence). However, establishing clear ways of measuring learner fluency using the components suggested above, such as coherence or uninterrupted flow, remained rather non-specific.

A key moment for beginning to see fluency research splitting into different domains can be seen in Lennon's (1990) distinction between a broad and a narrow sense of fluency. Lennon, perhaps partly motivated by the challenges of how to pin down definitions that could be more reliably assessed, noted a broad holistic view of fluency as a set of creative skills underpinning spoken communicative ability. He argued that this broad sense of fluency functions 'as a cover term for oral proficiency' or 'spoken command of a foreign language' (Lennon, 1990: 389) and is often assessed through perceptions or ratings of fluency by an L1 listener.

The second sense of fluency Lennon identified refers to the more objective and measurable aspects of speech where the speaker's speed of delivery, flow of speech and lack of hesitations and undue interruptions are valued. Fluency in this sense is objectively measured because amount of pause and frequency of interruptions could be reliably calculated. In this sense, fluency is seen as a question of how efficiently the speaker can construct an utterance using cognitive processes and linguistic knowledge available to them during the speech production process. Such speech efficiency is seen as evidence of developing automaticity – or speedy unbroken speech, identified as one of the most crucial aspects of fluency early on, for example, in the notion of creative automaticity (Gatbonton & Segalowitz, 1988, 2005).

1.2 What is Fluency? 7

While Lennon's seminal distinction has given researchers and practitioners a solid background to start examining and working with fluency, increasingly, there is growing awareness that this kind of distinction is limited for at least two reasons. First, some researchers have argued that by detaching cognitive-based fluency processes, measured in temporal rapidity and automaticity, from a more integrated sense of fluency as a component of fluency in interaction, we might be taking a reductionist approach to understanding fluency and researching it (Tavakoli, 2016; Nakatsuhara, Tavakoli & Awwad, 2019), missing the importance of fluency aiding communication across a range of contexts and cultures. Becoming fluent, in this interactional and more integrated sense of the term, can be challenging, even when broad and narrow senses of fluency have been fulfilled, as this quote from an international student living in the United Kingdom shows:

Sometimes I just sit silently with [local friends], and I am thinking very hard to find a topic but I just can't find one to chat with them very fluently, so, that's the problem.

Wright and Schartner (2013: 122)

The second reason Lennon's dichotomy has been considered limited in defining fluency has been highlighted by Tavakoli and Hunter (2018). The authors argue that more recently fluency is often understood and discussed at four different but interrelated levels: very broad, broad, narrow and very narrow (see Figure 1.1).

Tavakoli and Hunter (2018) consider fluency as a pyramid, at the bottom of which fluency is defined as a general view of L2 proficiency, including L2 ability in skills beyond L2 speaking. This is referred to as the *very broad* sense of fluency. The second level, the *broad* sense of fluency, reflects competent L2 speaking ability. A 'fluent person' in this sense of the term refers to a speaker who speaks confidently, communicating their intended message competently and coherently. Tavakoli and Hunter (2018) argue that fluency in this sense includes elements of pronunciation, intelligibility and ability to engage in a conversation. A *narrow* perspective is the third level of understanding fluency and highlights 'ease, flow and continuity of speech and sets fluency apart from other aspects of oral performance such as grammatical complexity and accuracy' (p. 343). The last level of understanding of fluency in Tavakoli and Hunter's (2018) model is the *very narrow* perspective, in which fluency of speech is considered in terms of its concrete and measurable features such as speed, silence and repair. This categorisation can also be valuable when considering the relationship between theoretical understandings of fluency and professional practice; for example, while researchers often engage with fluency at a *narrow* or

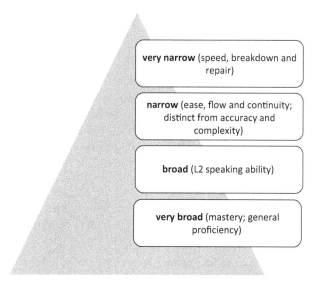

Figure 1.1 Four approaches to defining fluency
(from Tavakoli & Hunter, 2018: 343)

very narrow level, teachers may engage with it at *broad* and *narrow* levels, and non-specialists may benefit from understanding fluency at the *very broad* level.

In addition to the more nuanced four-way framework of fluency proposed by Tavakoli and Hunter above, other researchers have also sought to broaden out fluency beyond the unidimensional temporal sense of fluid, non-hesitant speech. Notably, Norman Segalowitz has been proposing a new model of speech fluency which calls for the kind of social dimension we offer here (Segalowitz, 2010, 2016).

1.3 Fluency As Multicomponent: Segalowitz's Triadic Framework

Segalowitz (2010, 2016) provides a fresh explanatory model for conceptualising and defining fluency; examining speech fluency from a cognitive and social perspective; and defining different aspects of fluency with regard to principles of language processing, language development, language use and individual differences in social experience and motivation. He acknowledges the multidimensional dynamic nature of fluency (originally noted by Goldman-Eisler, 1951), suggesting a triadic model of fluency, which is now widely used in different fields of study, particularly cognitive sciences and SLA. Segalowitz

(2010) identifies three elements of fluency as critically intertwined – cognitive, utterance and perceptual (see Chapter 2 for a detailed discussion). He argues that utterance fluency (observable features of fluency such as speed and pauses) must be seen alongside other aspects of fluency, particularly cognitive fluency (degree of automaticity within the speech process) and perceptual fluency (how fluency is perceived and rated).

We explore Segalowitz's model in more detail in Chapter 2 and aim to use his framework throughout the volume to show how this triadic framework can be used as a point of departure to set out to provide a more rounded perspective on understanding fluency as a cognitive, social and individual feature of second language speech. We argue that this wider perspective can be more directly applicable to a wider range of applied linguistics areas, such as Discourse Analysis, and relatable to practitioners' needs, for example, in bilingual education. But in order to understand the framework more clearly, we start here by explaining in a little more detail the speech production models which underpin the core temporal view of fluency as rapid and smooth speech production, measurable in the utterances which speakers produce.

1.4 The Relationship between Fluency and Speech Production Models

As researchers and practitioners have become more interested in trying to pin down how language learners can develop smooth, speedy speech similar to native speakers, they have drawn increasingly on research into speech processing among cognitive scientists, particularly the work of Levelt (1989, 1999). His seminal model of the three stages of speech production (conceptualisation, formulation, articulation) is illustrated in Figure 1.2.

Levelt's model (1989, 1999) identifies L1 speech production as a one-way flow step by step through three separate stages, from underlying conceptual planning, via grammatical/lexical formulation, to overt articulation. Speech is constructed using mainly subconscious (procedural) processes working in incremental sequences and each part of the system is separate or modular; for example, when a piece of information passes from the conceptualiser to the formulator, the conceptualiser starts working with the next part of the message. When such processes are highly developed as in L1 or proficient L2 speech, these processes are automatic and operate in parallel, taking place virtually simultaneously, and require little cognitive effort. These characteristics of L1 speech production account for speed and fluidity, that is, a speaker's fluency. If the processes are not yet fully

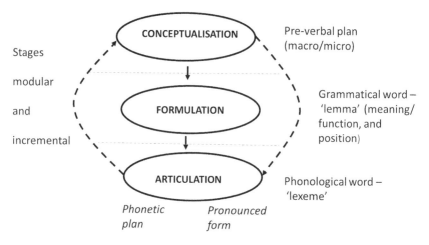

Figure 1.2 Illustration of Levelt's speech production model (modified from Levelt, 1989: 9, figure 1.1)

automatised, they will occur in a serial sequence, one after the other, and hence more slowly and effortfully.

The start of the speech process begins with the conceptualiser. Here the speaker creates the general intention of what to say (macro-planning) and what form to say it in, for example, question or statement (micro-planning). Macro-planning is the 'process by which the speaker decides what to say next' (Levelt, 1999: 92), further refined in micro-planning to select appropriate semantic information or 'perspective' (p. 94). Macro-planning is seen as language independent, while micro-planning may need to be language-encoded due to differences in ways of encoding semantic concepts, such as space or time, or pragmatic information to show relevance for the listener. This stage is pre-verbal, but can be open to conscious consideration (i.e., the speaker can be aware of the process of planning what to say).

The concept then automatically progresses through to the formulation stage, to be encoded in grammatical and lexical form as a 'lemma'. This stage involves unifying all the relevant grammatical features needed to create words and phrases (such as information about gender or plural marking on nouns, tense and aspect marking for verbs). The relevant processes for binding together syntactic, morphological and semantic information are assumed to be automatic (i.e., the speaker would not be aware of adding the necessary information for making a verb in past tense form, or obeying word order or subject-verb agreement rules). The grammatical/lexical speech plan is then ready to go to the next stage, in which morpho-phonological

1.4 Fluency and Speech Production Models   11

words are encoded with information about word form, syllable boundaries, intonation and prosodic information, known as a 'phonological score' (Levelt, 1999: 110). Finally, the formulation then progresses to articulatory encoding in morpho-phonological form or 'lexeme', ready to be articulated as overt speech within appropriate phonetic constraints (a phonetic plan), fitting expectations of pronunciation, speech rate, syllable duration and loudness. Throughout the cycle of speech production, there is an accompanying 'monitor' loop, whereby the processes at every stage can be monitored to check they are in line with the original intention, form or sound required, and reinitiated or repaired if needed. Dysfluencies can occur as the utterance moves through the system and is noted by the monitor loop – for example, if the 'wrong' morpho-phonological word is mapped on the syntactic lemma, as when we say a word with the same starting letter but the wrong meaning, or when we cannot retrieve a less frequent word we need to precisely encode the intention we have, and we slow down in our articulation rate, or if we stall for time using filled pauses.

Levelt's model focuses on the idea of fluency at the individual's level of production. It does not refer particularly to fluency in the context of socio-pragmatic demands in discourse and interaction, nor is it particularly related to L2 research (House, 1996; Shively, 2011). The model also does not take into account the variety of L1 speakers' individual speaking patterns, which can have an observable impact on L2 fluency (see, e.g., de Jong, Groenhout, Schoonen & Hulstijn (2015) and Derwing, Munro, Thomson & Rossiter (2009)).

However, the model was rapidly adopted as the basis for models of L2 speech production, for example, by de Bot (1992), Bock and Levelt (1994), and further expanded by Kormos (2006). De Bot (1992) lays out how speech becomes specifically encoded for each language (illustrated in schematic form in Figure 1.3), suggesting how the bilingual speaker can draw on separate but connected representations and processes at syntactic and morpho-phonological level. In bilingual speech production, semantic, syntactic, phonological and other linguistic information is language independent (Lx) at macro-level, but must be tagged for a specific language (L1 or L2) at the micro-planning level (de Bot, 1992; Bock & Levelt, 1994; Segalowitz, 2010). Thus, when an English speaker wishes to talk about fresh bread to a French speaker, for example, a general concept at macro-planning will need to be clarified, during micro-planning, between bread in general ('le pain', masculine gender), or a specific type ('la baguette', feminine gender). Formulation must be language-specific to allow the underlying subsystems for syntax and phonology to generate the correct information, such as gender, word order and agreement

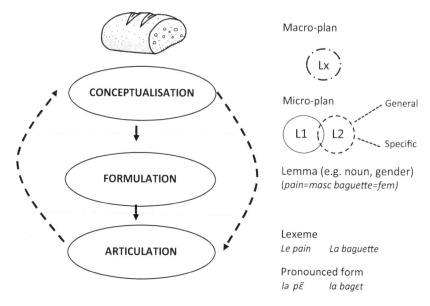

Figure 1.3 Bilingual speech model, following de Bot (1992), Bock and Levelt (1994: 951, figure 2)
(where the circles for Lx, L1 and L2 show overlapping or separated language planning and encoding)

for noun and adjective, and appropriate phonological encoding. However, the ultimate phonetic articulation may be constrained by articulatory limits on how target-like the L2 sounds can be produced, depending on accentedness.

At lemma level, articulation requires language-specific phonetic plans but will be constrained by a speaker's ability to pronounce relevant sounds. Fluency, in terms of smooth, speedy, effortless automaticity throughout all the stages of speech production, is only developed in highly proficient bilinguals. For learners at lower proficiency levels, it is assumed that gaps in linguistic knowledge, L1 transfer and lack of automaticity would lead to disfluencies at all stages. Most disfluencies may be seen to arise in the formulation stage, where binding together syntactic and lexical information may well need slow, conscious searching in memory for appropriate linguistic knowledge, or in articulation, trying to form L2 sounds in competition with long-established L1 phonetic habits. Fluency can also be seen affecting conceptualisation, where starting off in L1 and translating the thought into L2 leads to problems in planning and producing an utterance, whereas 'thinking in the L2' has been argued to help

1.4 Fluency and Speech Production Models   13

in building up speaking ability even at early levels of proficiency (Canale & Swain, 1980).

Kormos (2006) outlines the cognitive development processes of L2 fluency and its impact on L2 speech. For L2 learners, their underlying linguistic knowledge or repertoire of lexical, syntactic and phonological knowledge is still emerging and competes against the more easily acccessed L1. Much of their L2 knowledge may be explicitly taught, and stored as declarative knowledge, rather than as implicit procedural knowledge. In addition, access to that knowledge is not yet automatic (Kormos, 2006), making the process of retrieving linguistic knowledge slower and more cognitively demanding of attention. Disfluencies could thus emerge at every stage, but mainly at the formulation stage, where lexical-grammatical features may need to be connected using slow conscious serial processing, rather than using parallel automatic processing. However, disfluencies can also occur in conceptualisation and articulation stages – if a speaker has gaps in linguistic repertoire, then message planning has to fit round the gaps. Without much practice in speaking aloud, overt production will lead to slower and less efficient articulation. All these demands affect the ease with which the learner can access what knowledge they may have, and the ability to modify what they say to ensure their message is understood by their listener.

Greater fluency comes both by having access to a larger repertoire of lexical and grammatical knowledge, but primarily, as Kormos argues, by a more automatised access to that knowledge, developed through practice. Lack of automaticity or ability to maintain the message can lead to disfluency in terms of slower speech, breakdown or repair, either as silence, filled pausing, repetition or reformulation (Towell, Hawkins & Bazergui, 1996; Skehan, 2003; Tavakoli, 2011 – see more on fluency measures in Chapter 3).

For many researchers, using Leveltian speech production models provided a basis for reliable objective measures of fluent speech, particularly at articulatory or utterance level. One particularly influential framework is Peter Skehan's model for capturing aspects of utterance fluency (Skehan, 2003, 2009, 2014), by measuring speed, breakdown and repair. As will be discussed in Chapter 3, speed measures are features of speech that calculate the speed of delivery (e.g., articulation rate or length of run), breakdown measures are taken to indicate when speech flow is disrupted by pauses (e.g., silent or filled pausing) and repair measures reflect the monitoring process and use of strategies required to fix errors which may occur during the speech production process (e.g., false starts, reformulations or repetitions). However, as noted by Faerch et al. (1984) and highlighted by

14   *Introduction*

research since, fluency is not only just a question of measuring temporal speed of overt speech or cognitive automatic processes but also relates to the speaker's linguistic repertoire (in terms of syntactic and lexical accuracy and complexity), as well as to the semantic/pragmatic demands of different contexts and tasks. We explore these relationships in more depth in later chapters but introduce some of the key issues in these relationships now.

1.5 The Relationship among Fluency, Other Aspects of the Linguistic Repertoire and Task Demands

Fluency is seen as one of the components of language mastery, alongside accuracy of form and complexity of linguistic units (both syntactic and lexical) – brought together in the influential CALF (Complexity, Accuracy, Lexis, Fluency) framework for exploring language ability within a variety of task-based settings (discussed further in Chapter 4 in this volume).

As seen above, the processes involved in formulating and articulating an utterance, if not yet automatised, will be slow and effortful, particularly if the underlying linguistic repertoire is not very wide or easily accessed. Research has found that in some cases, even after years of language learning, or even immersion in the target language country, speakers may struggle to formulate utterances with reliable morpho-syntactic accuracy, particularly in dialogic interaction (e.g., Wright, 2013), or when facing unfamiliar or more demanding speech (e.g., Awwad, Tavakoli & Wright, 2017).

Not surprisingly then, fluency has often been assumed to operate in opposition to accuracy (e.g., Brumfit, 1984), an assumption which remains embedded in teachers' resources (British Council, 2019). However, as research has expanded into how fluency interacts with underpinning linguistic knowledge (see, e.g., Segalowitz, 2003), it has become clear that accuracy needs to be considered within both syntactic and lexical domains. Furthermore, while fluency has been conceptualised as more than greater ease in retrieving items of knowledge, it has also been connected to the ability to produce longer, more complex speech (Foster, Tonkyn & Wigglesworth, 2000; Skehan, 2003; Housen & Kuiken, 2009). The precise operationalisation of complexity remains somewhat open to debate (Pallotti, 2009), but most researchers (see Norris & Ortega, 2009; Housen, Kuiker & Vedder, 2012 for further details) agree that complexity includes a range of different measures both of overall length and more structurally complex language at phrasal/sub-clausal, clausal and sentence/utterance levels (e.g., coordination, subordination, use of relative clauses and adverbial phrases).

1.5 Fluency, Linguistic Repertoire & Task Demands   15

Finally, lexis has now emerged as a separate component of the CALF framework, as we begin to understand that fluency involves more than item-based rapid word retrieval, but can be impacted by frequency (de Jong et al., 2015; de Jong, 2016) and the use of chunks, formulaic sequences or multiword expressions (Wray, 2002; Tavakoli & Uchihara, 2020). The relationship between fluency and formulaic sequences (e.g., 'in front of', 'to be honest', 'as a matter of fact') has increasingly attracted L2 researchers' and practitioners' interest over the past decades (Wray, 2002; Wood, 2010). SLA research has shown that proficient L2 speakers, compared to low proficiency L2 speakers, have a more competent command of formulaic sequences, and that the use of formulaic sequences promotes fluency (Tavakoli, 2011; Tavakoli & Uchihara, 2019). The evidence supporting such claims has emerged from psycholinguistic research (see a summary in Siyanova-Chanturia & Van Lancker Sidtis, 2018), suggesting these sequences are stored and retrieved as individual units, thus freeing up attentional resources available to speakers and leading to an increase in the speed of processing (Kormos, 2006; Skehan, 2009). Second language teachers have also shown great interest in using formulaic sequences as the basis of their teaching, for example, the work of colleagues in using the Lexical Approach (Lewis, 1997) and other methodologies drawing on exemplar-based L2 instruction, all reporting positive effects on fluency (e.g., Boers et al., 2006).

Identifying complexity, accuracy and lexis as highly related to fluency has been useful to researchers particularly in a teaching or discourse setting, as it has provided a set of models to predict how speakers may perform in different task conditions. Currently, there are two primary approaches to task-effects on CALF: Skehan's Limited Attentional Capacity model (1998, 2015) and Robinson's Cognition Hypothesis (2001, 2007, 2015). Skehan's Limited Attentional Capacity model (1998, 2015) argues that the brain operates on limited cognitive resources and reduced attentional capacity is more obvious during less automatic and challenging tasks such as L2 speech production. He argues that when cognitive demands of a task increase (e.g., where there is a lot of information to process in a speaking task, or where the information is not well-structured), there will be a competition in allocating attention to different aspects of performance (i.e., complexity, accuracy, fluency and lexis). This competition will inevitably result in some trade-offs between the different aspects of performance; for example, a task requiring highly complex syntactic structures or low-frequency words will be less fluent or accurate.

Robinson's Cognition Hypothesis (2001, 2005), by contrast, hypothesises that the human brain operates on a multiple-resource

16   *Introduction*

attentional structure, in which raising the demand in one pool does not affect attentional demands in other pools. Therefore, raising the cognitive demands of task performance does not necessarily hinder performance; it is possible for L2 speakers to perform complex tasks and produce fluent language which is also accurate and complex. The impact of task design remains crucial for understanding fluency in and out of the classroom; therefore, we explore what we know from current research and applications to practice in more detail in Chapter 4. We also highlight where further work needs to be done to contextualise the CALF-based approach to fluency in different discourse and social settings.

1.6 Fluency in Different Contexts: A New Approach

The brief overview of findings from recent research covered above has identified that too narrow a focus on a temporal sense of fluency does not capture wider issues of how to operationalise fluency, particularly in different contexts and social settings (see, e.g., Mora & Valls-Ferrer, 2012; Nakatsuhara, 2012; Foster, 2013; Witkins, Morere & Geer, 2013; Nitta & Nakatsuhara, 2014; Wright & Tavakoli, 2016). We are beginning to see work in which fluency measures can be used to compare everyday spontaneous casual speech and other different functions, for example, with more or less planning or spontaneity (Yuan & Ellis, 2003), and between a monologic context and dialogic context (Tavakoli, 2016). Robinson and others have focused on context-based task demands affecting fluency (e.g., Robinson, 2003, 2007), including planning time (Skehan, 2014), using familiar topics (Bui, 2014) and under different performance conditions (Skehan & Shum, 2014).

Other researchers have focused on affective factors which may impact on developing fluent interaction (see, e.g., MacIntyre, Clément, Dörnyei & Noels, 1998; Dewaele & Furnham, 2000). Another crucial area of research impacting on fluency development addresses the purpose of speech – whether speech is transactional or interactional (Walsh, 2011; Seedhouse, 2013), or what the context is – whether formal (e.g., for an exam or in a classroom) or more informal (e.g., living in the target country, making local friends, Wright, 2010, 2018a).

Finally, as noted by Segalowitz (2010), researchers are increasingly addressing the importance of perceptions of fluency – how to judge speech as fluent (Bortfeld et al., 2001; Bosker et al., 2012), the role of prosody and intelligibility (Préfontaine & Kormos, 2016), perceptions of communicative adequacy and comprehensibility (see, e.g., Révész

1.6 Fluency in Different Contexts: A New Approach 17

et al., 2016), and the critical role played particularly in assessment by how fluency is rated (as addressed in Chapter 6 in this volume).

Such research has highlighted the need for a return to a more integrated approach to fluency, combining both creative communicative ability and specific aspects of fluent performance; in addition, it has signalled the value of moving away from the sense that L2 fluency has to be compared against an L1 norm. We will argue, indeed, that research into bilingual models of language can help us move to more meaningful ways of using bilingual norms as the basis for fluency development, rather than retaining a native-speaker goal for research and practice. Overall, we see existing research as highlighting the need to rethink what measures we use for fluency and the value of a more multidimensional view of the concept, combining both broad and narrow senses of fluency. This leads us to articulate the first disconnect that has inspired this book.

1.6.1 Disconnect between Research Disciplines

The first main disconnect we seek to address in this volume is a lack of communication between different disciplines that should in principle be interested in and inform fluency research, for example, SLA and Discourse Analysis. We argue that research in fluency has primarily taken a cognitive learner-internal focus and has thus tended to overlook the relationship between fluency as both a psycholinguistic construct and as a communicative social and pragmatic variable.

We would expect these different but neighbouring disciplines to contribute to the development of a more in-depth and comprehensive understanding of fluency, but they often seem to work rather independently with little attention to the benefits of an interdisciplinary examination of fluency. A good example of the kind of work that can potentially bridge the gap is Nakatsuhara et al. (2019), who have examined fluency from both SLA and Discourse Analysis perspectives. The work of Seedhouse and Nakatsuhara (2018) is another example of bridging the gap between Conversation Analysis and Language Testing. As we will discuss in Chapters 5 and 6, the findings of such interdisciplinary research on fluency will enrich our understanding of fluency and broaden our perspective to how fluency should be defined, operationalised, measured and practiced.

1.6.2 Disconnect between Research and Practice

The second disconnect we will discuss is between research in L2 fluency and practice in applied linguistics, specifically in language

18   *Introduction*

teaching and language testing, and how these different domains emphasise fluency differently. This has left gaps in the understanding of how speakers' fluency varies for different purposes (e.g., when giving good news vs. breaking bad news), in different settings (e.g., formal assessment vs. informal authentic interaction) and in different cultures (British English vs. American English). Throughout the volume, we highlight where current research can shed useful light on professional practice. We also identify limitations in current empirical investigations in teaching and assessment, so far dominated by research in English and European languages. We look at how new research is bringing insights into fluency development in non-European languages, allowing for a wider range of bilingual empirical comparisons, and informing fresh directions for conceptualising, teaching and assessing fluency. Addressing these disconnects is key to our approach throughout this volume, as we explain below, outlining the purpose and aims of the book.

1.7 Purpose and Aims of the Book

As Koponen and Riggenbach (2000) suggested in one of the first systematic explorations of the construct of L2 fluency, it may be almost impossible to develop a single catch-all definition of this word. However, this volume aims to respond to their challenge to clarify and refine how to use the term 'fluency' both for research and practice. Doing so within an agenda linking theory and empirical data will foster greater 'consistency among those exploring definitions and components of fluency' (p. 6). To drive that agenda forward, our chapters provide an accessible synthesis and evaluation of recent achievements of current research and practice. Questions combining cognitive, interactional and pedagogic issues are highlighted, with implications for future L2 fluency research and practice. The principal argument presented throughout is the need to examine fluency in broader social and multilingual contexts – without doing so, research on L2 fluency will become inadequate, unidirectional and disconnected across research paradigms and also will limit the effectiveness in linking research to practice. We seek to bring an innovative perspective on research on fluency in applied linguistics as an important feature of successful oral communication, shaped not only by the cognitive and psycholinguistic demands of L2 processing, or by formal testing constraints, but also by the communicative needs of speaking tasks and the social pragmatic demands of the context of communication.

This book therefore aims to address the two disconnects we identified above in existing research on speech fluency: between different disciplines that should, in principle, be interested in and inform speech fluency research, and between research and practice in the classroom and beyond. By reintegrating the questions which research can best address in conjunction to practice, we seek to better understand the relationship between fluency as a cognitive/psycholinguistic construct of speech utterance ability on the one hand, and as a social construct of conversational fluency and interaction on the other hand, where communicative adequacy and managing interactional demands at discourse-level also impact on fluency and its development. This view of speech fluency needs to encompass both broad and narrow aspects, which can be clearly delineated but must be understood as dynamically connected. We show how these connections can be improved, how to link to practice and why this can be of benefit to research and practice in a globalised world of multiple domains and functions for oral communication.

The book is based on our own research as well as our well-grounded synthesis of existing findings, in order to provide a practical and empirically based account of what these new directions in defining, examining and measuring fluency mean for researchers, language professionals and language educators in their professional practices. Because of its strong academic grounding and practical orientation, the book will be a valuable resource both for academics and post-graduate students as well as for language professionals in teaching and assessment, who would benefit from the empirical contributions of this book. We therefore hope this book will be a bridge between researchers and practitioners, conveying cutting-edge research in an accessible way for readers, highlighting what practical implications researching speech fluency has for pedagogy and language use, showing in what ways research and practice can mutually benefit, as well as pointing to new directions for research to go.

1.8 Structure of the Book

The chapters in the book move from theory to practice, reviewing first in more detail the psycholinguistic processes discussed earlier in this introduction, then moving to operationalisation and measurement, task-based issues, teaching practices and testing applications. We will look beyond the dominant L2 English global lingua franca model to discuss the implications of our reconceptualisation of cognitive-interactional fluency from a cross-linguistic perspective and identify remaining questions for future research. We aim to discuss whether such questions will enable us to eventually operationalise a multilingual L2 model of fluency, which incorporates a speaker's own

20   *Introduction*

individual differences in L1 speech habits as the basis for comparison against their L2 speech, and to reduce what we see as the current assumption of seeing L2 fluency as a deficit against the monolith of an idealised L1 speaker.

Chapter 2 provides a deeper and broader critical evaluation of the current dominant psycholinguistic paradigms in L2 speech fluency, which were briefly outlined here. We show how cognitive and psycho-social factors can affect fluency, including the role of the speaker's L1, which increasingly is seen as an influence on individual variation in fluency.

Chapter 3 provides the technical heart of the book, consisting of a synthesis of the most important research looking at operationalisation and measurement of fluency in different contexts, and covers different ways of operationalising and measuring fluency. This chapter will be of particular interest to researchers wanting a comprehensive and novel overview of the mechanics of how to investigate fluency across different social settings and cultural backgrounds.

Chapter 4 explores questions and insights from task-based approaches to researching language learning, particularly within the widely used CALF framework, in which effects of task design on fluency performance are investigated alongside complexity, accuracy and lexis.

Chapter 5 focuses on research in fluency in L2 pedagogy and provides an analysis of the importance of fluency in L2 curricula and teaching materials, exploring current research into teacher under-standing and classroom practices for developing fluency. The chapter will make a few suggestions about what can be done to help teachers, learners and material designers develop more effective ways of engaging with fluency in theory and practice.

Chapter 6 highlights the importance of fluency in the assessment of L2 speech, problematising the dearth of studies investigating dimen-sions of fluency in high-stake tests, arguing that the gap between fluency research and language testing should be bridged if a valid and reliable assessment of the construct of fluency is expected.

Chapter 7 reaches beyond Anglophone or Western European-based research and practices to explore implications of taking a more vari-able multilingual view of fluency for teaching and assessment, moving away from English-rooted paradigms, and standardised native-speaker norms. Looking at research into study abroad experiences and use of wider cross-linguistic corpora, new reference points can be identified for a more authentic perspective on fluency development in different contexts cross-linguistically.

In the final chapter, we pull together the themes and questions covered throughout the book, across cognitive, interactional, pedagogic and assessment dimensions of language use. We highlight opportunities for future research based on closer integration of fluency as a temporal construct and fluency in interaction taking into greater account influences from task, mode, context and communicative purpose. Using the broader reconceptualisation of fluency as we have done here, we seek to ensure this body of research can be applied more usefully to issues of real-life second language communication.

2 Fluency from a Psycholinguistic Perspective

2.1 Introduction

As we saw in Chapter 1, understanding what L2 speech fluency is and how it develops can be seen from a range of perspectives, broad and narrow (Lennon, 1990; Tavakoli & Hunter, 2018), indicating at one end of the spectrum a holistic sense of spoken mastery of a second language, through to demonstration of speedy, fluid cognitive-temporal processes in narrowly defined aspects of speech production.

Much of the research over the past three decades has largely focused on this latter psycholinguistic perspective of temporal evaluations of fluency. In this approach, L2 speech fluency is often seen as acquiring the kind of smooth, automatic processes used by native speakers in conceptualising, formulating and articulating speech. As such, fluency may often be researched as a separate phenomenon from L1 speech use. Such an approach inevitably results in many comparisons with L1 speech, often construed, rather negatively, as what the L2 user cannot do, or how their L2 speech may be related to what they can do in their own L1. In this chapter, we suggest that this deficit model of L2 speech misses important insights into what a bilingual speaker is doing as they develop their L2 fluency. To do so, we go into more depth of analysis of what the current body of psycholinguistic research reveals, where current limitations can be found and how it could be beneficial to take a more dynamic bilingual contextualised view of fluency.

The speech production models mentioned in Chapter 1 (e.g. Levelt, 1989; de Bot, 1992; Kormos, 2006) are explored to clarify their implications for L2 fluency development, and how they can be related to cognitive models of information processing and skill development (Anderson, 1983, 1993). We will expand on Segalowitz's (2010, 2016) differentiation between the three domains of cognitive fluency, utterance fluency and perceptions of fluency, to give the context for current conceptualisations of utterance fluency, in terms of speech rate, breakdown and disfluency (e.g. Skehan, 2003; Tavakoli & Skehan, 2005), which forms perhaps the most extensive aspect of current L2 fluency research. It can be seen how speed, silence and repair may be rated as both negative and positive aspects of fluency, and why current research may thus be limited by seeing L2 fluency as disconnected from L1 speech and language systems, rather than being seen part of a multicompetent whole (Cook, 2002). The role of the speaker's L1 is highlighted, in view of research from neurolinguistic and other perspectives which further emphasise the interdependence of individual speech processes across both L1 and L2 (Derwing, Munro & Thomson, 2008; de Jong, Groenhout, Schoonen & Hulstijn, 2015). We then examine how a more interconnected view of fluency can also be informed by research into the relationship between fluency and ease of access to different linguistic domains (particularly vocabulary and the role of formulaic sequences or multiword expressions).

We turn after that to look at factors related to individual differences, which have been argued as potentially affecting fluency; in particular, it has been suggested that working memory may facilitate or constrain fluency (Weissheimer & Mota, 2009; Wright, 2013). Key research on other psycho-social factors is examined for potential impacts on L2 speech fluency, for example, personality-traits (Dewaele & Furnham, 2000; Moyer, 2004), willingness to engage in interaction or not (Wright, Lin & Tsakalaki, forthcoming) and how fluency can thus be affected. We finish by broadening out further to review where the cognitive models of fluency can be connected with more interactional context-based views of fluency, by understanding fluency strategies as a kind of 'juggling act' (Ejzenberg, 2000) and returning to Segalowitz's model to look at his third component – perceptions of fluency.

2.2 A Historical Perspective on Cognitive Models of Speech and Fluency

Over many decades, psycholinguistic constructs of speech fluency have been developed in terms of procedural automaticity (e.g. Goldman-Eisler, 1951; Fillmore, 1979), in which 'the psycholinguistic processes of speech planning and speech production are functioning easily and efficiently' (Lennon, 1990: 391). Fluency can thus be explained as a sign of increasing implicit acquisition of linguistic forms as 'procedural knowledge' (Schmidt, 1992: 358), as well as growing automaticity in terms of 'speed of access and control over the available linguistic forms' (de Jong & Perfetti, 2011: 534). The next sections explore in

24   *Fluency from a Psycholinguistic Perspective*

more detail at how current research analyses both automaticity and development of available knowledge in relation to specific stages of speech production, particularly in formulation.

2.2.1 Fluency Development as Increased Automaticity

Our understanding of automaticity in skill-based views of fluent speech can be clarified by research into memory, attention, information processing and skill development (e.g. Anderson, 1983, 1993; Schmidt, 1992; Segalowitz, 2010; de Jong & Perfetti, 2011; Wright, 2018b).

Fluency, as we have seen, relies on ease of access to underlying linguistic knowledge held in memory. Most models of memory assume two types of long-term knowledge, accessed in real time via short-term or working memory processes (see summaries in Wright, 2010, 2018b – and see further discussion in relation to fluency below). The first type of knowledge is procedural, or knowledge 'how', which does not require conscious attention and is the basis of most routine activity – such as the well-rehearsed smooth operation of giving out a familiar telephone number. The second type is declarative, or knowledge 'that', which is stored via conscious noticing and explicit memorisation. Such knowledge typically requires more effort if not rehearsed or repeated – such as trying to recall complex spellings of rarely used technical vocabulary or constructing a complex argument in a debate. Since early models of processing (e.g. Schneider & Schiffrin, 1977), automatic processes are similarly considered to be those which operate on proceduralised knowledge. Automatic processing is thus characterised as:

(a) fast and efficient, (b) effortless, (c) not limited by short-term memory capacity, (d) not under voluntary control, (e) difficult to modify or inhibit, and (f) unavailable to introspection.

Schmidt (1992: 360)

In initial stages of learning a language, it requires controlled and focused attention to construct the required output (such as retrieving words or producing a spoken phrase). After sufficient practice, the repeated act of retrieving the relevant speech information creates strong enough neural networks to produce what is needed without attention. As Schmidt (1992) discusses, problems with how to substantiate this model, particularly in relation to fluent speech (Schmidt, 1992), led to proposals by Anderson (e.g. 1983, 1993) of a three-stage process of how cognitive skills can be acquired – his Adaptive Control of Thought (ACT) model. Anderson's ACT model suggests that in the

2.2 A Historical Perspective on Cognitive Models 25

first stage of skill development, cognitive processes rely on declarative knowledge, consciously accessed via serial processing (i.e. segment after segment) via working memory. Such controlled conscious processing carries a heavy cognitive cost in time, effort and working memory space (Schmidt, 1992: 363). The second stage creates the basis for emerging procedural knowledge by building up readily connected items or combinations of regular routines, usually through practice and rehearsal, so that frequently required knowledge can be retrieved directly from memory and does not need activation via working memory. In the final stage of 'tuning', (Schmidt, 1992: 363–364) processes to retrieve information are stronger and able to draw on more ready-stored routines, thus becoming automatic, subconscious, difficult to think about, modify or inhibit.

2.2.2 Where We Are Now

Understanding the role of automaticity in L2 fluency has been central in of models of L2 fluency, led by work by Segalowitz (from the 1980s to the present). Segalowitz's current (2010, 2016) fluency model has three parts: the L2 speaker's underlying cognitive processes in planning and formulating the utterance ('cognitive fluency'); the processes for smooth production, observed at surface or articulatory level ('utterance fluency'); and 'perceived fluency', in which the hearer's judgement of how easy it is to follow speech is seen as a crucial aspect of L2 fluency.

In considering cognitive fluency, Segalowitz is careful to differentiate the role of both general cognitive fluency implied by the kind of broad mechanisms of automatic processing described above, and also those he argues may be specific to L2 cognitive fluency. First, he distinguishes two aspects of automaticity, namely, speed of processing and the ease or stability of the processing involved (Segalowitz & Segalowitz, 1993; Segalowitz & Freed, 2004; Segalowitz, 2010), taking evidence from research on grammatical processing. L2 cognitive fluency also requires 'flexibility in the control of linguistic attention' (Segalowitz, 2016: 9), taking evidence from recent research that shifting between different types of tasks reveal an L2-specific attention cost. Therefore, he argues, L2-specific cognitive fluency should underpin utterance fluency, since 'speaking fluidly requires shifting attention focus continuously while packaging information to make the utterance unfold properly' (Segalowitz, 2016: 11). However, both aspects, he suggests, need further research for strong empirical support. In particular, he underscores the limitations on too simplistic a view that fluency is just a question of practice. Rehearsal and

26   *Fluency from a Psycholinguistic Perspective*

practice of familiar tasks can undoubtedly lessen cognitive load and lead to speedier surface performance, for example, through the 4–3–2 activity, practising story telling in increasingly short time bursts from 4 minutes to 2 minutes (Nation, 1989; de Jong & Perfetti, 2011). However, Segalowitz suggests that utterance-level practice may not bring about qualitative restructuring in underlying cognitive processes, and so will be limited in its application to new, more creative or more taxing speaking activities (also noted by DeKeyser, 2001, 2007).

Utterance fluency in observed speech can be evaluated by temporal measures such as syllable rate, duration and rate of hesitations, filled and silent pauses. These measures are the most used in other models of speech fluency, notably Skehan (2003), Tavakoli & Skehan (2005), and Tavakoli, Nakatsuhara and Hunter (2020) (see Chapter 3). Segalowitz, however, points out that there can be a number of ways to measure utterance fluency, and debate still exists over how best to operationalise it, as discussed in the next section.

2.2.3 Problems with Current Operationalisations of Fluency

One particularly challenging area in operationalising fluency relates to pausing. It has been suggested that simply using length or number of pauses may no longer be adequate to represent the complexity of the underlying processes (e.g. Tavakoli, 2011). Instead, the location of pauses can tell us more about how the speaker is succeeding in managing to produce speech. Pausing between clauses has long been assumed to relate to 'idea boundaries' or 'topic shifts' (Raupach, 1980; Tavakoli & Skehan, 2005), representing likely moments of thinking about meaning, where the conceptualiser is engaged in checking and creating the pre-verbal message. As Raupach (1980) noted, pausing at the end of a clause or juncture only indicates the speaker wants to change or improve on their original idea, not necessarily be unsure how to construct it. Pausing mid-clause is, however, more likely derived from monitoring how the output is formulated, checking if repairs are needed, and reformulating the structure of the grammar or lexis of the desired expression. However, as noted by Skehan, Foster and Shum (2016), it remains very difficult to identify how far mid-clause pausing does indeed reflect either gaps in proficiency or lack of underlying cognitive fluency.

Segalowitz's model is also important in reinforcing the hearer's role in fluency as an interactional construct and not just a learner-internal psycholinguistic construct. L2 perceived fluency harks back to Lennon's (1990) 'broad' definition, referring to the subjective judgements by listeners of L2 speakers' oral fluency (Segalowitz, 2016).

Rather than suggesting this is disconnected from objective temporal measures, Segalowitz points to research where perceptions of fluency have been found to correlate robustly with objective measures of overall proficiency (Derwing, Rossiter, Munro & Thomson, 2004; Bosker et al., 2012; Préfontaine, Kormos & Johnson, 2016; Wang, Na & Wright, 2018), as well as with speakers' own self-ratings of fluency (Préfontaine, 2013). There is extensive research into the challenges of operationalising perceptions of fluency, including using trained raters or not (e.g. Kormos & Denés, 2004; Préfontaine, 2013). However, since such research highlights the variability within such measures of perceived fluency, Segalowitz suggests it is not appropriate to see subjective perceptions of fluency as operationally connected to cognitive and utterance fluency.

Another problematic aspect of considering utterance fluency in terms of automaticity within L2 formulation can be found in understanding variation within individuals across tasks, or in terms of development over time. Such variance suggests that different speakers have different attitudes (conscious or not) as to how they handle any possible linguistic or processing gaps when speaking in their L2. Wright (2013) tracked thirty-two upper-intermediate adult Chinese learners of English over a year's period of study in the United Kingdom and found varying levels of fluency in their L2 at both times of testing. At time one, within four weeks of arrival, some individuals spoke very fast with many pauses and repairs, others spoke slowly with few repairs – overall, these speech patterns were repeated even after a year's immersion. Compared to a test of their L1 speech, there were non-significant but marked similarities in terms of speech rate in both languages. Similarly, in studies of adult English learners of Mandarin before and after a year abroad in China (Wright & Zhang, 2014; Wright, 2018a), those who spoke slowly or using filled pauses at Time 1 also did so at Time 2 (see further detailed discussion in Chapter 7). This evidence suggests that patterns of speed, pausing and repair are intrinsic to each speaker.

2.3 Interconnectedness in the Mind/Brain

Understanding L2 fluency has, even within models such as Segalowitz's discussed above, maintained the aim to understand how the L2 speech system works in terms of the ability – or inability – to access processes and knowledge that match the automaticity and lack of conscious control found in mature L1 speech. While in such models L2 speech has often been discussed in contrast to L1 speech as lacking the relevant systems and processes, recent cognitive and neural

28   *Fluency from a Psycholinguistic Perspective*

research emphasises the many areas of overlap in processing for L1 and L2, and therefore one of the more interesting questions we now turn to is how speakers handle both languages in real-time speech (Green, 1998). As Grosjean (1982, 2008) has long pointed out, it is a false assumption to see a bilingual or L2 speaker as being two monolinguals in one person. It is thus logical to assume that at least some of the interactions will combine knowledge and processes that are shared between a speaker's various languages (Kormos, 2006; Götz, 2013), and can thus impact on fluency.

Bilingual lexical studies using techniques such as rapid naming activities (see, e.g. Costa, 2005; Kroll, Bobb & Hoshino, 2014) have consistently showed that accessing a word in one language activates related words in another language, for example, when a French speaker sees the English word 'coin', the part of the brain which knows the French word 'coin' ('corner') is also activated (Kroll et al., 2014). This semantic co-activation phenomenon has also been shown to exist when the two languages are typologically more different than French and English, even with different writing systems like Chinese and English, or if one language is spoken and the other is signed (Kroll & Bialystok, 2013). The cognitive processes by which the chosen language is maintained and the other language is inhibited in fluent speech is still not yet fully understood. Much of the work on bilingual language control has been done at word level in relation to lexical access (Kroll et al., 2014), rather than to test fluency in discourse; further research would usefully extend our understanding of control and retrieval mechanisms across both languages part of effective communicative strategies in emerging bilingual speech (Kasper & Kellerman, 1997).

As well as overlapping linguistic knowledge, the psycholinguistic processes used in speaking have been found to overlap between L1 and L2 in terms of cognitive and neural processing for language (Stowe & Sabourin, 2005; Kroll & Bialystok, 2013). Stowe and Sabourin (2005) reviewed a large number of recent neuro-imaging studies, which all consistently found evidence that the same neural areas were activated when participants at different levels of proficiency were asked to do a range of tasks, including fluency-related tasks, such as rapid naming of words in both languages (including Chinese-English learners). Current neurolinguistic research throws up as many debates and questions as any other field relevant to L2 speech fluency, but we suggest that there is a reliable basis to persist with research based on how languages complement each other, rather than reiterate models and operationalisations based on fundamental differences between an L1 and an L2. We can therefore assume there is a basis for concluding that both neural and psycholinguistic factors are part of a continuum of linguistic and cognitive processes in which L1 speech patterns could in fact be supporting rather than hampering fluency in L2 speech.

2.4 Overlap between L1 and L2 Fluency

We now turn to how the actual processes involved in speech may overlap between languages. It has been claimed that 'L2 fluency behaviour can, to a large extent, be predicted on the basis of the L1 behaviour alone' (de Jong et al., 2015: 237). This hypothesis may be seen as somewhat contentious in light of standard separate views of L1 vs. L2 performance. Having seen the evidence for the level of psycholinguistic and neural similarities between linguistic representation and areas of activation and processing between both languages, perhaps this claim is less controversial than at first sight, indicating fluency could be seen as a kind of personality 'trait' rather than a 'state' or indication of proficiency (Derwing, Munro, Thomson & Rossiter, 2009: 534). Segalowitz argued for the importance of assessing 'sources of variability that are not related specifically to the disfluencies in L2 but that characterise a person's general performance in the given testing conditions' (Segalowitz, 2010: 40). We now look at some key studies that have led the way in establishing the evidence of L1 influence on L2 speech and setting out clear implications for considering L1 fluency when assessing L2 speaking performance.

In early work comparing L1 and L2 speech, Raupach (1980) noted that common phenomena assumed to indicate disfluencies in L2 speech were in fact often found in fluent L1 speech – where speakers rated as highly competent may employ filled and unfilled pauses and repairs as part of effective communication. He highlighted the likely trait links between L1 and L2, particularly in pausing patterns or dysfluencies, which were found to be systematically similar between the two languages. Clark's theory of speech performance (Clark & Fox Tree, 2002) highlights, for example, that filled pauses ('uh', 'um') are used in a consistent way (though varying in usage between individuals) as a signal for maintaining the floor, indicating the speaker's 'ongoing performance' (Clark & Fox Tree, 2002: 103).

However, evidence is not consistent with such trait-like similarities in all studies. Riazantseva (2001) looked in intermediate/upper-level Russian learners of English, in view of a consistent 'language-specific' (p. 522) pattern of longer pauses in her L1 Russian speakers. She found an effect of longer L1-Russian pauses in the intermediate-level speakers of English, though less effect in the more advanced learners,

30   *Fluency from a Psycholinguistic Perspective*

thus indicating a possibility that pausing is indeed simply a manifestation of proficiency level.

Given the discrepancy between such evidence for L1 effects on L2 fluency when limited to pausing, it is clearly important to include a greater range of L1s and a greater range of fluency measures. In a ground-breaking longitudinal study of fluency development, Derwing et al. (2009) compared two long-term resident L2 communities in Canada – one group of Slavic and another group of Mandarin speakers of English, assessed over a two-year period. The two groups performed the same narrative task in both L1 and L2, with the L2 performance measured two months after from the L1 performance to avoid any practice effects. The speakers' performance was measured by a battery of standard fluency measures, including raters' perceptions of fluency, as well as temporal measures such as speech rate, length of run, number and length of pauses (see Chapter 3 in this volume for more discussion on types of fluency measures). Derwing et al. (2009) found that there was a significant correlation between the L1 and L2 behaviour on measures both of production (speech rate and pruned syllables per second) and silence (number of pauses per second). Unlike Riazantseva's study, they found no change in the Slavic speakers' pauses in L2 English over the two-year period. For the Mandarin speakers, it seemed that those who were most fluent in their L1 also showed most improvement in the L2 over the period. Interestingly, for both groups, fluency ratings also correlated with the temporal measures, suggesting that qualitative perceptions of competent speech can accept a degree of pausing, repair and so on, just as is found in L1 fluent speech. Derwing et al. (2009) thus conclude there is a strong basis to assume that L2 fluency relies on L1 performance, even when measured longitudinally.

De Jong et al. (2015) adopted a broader experimental approach to comparing L1 and L2 fluency in their study of fifty-one Turkish and Dutch learners of English. They included a greater range of tasks (all were descriptive monologues, but varied by degree of complexity, formality and discourse type) and used three dimensions of fluency: speed fluency (syllable duration), breakdown fluency and repair fluency. All participants were less fluent in absolute terms across all three types of task and across all fluency dimensions in the L2 than the L1. However, there was a high degree of variability within each group, showing that there were more and less fluent speakers even in the L1. Allied to this, they found a consistent trend of positive correlations between the majority of the L1 and L2 measures, leading them to conclude that in general, 'the more fluently one speaks in the L1 with respect to one aspect, the more fluently one also tends to speak with

2.5 Fluency & Relationship to Linguistic Repertoire 31

respect to another aspect' (p. 232). Their study is also interesting in that this L1–L2 fluency connection was found across the different task types, suggesting that even non-fluent L2 speakers may be able to draw effectively on L1 discourse skills in different social contexts, for example, when requiring more complex, formal or persuasive types of talk.

De Jong has also extended our understanding of how L1 and L2 systems may overlap at various stages of the speech process. One recent study (Felker, Klockmann & de Jong, 2019) looks at whether conceptual planning affects L1 and L2 speech performance differently. Simple network connections (i.e. describing an object with one connection to another) were faster in the L1, whereas complex network connections, where multiple choices were randomly generated, slowed both L1 and L2 similarly, suggesting that even pre-verbal planning stages can draw on common cognitive resources (Felker et al., 2019). Having seen how L1 and L2 processes may interact to support or affect L2 fluency performance, we now turn to explore in more depth how access to underlying knowledge or repertoire can affect fluency.

2.5 Fluency and Relationship to Underlying Linguistic Repertoire

Chapter 1 discussed how fluency can interact with accuracy, complexity and lexis (CALF). Many studies into L2 fluency and breakdown, particularly at formulation level, have highlighted the significance of L2 accuracy and complexity as a bottleneck for formulation (e.g. Slabakova, 2012; Wright, 2013). As the store of implicit grammatical knowledge builds up, it can be assumed that accurate and more complex speech can be formulated more automatically. But research into L1 effects on L2 speech shows that accuracy and complexity may not necessarily act as such bottlenecks when viewed through the lens of individual preferences for speech speed and repair styles, or in relation to task effects, as will be seen in Chapter 4. However, work on how learners can access the lexicon in real-time speech, particularly understanding the use of chunked phrases, is essential to understanding how speech fluency develops.

The research on chunked phrases or formulaic sequences in L1 and L2 speech has been very influential in the past thirty years or so (e.g. Pawley & Syder, 1983, 2000; Schmidt, 1992; Wray, 2002; Götz, 2013; Myles & Cordier, 2017). As demonstrated in Chapter 1 and drawing on Tavakoli and Uchihara's (2020) findings, we now know how much of everyday speech uses pre-set sequences, collocations and phrases – to the extent that they are, effectively, seen as single lexical

32   Fluency from a Psycholinguistic Perspective

items, and are assumed to be retrieved automatically, similarly to a single word from the linguistic store. Many types of discourse, such as persuasive language in marketing or political argumentation, use formulaic sequences in the sense of fixed 'communication routines' (Berger, 2014: 19). We may be familiar with the kind of clichéd utterances which can be mocked in, for example, management discourse or sports commentaries (Berger, 2014). But even without using clichés, there is no doubt that we rely on many set 'multiword sequences' as we speak (Götz, 2013). The assumption is that many set forms are encountered in early acquisition and routinised in adult speech as lexical chunks. They are 'retrieved whole from memory' (Wray, 2002: 9) at the time of use; they require little or no attention or cognitive effort and can thus be used to lengthen the utterance without extra processing cost. More reliably, they reduce the need for pausing to construct the utterance word by word in real time. Research has robustly shown that 'the higher the number of prefabricated units in speech is, the fewer pauses and hesitations occur' (Götz, 2013: 27).

The benefit for fluent speakers in knowing and using chunks is clear. However, what a chunk actually is in L1 or L2 and how they are developed to be used suitably in different discourse settings remain poorly understood (Wray, 2002; Wray & Fitzpatrick, 2008; Wood, 2010; Götz, 2013). Formulaic language or chunks have been claimed to create an effective basis for development of L2 communicative ability or fluency since the time of audio-lingual drilling (Wray & Fitzpatrick, 2008). However, if the chunk is simply presented and memorised in one set construction or form, it can be mislearned or misused (Götz, 2013), making it extremely difficult to be adjusted by the individual to any differences required, for example, changing reference from singular to plural, or present to past (Myles, 2004).

The relationship between learned chunks and developing fluency in L2 speech is thus likely to be highly complex but will draw in varying ways on linguistic knowledge and cognitive processes and can also help improve speech effectiveness if chunks are appropriately used at pragmatic or discourse level (Götz, 2013). Greater naturalistic exposure to the target language, away from classroom drills, can help the individual build their own repertoire of sequences. In one recent study, Cordier (2013) examined a group of L2 French speakers before and after a period of a year's study abroad in France. She found they created their own personalised chunks – idiolectal sequences. Some of these chunks reflected standard instructed constructions, but some of them were more variable – they may have originally been not quite target-like in form, or they reflected the speakers' own personal preferences for how meaning could be conceptualised and phrased. Cordier found such idiolectal sequences to be very consistent over the year's immersion, again suggesting that the speakers' preferences for using such chunks resisted exposure to the target language and interaction with target language speakers, who would not necessarily have recognised these sequences.

A multitude of research perspectives seem to suggest that fluency does not operate in isolation. An individual's fluency patterns will be inherently based on many factors. What is sometimes assessed as disfluency in L2 research or in the classroom – pausing, slowing down, repairing or using non-standard chunks – may in fact be a demonstration of intrinsic speech strategies used for speech in either language, rather than a sign of a lack of L2 proficiency. The question then emerges how far such strategies can be understood as being subconscious, reflecting internal general cognitive capacities, such as working memory and processing speed, or how far they are conscious, representing choices and attitudes in response to an external social setting. We must therefore understand how the individual L2 speaker develops and uses such strategies, rather than assume one model of speech development fits all. In the next section, we turn to research that looks at such individual differences in terms of internal and external factors affecting speech.

2.6 Why Individual Differences Matter

This section looks at some of the most influential current research into how individual differences (e.g. psycho-social factors) are involved in speech production, with particular relevance to our focus on a socio-cognitive perspective on L2 fluency. We focus first on working memory and how individual differences in constraints on the storage/processing trade-off may affect speech, then on personality trait factors – including the popular assumption that extraverts are more fluent. We put such research into the context of motivation and willingness to communicate. We finish with how speakers handle the social demands of interacting, including the capacity to create the appearance of fluency.

As noted earlier, one of the factors most affecting the speech model's efficiency is assumed to be the cognitive balance between automatic processes of formulation and more deliberative aspects of creating and checking the speech production – which requires different aspects of working memory to handle the complex demands involved (Levelt, 1989; Temple, 1997). If we consider that individuals vary in their working memory capacities (Baddeley, 2007), we can predict that

34   *Fluency from a Psycholinguistic Perspective*

speech fluency will also vary according to working memory capacity (Daneman & Green, 1986; Daneman, 1991). In the speech models referred to earlier (such as Levelt's), the main load on working memory comes at the conceptualiser and monitoring phases to check meaning is clear and comprehensible (Daneman & Green, 1986; Levelt, 1989). We can assume that for many L2 speakers monitoring may be required both for meaning and form and therefore that working memory may be needed at the formulation stage as well (de Bot, 1992; Kormos, 2006; Wright, 2010) – i.e. 'at virtually every stage' of the speech cycle (Temple, 1997: 87). A growing body of research has begun to test the assumption that greater working memory capacity may foster speech performance in terms of fluency, accuracy, complexity, lexical density and so on, but findings are so far rather mixed (Fortkamp, 1999; Mizera, 2006). However, not much research has been done on the interface between L1 and L2 speech with regard to working memory nor on the possible effect of working memory on speech development.

As mentioned briefly earlier, Wright (2010, 2013) sought to address some of these issues by testing working memory in both L1 and L2 using a battery of working memory tasks (Digits Back and Story Recall) among a group of thirty-two Chinese learners of English resident for a year in the United Kingdom. Working memory scores using purely aural/oral mode were tested at the start and end of the year's immersion and then compared to an oral proficiency task in the L2 (producing questions to complete a picture). For the Digits Back span task, speakers heard sequences of numbers starting with sets of 3 digits, then 4, and so on, and were asked to repeat them in reverse order; for the story recall task, speakers heard a simple narrative lasting no more than fifty seconds (in the L1) or thirty seconds (in the L2), and were asked to repeat them using as far as possible the same words and phrases. Similar to other cross-linguistic comparisons of working memory (Osaka & Osaka, 1992), scores in Wright's cohort were significantly similar across languages ($p < .05$) – i.e. high scorers in the L1 scored highly in the L2, although L2 scores were in absolute terms lower than the L1 scores. As noted above, when the L1 and L2 speaking tasks were compared in terms of speech rate and repairs, again the speech rate was comparable (though non-significant statistically), suggesting that working memory capacity is non-language specific and in general supports speech production at a cognitive, rather than linguistic, level. Interestingly, working memory scores on the story task in the L1 were found to be the best predictor of L2 improvement on the oral question production task, at least in terms of degree of improvement in error-free speech. These results indicate

2.6 Why Individual Differences Matter 35

that the cognitive support of greater working memory may also facilitate L2 speech development.

By contrast, Weissheimer and Mota (2009) explored the question of working memory and speech development with a group of thirty-two adult Brazilian learners of English over a shorter period of eight weeks in an instructed foreign-language classroom setting. Participants took a speaking span test and were then divided into a high or low working memory group. Participants were then asked to create a narrative, using visual picture cues; this was untimed but generally around one minute, and narratives were measured for fluency (in terms of speech rate) twice, at the start and end of the eight-week period. Weissheimer and Mota failed to find clear evidence of working memory scores as a predictor of fluency gains over the period. While this could be due to the short time frame, it leaves the question open as to whether 'working memory is an efficient predictor of L2 speech performance' (2009: 109). Thus, the role of working memory within increasing automatisation of speech processes remains an area to be further explored.

Turning now to personality-focused research, we mentioned at the beginning of the chapter that it is possible to see fluency as a trait, rather than a state, and in doing so, we can incorporate both cognitive and personality dimensions as influencing individual speech patterns. One way to investigate this has been pursued in terms of extraversion/ introversion, led by Dewaele and colleagues over the past two decades. Dewaele and Furnham (2000) note that psychologists have found a link among personality, cognition and speech, in that extraverts are deemed to have higher short-term memory than introverts, tend to have lower social anxiety linked to communication, and lower language anxiety in terms of willingness to communicate in a foreign language particularly when handling different settings such as formal or informal settings (see also Chapters 6 and 7 for a discussion of the context of communication). They assume that personality traits such as extraversion are language-independent, and therefore extraverts should behave differently in tests of fluency regardless of language proficiency. To test these claims in relation to L2 speech performance, Dewaele and Furnham studied twenty-five Flemish adult classroom-learners of French, gathering speech data comparing a formal setting (stressed, exam-style) and informal setting (neutral general conversation). The data were measured for speech rate and filled pauses ('er') and complexity in terms of length of utterance among other factors and were then correlated with extraversion scores from a standard personality questionnaire. They found that the formality of the situation had 'the strongest effect on speech production'

36   *Fluency from a Psycholinguistic Perspective*

(Dewaele & Furnham, 2000: 363) across most of the variables they studied, especially speech rate, repeated filled pauses and utterance length, suggesting that stress combined with a high load on working memory can break the fluency of speech production. The limitation of this study is that it did not compare similar performance in L1; thus, this remains to be addressed by future research.

Linked to personality-related factors affecting fluency, it has long been assumed that attitudes, strategies and motivation may have a facilitating effect on oral proficiency in performance (e.g. Horwitz, Horwitz & Cope, 1986; Oxford, 1990; Cohen & Macaro, 2007; Dörnyei & Ushioda, 2013). Here, we discuss one particular aspect of motivation as willingness to engage in communication (MacIntyre, Clément, Dörnyei & Noels, 1998; MacIntyre & Doucette, 2010). It is assumed that the socio-affective aspect of willingness to engage and interact is connected to the underlying drivers of cognitive fluency (Segalowitz, 2010), as well as being bound up in issues to do with identity as a successful L2 speaker (Moyer, 2004; Norton, 2013; Magne et al., 2019) – these factors are thus highly relevant to our multiperspective approach to fluency development in social contexts.

MacIntyre and Doucette (2010) note that willingness to interact is a sign of communicative competence that may transfer from mother tongue to L2, rather than simply the choice of whether or not to use an L2 in a specific context. Not much research has examined fluency specifically within the context of willingness to speak, particularly in comparing L1 and L2, making this an area that requires considerable further investigation. However, there is a line of research which sheds some light on a plausible psychological underlay between L1 and L2 willingness to communicate and which would serve as a way forward for future research into the fluency/willingness to communicate interface. MacIntyre and Doucette (2010) look at willingness to communicate from the perspective of Kuhl's (1994) Action Control model – in this model, an individual's action (such as speaking) is seen as the 'tendency to approach or avoid a goal' (MacIntyre & Doucette, 2010: 163). The three factors inhibiting that intention, or action control, are hesitation, preoccupation and volatility. Hesitation can be seen as a kind of vacillation over the decision-making process; preoccupation is based on the extent to which previous experience, perception of risk or other unpleasant aspect, is attached to the potential behaviour, thus stopping the intent from becoming action; volatility refers to the capacity to sustain or abandon the intended behaviour. MacIntyre and Doucette's (2010) study of 238 English-speaking high-school students of French examined the students' action control self-ratings on the three dimensions of hesitation, preoccupation and volatility,

2.7 Fluency Strategies: The Juggling Act 37

and their perceived communication competence in both languages, including willingness to communicate and anxiety about speaking. They then compared these scores with students' self-ratings for speaking in and out of the classroom in L2 French. They found strong significant correlations between willingness to communicate and communication competence in both L1 and L2. In addition, the results suggested that anxiety in speaking in either language associated strongly with hesitation, as well as with lower perceived communication competence in either language. This study provides a good evidence base for the intuition that good communication strategies, for example, in managing turn-taking and handling different types of speaking situations, should reduce anxiety or hesitation in handling communication, and should be incorporated into models of L2 communication in general, and for considering root causes of speech fluency specifically.

Further research has also identified that speaker stance can play a role in engaging in interaction – if speakers prefer a 'safer' speaker stance (Faulkner, Littleton & Woodhead, 2013), they may avoid risks, be self-oriented rather than other-oriented in paying attention to their interlocutor (Wang, Bristol, Mowen & Chakraborty, 2000) or find it difficult to take the initiative in constructing a meaningful effective dialogue. In relation to this, they may struggle to develop meaning-focused communicative strategies, needed for maintaining fluency and interaction (Nakatani, 2006; Wright et al., forthcoming). Wright et al. (forthcoming) conducted longitudinal studies over both short-term (four week) and longer-term (nine month) English Academic (EAP) language programmes in the United Kingdom. The findings showed that students struggled to develop strategies designed to foster fluent interaction, including being able to adjust their message if not easily understood, listening well, being confident in taking risks even if they were not sure of being accurate, and keeping the flow of conversation going. The strategy patterns suggested that students relied more on a 'transmission' approach to speech (Seedhouse, 2013), in which they preferred being able to prepare their own ideas in L1 and translating using familiar words and phrases, relying on being a 'safer speaker', rather than maintaining the conversation, being 'other-oriented' and taking risks.

2.7 Fluency Strategies: The Juggling Act

Connected to the notion that fluent speakers require good communication competence, we finish with a brief look at speakers who develop effective strategies to 'appear' fluent, particularly as this

38 Fluency from a Psycholinguistic Perspective

informs our emphasis throughout this volume on the social dimensions of fluency, i.e. the ability to handle different discourse contexts. Ejzenberg (2000) discusses speaking as a 'juggling act' (p. 288) because speech is not just about using linguistic elements such as more words or faster speech, but rhythm and effectiveness also count in projecting 'an image of fluency' (ibid) to a speaker's audience. Ejzenberg investigated a range of fluency measures in an in-depth study of forty-six learners of L2 English and highlights several strategies used by the most fluent speakers that were not specifically due to L2 proficiency but more about the way they handled the discourse. One strategy was the ability to interact with an interlocutor well – such as repeating words and phrases to 'capitalise' (Ejzenberg, 2000: 293) on these cues to help enrich their own linguistic resources. Another strategy was higher use of repetition and formulaic speech, noted by Tannen (1984) as a way of facilitating fluent language, and interpreted by Ejzenberg as a means of connecting and reinforcing the discourse thread, to keep the dialogue moving forward. In this way, successful speakers could cover over underlying gaps in knowledge which could have involved 'losing face' (ibid: 203) with the interlocutor. The limitation of this study is that the speakers' L1 speech patterns were not considered alongside their L2 performance, but Ejzenberg sees such strategies as individually and discourse-based rather than specific to the knowledge or use of the L2. She concludes that it is essential to consider fluency less as a context-dependent phenomenon and more in terms of the speaker's ability to convey an image of ease to their interlocutor. Thus, fluency seems to belong to the realms of sociolinguistic and discourse competence as much as to psycholinguistic competence.

But not all speakers may wish to adapt to L2 sociolinguistic norms, of course. There is an extensive literature on L2 identity, relating to issues of integration and acculturation (Schumann, 1986; Moyer, 2004; Norton, 2013), often with highly emotional factors involved. The main issues and detailed overview of this research are beyond the scope of this volume. However, it is helpful to mention some key findings briefly to grasp the complex balance between an emerging L2 speaker's desire to sound fluent, particularly in managing smooth articulation and accent, and wanting to keep a unique, even non-proficient, identity. Moyer's (2004) study of learners of German and their experiences in developing more or less target-like pronunciation and fluency highlights the multiple connections between the many linguistic, contextual and emotional/affective factors involved. She highlights the dynamic aspect of a speaker's wish to sound 'more' or 'less' foreign in different contexts, depending often on who they are speaking with or what they are speaking about. The main point of this important study is that even something as apparently linguistically clear and measurable as target-like pronunciation or speech rate can be individually controlled, even if not always systematically. Taken overall, these studies suggest it is important to understand that psychosocial impact on fluency development may be related to longer-term states and traits, not just short-term pressures on performance arising from social context and discourse demand.

2.8 Perceptions of Fluency

Another aspect of fluency which is inevitably entangled with internal and external factors affecting performance is how fluency is perceived. In previous sections, we have looked at cognitive and psycho-social aspects affecting a learner's development of fluency. We finish this chapter by considering some recent research taking forward Segalowitz's third element of fluency, that of perceptions of fluency; we argue that fluency perception needs to be reconsidered in a new emerging perspective of fluency in terms of communicative adequacy (addressed in our final chapter).

As noted above, for holistic and broad senses of fluency (Lennon, 1990), the way in which listeners perceive speech is key to a full understanding of the interactive success of fluent speech. This matters for the L2 learner, who is keen to be fluent enough to be understood in the target language environment, or is working hard to get a good score on an oral assessment. Given the specialisation in fluency research within learner-internal cognitive domains of narrow, temporal fluency, the listener has been to some extent seen as irrelevant, or at least part of a separate operationalisation of fluency. However, within our more unified socio-cognitive take on fluency, we believe it is essential to connect research into how fluency is perceived with research into how fluency is achieved, not least as a way of triangulating whether subjective listener perceptions match objective temporal and empirical cognitive measures (e.g. Ejzenberg, 2000; Freed, 2000; Kim et al., 2015; Wang et al., 2018). Segalowitz (2010: 48) defines perceived fluency as the 'inferences listeners make about a speaker's cognitive fluency based on their perception of utterance fluency'. Measuring such listeners' inferences is often done using quantitative rating scales asking for a numerical judgement on a scale from non-fluent to fluent; other studies may ask for qualitative comments on what affected their judgement. Studies also may ask non-expert raters for judgements, to compare to more expert raters, and find that untrained raters can provide rich insights into specific elements of

40   *Fluency from a Psycholinguistic Perspective*

fluency, whether weighed against grammatical accuracy, or against other factors (e.g. Freed, 2000; Préfontaine & Kormos, 2016; Dijum, Schoonen & Hulstijn, 2018). Dijum et al. (2018) studied ratings of exam performance in L2 Dutch and found that non-trained raters tended focused on fluency, while linguistically trained raters were relatively more affected by morpho-syntactic accuracy in overall judgements of fluency. Even untrained raters can provide very rich and specific insights into different elements of fluency – Freed (2000) combined quantitative and qualitative listener ratings of improvements of fluency in French in intermediate-level learners before and after a period of study abroad. Raters were given specific temporal features relating to fluidity, such as speech rate, unfilled and filled pauses, length of run, and repairs, and were asked to rank them by level of importance in reaching their judgement. While more than half of the raters identified speech rate as crucial to improved fluency, others did not mention such fluidity phenomena, highlighting instead better grammar and vocabulary, accent, confidence or even tone of voice. Thus, L2 fluency ratings can clearly be influenced by a 'far broader' (Freed, 2000: 262) set of phenomena than the usual narrow temporal measures.

Following up on this study, Préfontaine and Kormos (2016) aimed to uncover the range of linguistic processing involved when listeners evaluate L2 speech as if 'in the real world' (p. 159). Unlike Freed's study, they gave no prior list of factors to consider, but analysed the raters' comments and reactions to a heterogenous group of L2 learners of French (n = 40), narrating three different types of stories. Clear themes emerging from the raters' analyses highlighted some elements of temporal fluidity, in that pausing or some kind temporary interruption of the stream was identified by all raters as a frequent marker of disfluency, but overall their main comment related to ease and efficiency (i.e. the sense in which the speech seemed effortless), while self-correction or amount of repair was mentioned the least. Good linguistic knowledge, particularly vocabulary, was rated similarly or more importantly than speed. Préfontaine and Kormos particularly note that hesitation should not necessarily indicate disfluency – indeed one rater notes of a speaker, "His hesitations seem normal because francophones use the same filler trick" (p. 161). Confidence was also highlighted, along with appropriate rhythm, so that even a very accurate and temporally fluent speaker was rated down for speaking in 'the music of the English language' (p. 162). Clearly it is not enough to teach learners simply to produce utterances encoded correctly and efficiently, but for effective communication they need also to interact with appropriate prosodic style and grasp of appropriate intonational cues (Wennerstrom, 2000).

2.9 Conclusions

This chapter has explained some of the key elements of cognitive perspectives on L2 fluency, how current models operationalise different aspects of the speech production process, and the implications for understanding fluency as a set of automatised procedural skills. Nevertheless, as set out by Segalowitz (2010, 2016), it is crucial to understand how other contextual factors impact on fluency. Comparing a fluent L1 with a disfluent L2 needs to be done with care, to avoid misunderstanding the extent to which L1 and L2 speech fluency are related. Research has revealed ways in which linguistic knowledge and processing overlap across L1 and the L2, including how speech patterns vary among individuals and can carry over from L1 speech into L2 speech. Psycho-social research on individual differences and their effect on L2 speech fluency has emphasised the need to take into account issues such as working memory capacity, extraversion and motivational factors, including willingness to communicate in L1 and L2. L2 users have been shown to retain a dynamic capacity to vary their speech depending on who they are talking to, what they are talking about, how they feel or what are the task demands. We also have seen how fluency is a two-way process, in which perceptions of fluency by the listener can also be highly variable, for example, depending on the context, or on the experience of the listener.

Our understanding and explanations of L2 fluency performance and development must therefore be able to account for such differences, even in cognitive learner-internal definitions of fluency. We believe that reliability, validity and clear operationalisation must factor in a degree of variability, not just in linguistic temporal terms, but also social and emotional context, interlocutor and task. Instead of a comparative deficit view of L2 speech, an approach should be adopted that all L2 users at any stage of development will rely on their L1 knowledge about communication, which can foster fluency, rather than hamper it. Likewise, fluency in performance or in development must be seen as a separate phenomenon from specific levels of L2 linguistic knowledge or proficiency (Ejzenberg, 2000). In this sense, we stress the value of seeing all L2 learners as bilingual multicompetent users along a continuum (Cook, 2002), rather than trying to pin down a level of proficiency which would distinguish the L1 from the bilingual (de Bot & Jaensch, 2015). We note the value of Selinker's (1972) classic definition of interlanguage to account for systematic and testable stages of linguistic development and suggest that there may be value in the notion of 'interfluency', as a way of avoiding a binary distinction between fluent or disfluent, to include a more interconnected

42 *Fluency from a Psycholinguistic Perspective*

approach between L1 and L2 fluency, and to allow for more systematic understanding of how fluency varies across contexts and functions.

There are, however, many gaps limiting the application of a rigorous 'interfluency' approach to evaluating fluency development. Much of the research covered above does not systematically relate the various linguistic, cognitive, psycho-social and pragmatic factors involved in comparisons of individuals' L1 and L2 speech practices. In particular, very little attention is paid to the social and communicative factors that contribute to fluency when comparing L1 and L2 speech. These gaps are especially relevant for teachers and learners who are keen to understand what factors may reliably improve L2 speech fluency development. Our next chapter thus addresses how fluency is measured and the challenges we find in trying to establish the most reliable operationalisations of fluency in different social or communicative contexts.

3 *Measuring Fluency*

In previous chapters, we discussed the importance of fluency in the second language (L2) processing and production and explained the underlying principles and concepts that inform theoretical perspectives in L2 oral fluency. These theoretical perspectives and principles will inform researchers' decisions about which measures of fluency they need to use in their work. Whether one should use a measure of speed, breakdown, repair or whether they need other measures will certainly depend on their research aims and questions. Whatever aims researchers pursue in their work, they are likely to use a range of different measures to investigate fluency.

A lack of agreement about what measures best characterise fluency is not new in language studies. Fluency has historically been operationalised variedly by different disciplines, different research groups and different individual researchers. The measures used range from temporal features of speech such as speech rate and frequency of pauses to prosodic features of speech such as intonation and stress patterns and sociolinguistic features of turn-taking and degree of dominance in a conversation. Although the diversity of fluency measures used in different studies is one of the intriguing characteristics of fluency research (Lennon, 1990; Koponen & Riggenbach, 2000; Skehan, 2003; de Jong, Groenhout, Schoonen & Hulstijn, 2015), it can also create problems when results of the different studies are compared, or when understanding and interpreting conflicting results act as a barrier to the development of research in these disciplines.

The purpose of this chapter is not to make recommendations about which measures should or should not be used. In effect, multiple measures can have their uses depending on specific research purposes and questions. Knowing the value of each type of measure is, however, essential to improve the current risk of non-comparability. Therefore, the current chapter aims to provide an overview of utterance fluency measures used in L2 fluency studies and to highlight the complexities

44   *Measuring Fluency*

involved in measuring L2 fluency. By providing a synthesis of the most common ways of operationalising and measuring fluency, this chapter acts as the technical heart of the book offering a historical overview of the measurement of fluency, and the changes that have occurred in its operationalisation and measurement over time. After providing a historical perspective to the measurement of fluency, we will present a summary of the most frequently used fluency features in second language acquisition (SLA) studies, and conclude by offering a list of measures that have been suggested as more reliable representatives of utterance fluency.

3.1 A Historical Perspective to Measuring Fluency

3.1.1 Influence from Other Disciplines

The earliest studies reporting measurement of fluency in L2 research go back to the 1980s (Brumfit, 1984; Mohle, 1984). These studies were drawn on the analysis of fluency in first language (L1) and often referred to native speaker fluency as the norm against which L2 fluency was discussed (e.g. Fillmore, 1979). The existing evidence suggests that the earlier methods of measuring L2 fluency, both subjectively and objectively, relied at least to some extent on the development of fluency research in other disciplines interested in L1 fluency. One such discipline has been speech-language pathology, in which assessment of speech fluency, e.g. for diagnosing aphasia, was based on examiners' judgment of the patient's spontaneous speaking performance. These subjective judgments, based on pathologists listening to the patient's speech, informed their decision about whether the patient was *fluent* or *non-fluent* (in applied linguistics' terms *disfluent*). Objective measures for fluency were also common in these other disciplines. In such cases, pathologists considered a range of objective speech features such as 'speech rate, length of utterance, prosody, articulation ability and word-finding difficulty' (Marshall, 2000: 78). For speed, the number of words per minute informed decisions about whether a patient was aphasic or not since aphasic patients are reported to produce fewer words per minute. Given the clinical nature of the work, threshold levels had been set to inform the pathologist's decisions. A fluent speaker, e.g. was expected to produce about 130 words per minute, whereas an aphasic patient could produce fewer than 30 words per minute (Prins, Snow & Wagenaar, 1978). In terms of mean length of utterance, Prins et al. (1978) suggested that non-fluent patients had a mean length of utterance of 3.51 words, whereas fluent patients' mean length of run was 10.26 words per uninterrupted string of speech.

3.1 A Historical Perspective to Measuring Fluency   45

In the next section, we will discuss a more current perspective to measuring fluency in SLA. However, before that, it is necessary to highlight some important differences between measurement of fluency in these earlier clinical language studies and those currently used in SLA. While in clinical studies measurements were based on a count of words, in SLA syllable counts are used instead since words are complex constructs that are difficult to define and agree about in different languages. For example, in an agglutinative language like Turkish or Finnish, a word can accept several affixes and prefixes to convey different morphological and syntactic information. Another problem is that syllable insertion or deletion in words, common among second-language speakers, will have an impact on the speed with which they speak. Therefore, it seems more systematic to use number of syllables than words in measuring speed. The other key difference is that, given the importance of making a medical diagnosis, clinicians had to put thresholds for healthy and unhealthy patients. In most SLA studies, such thresholds do and of course, should not exist. As discussed earlier, native speaker norms provide the baseline for the measurement of fluency in clinical studies. In more recent accounts of SLA, however, proficient L2 speakers, rather than native speakers, are considered as the baseline norm.

Another discipline influencing the measurement of fluency has been the field of language testing. As will be discussed in detail in Chapter 6, for a long time international test providers have considered fluency as one of the key aspects of the speaking construct. In this sense, fluency often represents a subjective sense of the speaker's overall fluidity. Although assessment practises vary widely among different test providers, fluency is considered as a feature of delivery, coherence or communicative ability, and therefore, it is often assessed subjectively by the examiners and raters using rating scales and rating descriptors. Despite its subjective nature, language testing organisations have tried to assess fluency more objectively by having two or more raters, providing ongoing training to the examiners and raters, thereby, carefully defining and discussing fluency descriptors and using automated assessment technology. These points will be discussed in further detail in Chapter 6. For our discussion about the measurement of fluency, however, it is important to highlight that the language testing discipline has provided a new perspective to the measurement of fluency, i.e. how fluency is perceived by trained professionals, and what principles and assumptions inform their subjective assessment of fluency. To sum up, the measurement of fluency has been influenced by work conducted in other neighbouring disciplines such as clinical language sciences and professional language testing. As will be

46   *Measuring Fluency*

discussed in this chapter and the rest of the book, however, the important change in the measurement of fluency would emerge as a result of interdisciplinary research in this area (e.g. SLA and language testing).

3.1.2 Measuring Fluency in Second Language Studies

One of the first summaries of measurement of fluency in L2 studies is that of Oppenheim (2000: 220), providing a list of five features that are considered as criteria for native-like fluency of American English. These features were the *rate of delivery* of 150–200 words per minute, *pauses of less than half a second* between stretches of talk, *stretches of talk between four and ten words*, *a jump-up step-down intonation pattern* and *stressed time delivery*. According to Oppenheim, these features are proposed by different researchers as criteria for fluent and native-like performance in American English. Oppenheim (2000) further concluded that fluent speakers who had lived abroad spoke more and at a faster rate, had longer speech runs, produced fewer silent and non-lexically filled pauses, fewer clusters of disfluent speech (i.e. filled pauses in combination with other disfluency markers such as repairs) and more false starts and reformulations to change the linguistic expressions that do not work. Oppenheim's (2000) findings were then the starting point for many studies interested in L2 fluency.

Among L2 studies, Lennon's (1990) study is considered as a milestone in conceptualising and measuring fluency. In his seminal work, Lennon (1990) problematised the use of fluency in its broad and narrow sense and its inconsistent measurement across different studies. Calling for a more objective and systematic approach to measuring fluency to be used by language teachers and testers, he argued that:

> It would be advantageous if we could assemble a set of variables that functioned as good indicators of what expert judges, such as experienced native-speaker English as a Foreign Language (EFL) teachers, are reacting to when subjectively assessing fluency. This would advance our knowledge of what constitutes fluency and especially what makes for perceived fluency differences among learners and how an individual learner improves in fluency over time.
>
> Lennon (1990: 387)

In addition to highlighting the relationship between perceived fluency and measures that can reflect it, Lennon contended that perceived fluency is rather subjective, and what was needed in the field was objective measures that reflect speakers' fluency rather than listeners' perceptions of it. Drawing on Mohle (1984), Lennon argued that assessment of learner fluency should be based on a variety of temporal

3.1 A Historical Perspective to Measuring Fluency   47

measures, e.g. speech rate, length of run and number and positioning of silent pauses. He also argued that the frequency and distribution of such temporal measures can distinguish between L2 and native speakers' performances. Interestingly, Lennon (1990) also asked for a distinction to be made between lexical and syntactic fluency, i.e. whether pauses are made because of lexical retrieval or because of syntactic planning, which has not been addressed by researchers so far. Working with a small sample of four L2 learners who developed their proficiency while living abroad, Lennon proposed the following measures as reliable representations of fluency. The following measures will be discussed in further detail later in this chapter:

- words per minute (both pruned and unpruned)
- repetition per T-Unit
- self-corrections per T-Unit
- filled pauses per T-Unit
- percentage of repetitions and self-corrections
- percentage of unfilled pause time of total speaking time
- percentage of filled pause time of total speaking time
- mean length of speech 'runs' between pauses (in words)
- percentage of T-Units followed by pauses (filled and unfilled)
- percentage of total pause time at T-Unit boundaries
- mean pause time at T-Unit boundaries.

Following Lennon (1990), several researchers worked on measurement of fluency to streamline the rationale for using fluency measures (e.g. Foster & Skehan, 1996; Freed, 2000; Freed, Segalowitz & Dewey, 2004; Tavakoli & Skehan, 2005; Foster & Tavakoli, 2009). As a result of such attempts, an influential perspective emerged from Skehan's (2003) and Tavakoli and Skehan (2005) suggesting that fluency should be evaluated in terms of three groups of measures that best characterise fluency level: (a) speed fluency, i.e. measures that characterise the flow and continuity of speech, (b) breakdown fluency, i.e. measures that show pauses and silences that break down the flow of speech and (c) repair fluency, i.e. measures that reflect monitoring and repair processes such as hesitations, repetitions and reformulations that are used to repair speech during the production process. The introduction of this triadic perspective is perceived as a valuable framework that lends itself well towards measuring fluency and is treated as a fresh start in the measurement of fluency in L2 studies. Since 2003 when this framework was introduced, a large number of researchers have adopted it while analysing fluency, providing evidence that the framework can potentially help develop a better understanding of the relationship between fluency and L2 speech

48   *Measuring Fluency*

production. Skehan's triadic framework will be discussed in further detail below.

3.2 Recent Developments in Measuring Fluency

In line with Skehan's framework discussed above, L2 fluency research is now adopting a more systematic approach to measuring fluency. While the new perspective towards measuring fluency is based on solid research evidence emerging over the past decades, it would be unrealistic to claim that the measurement of L2 fluency is now totally systematic. As we will see in the discussion below, there are still many aspects of fluency measurements that need improvement. Before discussing the specific measures that are used to examine different aspects of fluency, however, we will provide a summary of the major changes L2 fluency research has witnessed in the past two decades. As discussed earlier, one of the major shifts has been awareness about the need to measure fluency along the three dimensions of speed, breakdown and repair.

One of the changes we have witnessed in measuring fluency is a distinction between 'pure' and 'composite' measures. Pure measures are those that relate to only one of the three aspects of fluency: speed, breakdown and repair, whereas composite measures combine two aspects of fluency, e.g. speed and breakdown, or repair and breakdown. Articulation rate, e.g. is a pure measure of speed that provides information about how fast a speaker speaks regardless of how much silence or repair is there in their speech. Frequency of pauses or frequency of repetitions are examples of pure measures of breakdown and repair, respectively. On the other hand, a composite measure like the mean length of run, i.e. the average number of syllables produced in runs of speech between silences, provides us with some information about the amount of silence (breakdown fluency) and the number of syllables (speed fluency). In effect, a speaker with a high mean length of the run may have paused infrequently and/or produced a high number of syllables between pauses. An example of a composite measure combining all three aspects of fluency is unpruned speech rate in which repair measures (e.g. reformulations and repetitions), pause and number of syllables all play a role.

Another major shift in the measurement of fluency has been the definition of the linguistic unit of speech analysis. Previous research, e.g. Lennon (1990), used T-Unit and C-Unit as the linguistic unit for analysing speech. T-Unit (Hunt, 1965) is defined as a main clause plus any other clauses that are dependent on it, but it excludes *non-clausal structures* and *sentence fragments*. The use of T-Unit in the analysis of

3.2 Recent Developments in Measuring Fluency 49

speech has been criticised by several researchers (e.g. Foster, Tonkyn & Wigglesworth, 2000) since the exclusion of non-clausal structures and sentence fragments would have an impact on the measurement of different aspects of speech. C-Unit, used in some other studies (e.g. Mehnert, 1998), is defined as an utterance providing referential or pragmatic meaning, consisting of either a simple clause or an independent subclause, together with subordinate clauses associated with it. As such, C-Unit is dependent on the semantic load of utterance ignoring the role of grammatical and intonational units and therefore, does not lend itself well to real-life speech. Criticising the use of the two previous units in speech analysis, Foster et al. (2000) proposed Analysis of Speech Unit (AS-Unit) as a more appropriate linguistic unit that considers inherent characteristics of speech including its syntactic, semantic and prosodic features (e.g. intonation and pause). AS-Unit has proved to be a more suitable and authentic unit of analysis for spoken data, and most recent L2 fluency studies have used it in their analysis. In what follows, we will discuss other changes that have occurred in each of the three aspects of fluency.

3.2.1 Speed Fluency

The field of SLA has witnessed several key changes in the operationalisation and measurement of speed fluency, but the most important shift has perhaps happened to the way we now understand speed fluency. For example, it is known that speed can reflect how the articulatory processes function (Huensch & Tracy-Ventura, 2017); it may indicate the extent to which the speaker 'buys time' by lengthening sounds (Hunter, 2017); and it can show whether the production process is interrupted by monitoring processes. Besides, nowadays there is a more in-depth understanding of speed fluency in terms of what can be expected from the speakers at different proficiency levels. For example, Tavakoli, Nakatsuhara and Hunter (2017, 2020) demonstrated that L2 speakers' speed improves along with proficiency level, but there is a ceiling effect wherein speed tends not to develop any further after the speakers reach a certain level of proficiency, e.g. B2 or C1 at the Common European Framework of Reference for Languages (CEFR) level. These results were replicated by Tavakoli, Kendon, Hunter and Slaght's (forthcoming) study, examining the Test of English for Educational Purposes (TEEP) Speaking test implying that L2 speakers' speed developed from lower levels to intermediate level of proficiency, but their speed did not develop any further as the speakers moved to an upper-intermediate level. It seems that there is a ceiling effect for speed fluency, i.e. speed improves only

50   *Measuring Fluency*

to a certain extent before it remains constant. The more in-depth understanding of speed fluency is also associated with a more valid understanding of how speed and breakdown measures interact. Fluency research has recognised the value of speed measures that only reflect speed, i.e. pure measures of speed such as articulation rate, and measures that combine speed and pausing, i.e. composite measures of speed such as speech rate and mean length of run. This difference is particularly important as with a pure measure of speed (i.e. articulation rate), we are focusing on the speaker's speed of speech production regardless of their pauses, while the composite measures of speed highlight the speakers' performance when speed and pauses are combined. This is important because pausing behaviour is only one reason for a slow speed while other factors affecting speed include personal style, individual differences and elongation. Given the emerging evidence about the relationship between L1 and L2 pauses, it seems necessary to include a pure measure of speed while studying L2 speakers' fluency behaviour.

Another methodological shift in measuring speed fluency came about by the introduction of digital technology that made it possible for researchers to measure temporal aspects of fluency with higher levels of precision and efficiency. Previously, the more mechanical measurement of fluency by using a chronometer and calculating silence on a scale of one second, allowed for a degree of measurement error when measuring fluency. Nowadays, there are different kinds of digital software (e.g. Audacity, GoldWave Digital Editor, CLAN/ELAN, WEBMAUS and PRAAT) that help researchers measure the temporal aspects of fluency more accurately. A commonly used programme in L2 studies is PRAAT (Boersma & Weenik, 2013) that allows for not only analysing speech but annotating files and developing scripts that provide the opportunity for working with background noise and exporting data to other software.

To sum up, measurement of speed fluency has developed to become more accurate, more sophisticated and more comprehensive. This, however, does not suggest whether speed fluency is fully understood or appropriately measured. Some of the key questions to answer while measuring speed include whether pure or composite measures of speed provide a more reliable picture of fluency, whether different speech acts encourage different rates of speech and whether technological advancement can facilitate measurement of fluency.

3.2.2 Breakdown Fluency

Measurement of pause and silence has also witnessed new developments over the past decades. For a long time, we have been aware of

3.2 Recent Developments in Measuring Fluency 51

the significant role of pauses during speech production, but more importantly, we have been aware of the different functions (e.g. buying time, rhetorical, personal styles, etc.) that pauses may serve (Fillmore, 1979). In addition to developing a more in-depth understanding of what functions pauses have, there have been several changes in the operationalisation and measurement of pauses. These can be divided into three key areas.

First, fluency research has managed to establish several thresholds for how long a pause is. While a pause in the 1990s was as long as 1 second (Foster & Skehan, 1996), and in the 2000s as long as 0.4 s or 0.5 s (Freed, 2000 and Oppenheim, 2000, respectively), most recent L2 fluency studies set a much lower threshold of 0.25 ms or even 0.20 ms as a noticeable pause that affects listeners' perceptions of fluency. This shift in the measurement emerged from the findings of studies (e.g. de Jong & Bosker, 2013) that reported a pause of longer than 0.25 ms can affect native speakers' perceptions of fluency.

Many researchers measure fluency in terms of both length and frequency of pauses. From a research perspective, it seems important to look at how long someone pauses as well as how frequently she/he may pause. *Amount* of pause is usually measured by calculating phonation time ratio, i.e. the proportion of time spent speaking compared to the total amount of time spent on the task. Drawing on the findings of their study, Bosker et al. (2013) argued that pause frequency is a more crucial indicator of breakdown fluency than pause length. However, several other studies have reported that both length and frequency of pauses are important as they affect perceptions of fluency. Studies investigating perceived fluency (e.g. Préfontaine, 2013; Préfontaine & Kormos, 2016) have also reported that listeners are not affected by the length of pause if they occur at clause boundaries.

Another important shift in the measurement of breakdown fluency has emerged as a result of recognising the importance of pause location, i.e. whether pauses occur in mid-clause or end-clause position. Studies in this area (Tavakoli, 2011; Kahng, 2014) have shown that a key distinction between fluent and dysfluent speech is that in the former speakers pause more frequently in mid-clause positions, whereas in the latter speakers pause more regularly at clause junctures. As discussed in Chapter 2, this can be usually assumed to reflect the differences between speakers with controlled versus automatic language processing ability. Speakers at earlier stages of interlanguage development whose language processing is largely dependent on controlled processes may need more mid-clause and mid-unit pauses to deal with the linguistic demands of the speech production process, e.g. lexical and morphosyntactic units retrieval. Some researchers have argued that mid-clause pauses are linked to Levelt's *formulation* stage, whereas end-clause pauses are related to the *conceptualisation* stage (Skehan, Foster & Shum, 2016).

Considering pause quality, or as some may call it to *pause character*, i.e. whether pauses are silent or filled, has been another change in the measurement of pauses. Researchers in L1 studies (Clark & Fox Tree, 2002; Schmidt & Fägersten, 2010) had for long argued that although both types may highlight the effects of language processing demands, filled pauses are often used for emphasis and discourse organisation. Filled pauses can also be considered as communication strategies that help speakers achieve their intended meaning (Dewaele, 1996; Schmidt & Fägersten, 2010). While measuring filled pauses has been used in L1 studies for some time, its importance seems to be more recent in L2 studies. It is necessary to note that while filled pauses seem to be a universal feature of spoken language use across different languages, they may affect communication in certain ways in different languages (Tian, Maruyama & Ginzburg, 2017). The key point in this argument is that filled pauses have a communicative function, e.g. suggesting difficulty in retrieving ideas or lexical items or showing hesitation and reflection. They may also signal a complex lexical item or linguistic constituent that is going to be produced (Arnold, Fagnano & Tanenhaus, 2003; Watanabe, Hirose, Den & Minematsu, 2008). Clark and Fox Tree (2002) argued that filled pauses are communicatively significant, but different fillers, e.g. 'er', 'um', 'uh', may have different communicative functions and meanings.

In a cross-cultural study of American English, British English, Chinese and Japanese, Tian et al. (2017) found that the use of filled pauses varies in different cultures and may serve different functions. They report that while 'British but not American English uses "um" to signal a more severe problem than "uh"', the Chinese language encourages the use of different filled pauses 'to signal the syntactic category of the problem constituent', and the Japanese language allows the use of different filled pauses 'to signal levels of interaction with the interlocutor' (p. 905). These findings suggest that filled pauses are culturally oriented, and as such, they should be studied across different languages and cultures if a valid understanding and measurement of pausing patterns is intended in fluency studies.

3.2.3 Repair Fluency

Compared to speed and breakdown aspects, the measurement of repair fluency seems to have changed the least over the past decades. Repair measures are assumed to be linked to self-monitoring processes of speech production (Huensch & Tracy-Ventura, 2017; Hunter, 2017) as making repairs shows the speaker's effort in monitoring his/her output to make some amendments to the original message. Repair measures or dysfluency measures as called by some researchers are most often calculated by finding the average number of reformulations, false starts, self-corrections, repetitions, replacements and hesitations in the speaker's performance (per sixty seconds). It can even be calculated as a single measure in some software such as CLAN. Although this approach is still widely used to measure repair fluency, we express a few concerns about it. Firstly, some of the repair measures overlap with one another or with other aspects of performance. False starts, e.g. are often followed by reformulations, and therefore, the number of false starts and reformulations are internally dependent. Similarly, hesitations (filled or silent) often precede or co-occur with other repair measures such as repetitions and replacements, and therefore, may not provide an independent representation of the repair phenomenon in fluency.

Secondly, verbatim repetitions do not necessarily reflect 'repair', as use of repetition may denote a communicative strategy or a personal style (Dörnyei & Kormos, 1998; Witton-Davies, 2014). There is emerging research evidence to imply that L2 use of repair measures (as well as other aspects of fluency) are related to personal speaking styles (Peltonen, 2018). For example, Duran-Karaoz and Tavakoli (2020) report that L2 repair behaviour is at least to some extent predicted from L1 repair patterns. While L2 repair is often motivated by the need to ensure the form reflects the intended meaning; in L1 repair is often used to make the message clearer, to provide more appropriate and accurate information or to ensure more impact. So far, only a few studies have looked into the relationship between L2 repair measures and monitoring processes (Kormos, 1999; Ahmadian, 2011); nor has there been sufficient evidence about whether L1 repair and monitoring behaviours are linked to L2 repair and monitoring behaviours. More research is needed to examine the nature of repair measures and its relationship with monitoring processes in L2 production.

3.3 Measuring Fluency: Speed, Breakdown, Repair and Composite Indices

This section's main aim is to introduce and discuss how fluency is measured in practise. Although measuring fluency is central to most research investigating fluency, most research papers, peer-reviewed articles and book chapters do not usually have space to discuss it.

54   *Measuring Fluency*

As such, we have seen many researchers and PhD students approaching us asking what the measurement procedures involve.

For many studies examining aspects of spoken language, a careful analysis of fluency seems to be a very important first step. This analysis is normally preceded by an attentive selection of the measures that can help demonstrate the construct of fluency under investigation and/or explain its nature. In this section, we will first introduce the common fluency measures regularly used in different studies in the field. Based on recent research findings, we provide a list of fluency measures and a brief description of how each measure is calculated for each of the three aspects of fluency. Before presenting the list, however, it is necessary to discuss a few important operational points. First, fluency measures should be based on averages, percentages or ratios so that they allow for comparison across different studies and data sets. Second, breakdown measures rely on pauses, but what constitutes a pause is something researchers make a decision about for each study. Pause length varies among different studies, ranging from 0.2 to 1 second, and the length considered as a reliable indicator of silence in one study may be assumed inappropriately for other studies. We consider pause location to be a crucial measure than can shed light on aspects of language processing and production. While most SLA researchers distinguish between pauses that happen at clause junctures and those inside a clause, some researchers distinguish between pauses at utterance junctures or inside utterances (Huensch & Tracy-Ventura, 2017). Moreover, the inconsistency in the use of terminology in our discipline is a point that invites a careful consideration. For example, pause *length* and *duration* refer to how long a pause is, and pause *frequency* and *number* are interchangeably used to show how many times a speaker stops speaking. It also should be noted that some of these measures are inverse of one another. For example, *phonation time ratio* and *pause ratio* are reverses of each other. In fact, by calculating *phonation time ratio*, e.g. dividing the total phonation time by the total amount of time multiplied by 100, if a figure of 65 per cent[1] is achieved, this figure tells us that there was 65 per cent phonation time ratio and a 35 per cent silence ratio in the speaker's speech. Finally, researchers will need to decide whether they want to work with pruned or unpruned data or both. Many studies use pruned data, i.e. removing all the repetitions, hesitations and repair features, for calculating speed, but they will need to work with unpruned data to calculate repair measures.

---

[1] Please note that in some studies the PTR is presented as a ratio while in others it is presented as a percentage.

3.3 Speed, Breakdown, Repair and Composite Indices   55

In what follows, we provide a list of most commonly used fluency measures in L2 studies along with a simple explanation of how they are calculated.

Base measures:

- performance time: total duration of time allocated to the speaking task
- phonation time: the time from when the speaker begins speaking the first phoneme until after the last syllable of speech produced
- total number of syllables (or words in case the counts are based on words) per minute or performance

Speed measures:

- speech rate: total number of syllables divided by the total amount of phonation (including pauses)
- articulation rate: total number of syllables divided by the total amount of phonation time (excluding pauses)
- mean length of run: the mean number of syllables between two pauses
- mean syllable length: total phonation time divided by the number of syllables
- phonation run: seconds of phonation between two pauses

Breakdown measures:

- phonation time ratio: percentage of time spent speaking
- mean length of all silent or filled pauses: the total amount of silent or filled pauses divided by the number of silent or filled pauses
- mean length of silent pauses at mid-clause and end-clause positions
- mean length of filled pauses at mid-clause and end-clause positions
- frequency of silent/filled pauses: mean number of silent/filled pauses per minute
- frequency of silent pauses at mid-clause and end-clause positions
- frequency of filled pauses at mid-clause and end-clause positions
- frequency of filled pauses at mid-clause and end-clause positions

Repair measures:

- frequency of all repairs
- frequency of false starts and reformulations
- frequency of partial or complete repetitions
- frequency of self-corrections

Prosodic measures

- pace: the number of stressed words per minute (Vanderplank, 1993; Kormos, 2006)

56   *Measuring Fluency*

- space: the proportion of stressed words to the total number of words (Vanderplank, 1993)
- prominence and pitch: prominent syllables per tone unit (also per cent of tone units containing at least one prominent syllable) (Kang & Johnson, 2018)

In addition to the measures presented above, some studies have looked into other fluency indices. For example, lengthening, also called elongation or prolongation, is an aspect of fluency that only a few researchers have examined (Witton-Davies, 2014; Hunter, 2017). Lengthening, i.e. 'the stretching out of speech segments inside words' (Rodriguez & Torres, 2006: 338) is often examined in L1 studies and assumed to play the same role as filled pauses, e.g. to express hesitation, signal a repair or hold the floor. In L2 studies, lengthening has not been studied sufficiently yet, there is an assumption that lengthening can indicate hesitation, or is used as a 'time-buying' strategy, a function similar to what filled and silent pauses serve.

3.4 Measuring Fluency in Different Modes of Speech (e.g. Monologue, Dialogue, Computer-Mediated)

Speech occurs in different modes from monologic to dialogic and small and large group conversations.[2] With the advancement of technology, we have also witnessed new modes of oral interaction mediated by digital technology when speech occurs in computer-mediated of both synchronous and asynchronous forms. These different modes of speech are known to affect oral fluency in different ways. Given the abundance and diversity of speech in these different modes, it is surprising that studies measuring L2 fluency have predominantly focused on monologic speech often in a face-to-face mode. The interest in measuring monologic speech can perhaps be explained in light of the advantages offered by analysing fluency in a monologic mode. Firstly, measuring fluency in a monologue offers researchers the opportunity to examine an extended stretch of talk in its full capacity without the speaker being assisted or interrupted by other interlocutors. Besides, there is often a high degree of control over the output and a more clearly anticipated outcome in monologic performance; these two factors, i.e. the degree of control and the predictability of the outcome, are indeed very useful for research purposes, especially when comparing speakers with each other or with the expected norm if there

---

[2] For the purpose of this discussion, we consider a dialogue a talk involving more than one person, with the speakers taking turns to talk.

3.4 Measuring Fluency in Different Modes of Speech   57

is one. The controlled and predictable nature of the output also enables SLA researchers to link fluency features to different aspects of language processing and production, e.g. lexical retrieval, conceptualisation and articulation.

In comparison to dialogue, measuring fluency in a monologue is also more straightforward since the measurement does not involve examining interactional features of fluency, such as between-speaker pauses, overlap and turn-taking. The following are excerpts from a monologic and a dialogic version of the same task L2 learners have performed in one of our research studies in a classroom context. The topic of the task is 'Which one do you prefer: Travelling alone or travelling in a group? Discuss your preferred method of travelling and provide reasons'. While in the monologic form, one student performed the task and produced a long stretch of talk, in the dialogue two learners interacted with each other to discuss their preference.

The following is an excerpt from the monologic task performance:

I think ¬ travel alone ¬ travelling alone is a ¬ in a foreign country is better than travelling in a group because ¬ some people want to ¬ go to ¬ some different ¬ places maybe a castle maybe bridge ¬ but some people want to stay home ¬ and ¬ every person has different aims ¬ or ¬ purposes for travelling ¬ some people very active and some people very passive and ¬ for travelling and ¬ I think it is good to ¬ travel alone

If you ¬ if you travelling in a group you ¬ can ¬ you can ¬ you can to learn maybe a foreign language because a lot friends ¬ among you ~ among a lot of friends, and ¬, of course, ¬ also ¬ you you ¬ you can lost each other because group in a group may be a lot of people and ¬ if you ¬ travel alone you can ¬ use just yourself and ¬ more learn a foreign language may be ¬ and ¬ you can do something you want

The following is an excerpt from the dialogic task performance:

A: Hello, Joe!
B: Hello, Aren!

¬ ¬ ¬ ¬

A: ¬ I want ¬ I'm I want to talk about ¬ ¬ why people ¬ prefer to go ¬ prefer to travel alone ¬ I think ¬ it's ¬ better ¬ it's better than travel in group because ¬ first, ¬ we can decide what you want to do <B: yeah> we can ¬ arrange or emm <B: oh, so> our plan
B: oh so ¬ sorry sorry <A: yeah, OK> to interrupt you <A: OK> sorry to interrupt you because I have the opposite idea <A: yeah> from you <A: yeah> In my ¬ opinion ¬ I see the travelling with a group it's better <A: yeah> ¬ than ¬ travelling alone <A: yeah> for many reasons <A: OK>

58   *Measuring Fluency*

> One of them you can share the experience from ¬ another group ¬ you can to have a fun with the group, so you can't have <A: you mean> fun for example <A: sorry > yeah
> A: sorry I interrupt you because ¬ I disagree with you ¬ If we want ¬ if you would like to share experience you can interact ¬ we can ¬ talk or speak or interact ¬ make interaction with the local people like. . .
> B: But what about fun? <A: Yeah yeah> I mean you will have fun alone?
> A: I think you misunderstand some point ¬ because we talking about foreign country <B: Yes I know> sometimes you you you aren't able to to speak this ¬ the language[3]

As can be seen in the excerpts above, there is an extended stretch of talk in the monologic task performance during which the speaker is neither supported nor interrupted by the other speaker/hearer. The speaker seems to be in full control of what is being said without much influence or assistance from other speakers. As indicated in the transcript, the speaker may have several opportunities for repair and correction but because they do not receive immediate feedback from an interlocutor, the need for repair is self-motivated and is perhaps mainly, but not exclusively, driven by a need for corrections. Some several repetitions and pauses may be primarily used to 'buy time' to help with retrieval and access processes.

On the other hand, the dialogue is an act of collaborative construction of meaning performed by the two speakers as the dialogue develops. In a dialogue, typically there are several turns, interruptions, overlaps and back channelling that interrupt the flow of speech. Although these are natural features of human conversations, they complicate the measurement process of fluency. Besides, there are unclaimed pauses between the two speakers (e.g. the long pause after the speakers exchanged greetings in this conversation). There are several overlaps, such as 'yes, I know' and 'sorry' that is not clear whether they are just an overlap or a new turn. The presence of back channelling, e.g. 'yeah' and 'OK', although makes the conversation more engaging and meaningful, adds to the complexity involved in measuring fluency. These are important factors that affect the measurement of fluency, and therefore, researchers' measurement is expected to be influenced by the decisions they make about these. There are a few key questions researchers need to ask when measuring fluency in a dialogue such as:

---

[3] In these transcripts the symbol ¬ shows a pause longer than 0.250 ms, while <> shows an overlap where the two speakers speak at the same time. For clarity and simplicity, we have not provided any coding for other measures of fluency.

3.4 Measuring Fluency in Different Modes of Speech   59

- How to deal with speech overlap? Should the overlap be divided between the two speakers? Should it be removed from the analysis?
- How to measure between-turn pauses? Who is responsible for these when neither Speaker A nor Speaker B claims the pause? Should the pause be assigned to one speaker or divided between the two? Should they be removed from the analysis?
- Should the back channelling, especially when word fillers such as 'OK' and 'right' are used, be considered as a new turn by the other speaker?

These are only some of the questions researchers working with dialogic data ask when measuring fluency. While there is no one-answer-fits-all approach to answering such questions, each study should decide between them in the light of their research aims and questions.

It may be true that the advantages of working with monologic data have inspired many researchers to focus on fluency in monologues. However, the significance of investigating other modes of speech has not been denied. Dialogues, which are typical of everyday interactions, shed light on a range of sociolinguistic, discourse and interpersonal aspects of communication, and enable researchers to develop a model of fluency that accounts for factors beyond the individual speaker. The complexities involved in measuring fluency in a dialogue discussed above have not yet been considered in models of measuring fluency. For example, none of the models of fluency discussed in earlier chapters has explicitly considered a role for the interactive features of speech (e.g. turn-taking and back channelling). This is surprising since investigating these interactive features has been an expanding area of research in other disciplines, e.g. Conversation Analysis and Speech Therapy. To understand such features of language use and to help develop an insight into what aspects of fluency are more central in each mode, it is necessary to discuss the differences between monologic and dialogic speech.

3.4.1 Differences between Fluency in a Monologue and a Dialogue

According to Edwards (2008), the key features of speech that make a dialogue different from a monologue include simultaneous talk (overlap), between-turn pauses and interruptions by the second speakers. Inherent in real-life dialogues are also other features of dialogue including silence, back channelling, self-selecting or selecting others as the next speaker, keeping the floor and signalling a change of turn-taking. Given the collaborative nature of a dialogue, the meaning is

60 Measuring Fluency

being constructed by the interlocutors. Speakers' speech is influenced by the interlocutor's performance in a range of different ways including lexical and grammatical choices, their degree of dominance and their interactional patterns. As regards fluency, the speaker's fluency depends at least to some extent on the interlocutor's speaking and conversational skills, such as their willingness to communicate, interactional skills (e.g. how often they interrupt other speakers), turn-taking patterns, speed and use of pragmatic features (e.g. discourse markers). As a result, it is reasonable to argue that in a dialogue a careful measurement of fluency will depend at least to some extent on the fluency behaviour of the interlocutor. From a speaker's point of view, researchers (Michel, 2011; Tavakoli, 2016) have argued that dialogues are cognitively less demanding as the speakers often share ideas and linguistic units (priming effect[4]), and use the interlocutor's turn to plan their subsequent performance. This normally leads to higher speech rates, less pausing and fewer repair measures.

The earliest evidence about the differences between fluency in monologic and dialogic performance seems to have come from L1 studies and clinical language sciences. In L1 studies, e.g. research has shown that more filled pauses are found in dialogues than in monologues (Siegman & Pope, 1966). Patients with specific mental health problems were reported to produce more silent pauses and fewer filled pauses (Pope, Blass, Siegman & Raher, 1970), and that speed of performance was faster when speakers were involved in a dialogue than a monologue. Some earlier studies had reported that more dysfluencies (e.g. empty fillers and repairs) were observed in dialogues than monologues (Bavelas, Gerwing, Sutton & Prevost, 2008). However, more recent research suggests that producing dysfluencies is a highly complex phenomenon that needs further research (Finlayson & Corley, 2008). Other researchers have argued that the rate of dysfluency features in a dialogue depends on a range of factors including age, relationship with the interlocutor, topic and gender (Bortfeld et al., 2001).

The most common fluency measures examined in L1 studies, whether for communication purposes or clinical reasons, are filled and silent pauses, repair measures and syllable lengthening (Rodriguez & Torres, 2006; Fusaroli & Tylen, 2016). This body of research has shown that silent pauses fulfil a range of communicative functions, e.g. checking the interlocutor's understanding, or allowing them either to interrupt the speaker or to signal the next turn can be

---

[4] Priming effect is a concept in psycholinguistic research that suggests that exposure to a linguistic element, e.g. syntactic or lexical unit, influences the response in a following stimulus without conscious intention.

3.4 Measuring Fluency in Different Modes of Speech   61

taken (Rodriguez & Torres, 2006). In addition to the typical measures of breakdown, speed and repair frequently employed in L2 studies, L1 studies have paid more attention to prosodic features of speech in dialogue. Fusaroli and Tylen (2016), e.g. argue that in a dialogue prosody and speech/pause rhythm are two crucial aspects of inter-action. They claim that prosodic patterns are important as they carry pragmatic meaning (e.g. placing emphasis), whereas speed/pause rhythm indicates disruption or ease of the discourse. They also argue that interlocutors tend to adapt to each other's prosodic patterns, and rhythms of speech and pauses (McFarland, 2001; Wilson & Wilson, 2005). Taking prosody into the measurement of L2 fluency, although a necessity, will inevitably throw new challenges to researchers since prosodic features of L2 often develop at a later stage in the process of acquisition, and therefore, they are not easy to account for in earlier stages of L2 acquisition. Furthermore, L1 pronunciation patterns have a direct impact on L2 pronunciation, and as such, it might be difficult if not impossible to distinguish L1 influences from L2 fluency behaviour.

As mentioned previously, in L2 research there are a few studies that have systematically examined fluency in dialogic performance. Tavakoli (2016), e.g. examined several interactive aspects of fluency in dialogic performance, e.g. interruptions, overlap and unclaimed between-turn, to understand in what ways measurement of fluency would be different in monologues versus dialogues. Highlighting the importance of between-turn pauses, she argued that L2 fluency research has not provided a clear description of how such fluency features can be measured in a dialogue, and maintained that fluency measurement in dialogue seems less systematic and research-oriented than that in a monologue. The results of Tavakoli (2016) underlined the importance of a more unified approach to measuring fluency in dialogues as the decisions researchers make about how to measure the interactive aspects of fluency would have an impact on the outcome of measurements of fluency.

3.4.2 Fluency in Face-to-Face versus Computer-Mediated Interaction

More recently, researchers have shown interest in measuring fluency in computer-mediated speech (Rodriguez & Torres, 2006; Huifen, 2015; Blake, 2009; Kang & Johnson, 2018). The key point of interest in this body of research is to find out whether computer-mediated interaction and communication has a positive impact on the development of oral proficiency (including oral fluency). With this chapter's interest in the measurement of fluency, however, we turn our discussion to fluency measurement in the computer-mediated mode of interaction.

Several studies analysing fluency in computer-mediated interaction, whether synchronous or asynchronous, have used typical measures of pause length, speech rate and phonation time ratio as their measures of analysis (e.g. Blake, 2009; Razagifard, 2013). In other studies, researchers have used raters' judgment of fluency to examine the impact of computer-mediated interaction on the development of fluency (Payne & Whitney, 2002; Sun, 2012). To our knowledge, no studies have so far considered a particular measure or set of measures that are specifically used to demonstrate characteristics of computer-mediated oral fluency. This is the same problem measurement of fluency encounters when examining speech in any non-monologic modes.

In terms of findings, some interesting patterns of fluency are reported. While different studies have reported various findings of this potential impact, a meta-analysis of studies investigating the effects of computer-mediated communication on oral proficiency (Lin, 2014) surprisingly reports a relatively negative impact on fluency (and accuracy) when compared with face-to-face interaction. Research in this area has also shed light on the similarities and differences observed between fluency in face-to-face and computer-mediated modes of speech. For example, face-to-face conversations commonly contain more repair and breakdown than human-computer conversations where there is no immediate feedback to be addressed.

3.5 Remaining Challenges and Limitations of Fluency Measurement

Measuring fluency has seen several major changes and developments over the past three decades, including shifts in understanding, operationalising and measuring fluency. Despite the great achievements SLA research has made in measuring fluency over the past decades, this body of research faces significant challenges to accomplish a reliable and objective measurement of fluency. We will summarise a few of these below.

Fluency research needs to develop a more reliable operationalisation and measurement of fluency in different modes. We know very little about how to measure fluency in dialogues and a range of computer-mediated interactions. As discussed earlier, to deal with the complex structure of the dialogue, researchers will have to make some important decisions about the dialogues (e.g. who owns a pause, or how to measure an overlap) which will have a direct impact on the results.

3.5 Remaining Challenges and Limitations   63

The lack of consistency in what different researchers may do will pose a challenge when it comes to comparing results from different studies.

Measuring fluency in other languages is also another challenge the research community will need to address. So far, L2 fluency has been examined in perhaps a dozen languages, many of them from the same typological category. We will need to expand our knowledge of what fluency features are common across different languages, and whether there are fluency features that are unique to certain languages.

While the existing computerised programmes have made measuring fluency more accurate, reliable and accessible, measuring fluency is still time-consuming, labour-intensive and not cost-effective. Those who have used PRAAT, Audacity and GoldWave can only confirm how much time and effort goes into measuring fluency. We are optimistic that the development of technology can make the measurement of fluency more convenient and cost-effective.

4 *Fluency in Second Language Task-Based Research*

This chapter will demonstrate that by the development of a task-based approach to researching language learning, a large number of studies investigating fluency have examined it as a variable that is affected by task design and implementation conditions (also known as performance conditions). We will then focus on how the immediate context of the speech, e.g. task design, implementation conditions and the role of interlocutors, influences speech fluency during the performance (e.g. Foster & Skehan, 1996; O'Sullivan, 2002; Robinson, 2003, 2007; Tavakoli & Foster, 2008), and to what extent research findings in this area produce convincing results that can be used in practical contexts such as language testing and teaching (Samuda & Bygate, 2008; de Jong & Perfetti, 2011; de Jong & Vercellotti, 2015). Although the primary aim of this chapter will be evaluating the effects of task design on fluency, the interaction between fluency and other aspects of language performance will also be briefly evaluated.

In this volume, we have so far consistently discussed the need for adopting a broader perspective on researching fluency that allows for combining the evidence from cognitive and information-processing research with findings from other potentially interested sub-disciplines, e.g. pragmatics, with the ultimate aim to develop a broader multidisciplinary understanding of fluency. We argue that the contexts in which this broader understanding can emerge should go beyond a predominantly lab-based setting and include speaking activities that are conducted for various purposes and defined by a range of different factors, including communicative purposes, speech acts and cultural norms.

The key tenet of using tasks in language learning and teaching is that if tasks are well-designed and implemented, they will trigger authentic second language (L2) acquisitional processes and facilitate the development of learner interlanguage, boosting syntactic and lexical knowledge, as well as the development of interactional skills

(Long & Crookes, 1992; Skehan, 1996; Robinson, 2001, 2011). Hence, using tasks that involve real-life communication and interaction, with a focus on getting the meaning across, is believed to promote language learning in general, and fluent use of language in particular (Skehan, 1998; Ellis, 2003, 2005).

Recently, therefore, research has turned to the notion of the task itself in more nuanced detail by considering the varied pressures that may arise from different task types and designs. It has been claimed that task design is critical in influencing both language performance and language acquisition, and tasks themselves need to be much more broadly conceived. While this was considered a bold, almost contentious, claim a few decades ago (see e.g. Sheen, 2003, 2005), currently there is growing agreement about the impact of task design on L2 performance and even on the acquisition itself (Ellis, 2009; Skehan, 2014). Drawing on convincing research evidence in this area, we aim to provide an insight into how task design influences speech fluency during L2 performance and L2 development. We look at how task design and implementation conditions are identified and explored from linguistic and cognitive perspectives. We identify areas that clearly need further investigation, such as exploring how tasks can help speakers' culturally-mediated beliefs about fluency in different discourse or professional settings (e.g. when hesitation can be appropriate). We suggest ways in which tasks can be better used to investigate fluency, not only from an information processing perspective but through an interactional lens, exploring speakers' communicative strategies in fulfilling listeners' expectations and communicative needs.

4.1 Task and Fluency

Since the 1980s, *task* has been the focus of a substantial interest in both second language acquisition (SLA) research and L2 pedagogy. This interest has been instigated by three important and interrelated reasons. Firstly, it has been hypothesised (Swain, 1995; Ellis, 2003) that task performance can drive interlanguage development forward by creating authentic opportunities for communication, and by motivating learners to retrieve and use L2 structures and lexis while performing a task. Secondly, the interest in *task* has been motivated by its appeal to L2 pedagogy as L2 educators are keen to employ tasks to develop a more effective pedagogic approach to L2 teaching and testing. Thirdly, *task* has become an interesting research instrument that lends itself well to various design and operationalisation methods researchers need when exploring the cognitive processes involved in language production.

66   *Fluency in Second Language Task-Based Research*

From a pedagogic perspective, tasks can be used in a general sense referring to 'the activities and the materials that teachers and/or students work on in the classroom' (Long, 2015: 6), or a specific sense when the L2 activity is communicatively oriented. In this case, the focus is on exchanging meaning, and to complete it, learners have to draw on their linguistic and non-linguistic resources (Ellis & Shintani, 2014). From a research perspective, however, *task* includes a broader spectrum of concepts and definitions. For many, any activity participants are involved in as stimuli for data collection can be called a *task*, from sentence repetition to fill-in-the gap, to communicative and authentic activities that resemble life outside the classroom. Nevertheless, for many researchers examining fluency in task-based language teaching (TBLT), *task* is used in a specific sense in which the participants are engaged in a meaning-oriented communicative and authentic activity. The diversity of the concept of a task in SLA research makes it difficult to analyse it thoroughly in a chapter like this. However, for this chapter, we report on studies in which task as a research instrument is used in its more specific sense where 'meaning is primary; there is some communication problem to solve; there is some sort of relationship to comparable real-world activities; task completion has some priority and the assessment of the task is in terms of outcome' (Skehan, 1998: 38).

4.2 Task Design and Fluency

Task design is a potentially rich area of research when investigating processes related to L2 performance and acquisition in general and different aspects of fluency in particular. Task design offers a promising opportunity to investigate the effects of a range of different task design features and implementation conditions that influence the shape and enhance L2 performance and acquisition. To date, research on task design has been very useful in casting light on some aspects of SLA, specifically about developing a model of L2 speech production (see Chapters 1 and 2). Although task design and its impact on L2 performance and SLA have been extensively researched over the past decades, to date, no clear definition has been provided for task design, its key components or how its different aspects relate to and interact with one another.

In this chapter, we are presenting a new classification of task design features and will discuss in what ways the various aspects of task design (e.g. task content, task type and implementation conditions) contribute to fluency. More central to our discussion will be an analysis of how these features interact with one another to influence L2 production processes involved in task performance, and to what extent they promote or inhibit fluency. Our discussion will also highlight the complex and multifaceted nature of task design, which partly explains why research in this area has not generally been conclusive.

4.3 Task Design Features

One way to investigate the effects of task design on fluency is to consider two main dimensions to it: (a) task design features, e.g. number of elements or information type that are inherent in a task, and (b) implementation conditions, e.g. the social environments under which a task is performed. By this categorisation, features such as cognitive demand, organisation of information and kinds of outcomes are grouped under task design features, and factors such as task mode, presence or absence of planning time and communicative purpose are classified as implementation condition features.

4.3.1 Organisation of Information: Task Structure

The structure of the information provided in a task is one of the key task design features examined in TBLT research. A summary of studies on task structure suggests that it has been defined and operationalised in an inconsistent and unsystematic manner. On the other hand, a more positive point about this body of research is that task structure is one of the few features that has convincingly and consistently been shown to have an impact on speech fluency. The main rationale behind researching structure is that the presence of a clear macrostructure in a task, operationalised in terms of amount, kind and organisation of information, would help reduce the processing load associated with performing a task in L2. A reduction in the processing load would help release attentional resources that the learner will need for planning and performing the task.

Studies conducted by Foster and Skehan (1996) and Skehan and Foster (1997) were two of the first studies looking into the effects of task structure and defined it in terms of the degree of organisation of input material and its time sequencing. They considered a personal instruction-giving task, i.e. 'give instructions to a friend to go to your home and turn the oven off', a well-structured task since the input was based on familiar content, and the information had to follow a non-arbitrary sequence of events. In their oral narrative task, involving the narration of a short picture story to a partner, they defined structure in terms of having a clear sequential relationship between the different events in a task, or a clear representation of its macrostructure.

68   Fluency in Second Language Task-Based Research

In other words, their studies suggest that familiar content and a clear sequence of events were the key factors that made a task well-structured. In these studies, performance in well-structured tasks was associated with more fluent language.

Tavakoli (2004) set out to provide a more systematic framework for defining and operationalising structure in oral narrative tasks. Drawing on the literature on knowledge and information structures (Hoey, 1983; Mohan, 1991), Tavakoli argued that learner familiarity with knowledge structures would have a facilitative role in comprehending what should be done, and would assist the process of L2 production. Acknowledging the possibility of the diversity of representation and conceptualisation of knowledge structures in different cultures, she defined a *schematic sequential structure* in an oral narrative in terms of following a clear timeline of when events happen, in an organised temporal sequence, where the order of events cannot be rearranged without the core of the story being compromised. Another kind of structure defined in this study was a problem-solution structure, i.e. a structure in which besides the sequential structure, the task contains a problem for which a solution is suggested or sought, and an evaluation of the situation is required. Tasks without a problem-solution structure, without a clear timeline underlying the events or with an arbitrary sequence of events were considered as less structured. Investigating these tasks with 140 L2 learners, Tavakoli (2004) reported that the presence of structure in an oral narrative promoted learner language performance in terms of its fluency and accuracy. Learners produced longer runs, less silence and fewer pauses in more structured tasks, implying that the presence of a set structure released learners' attentional resources at the *conceptualisation stage* (Levelt's model, 1989), making it possible for them to attend to communicating the message with less disruption and hesitation. This hypothesis was further put to trial in studies by Tavakoli and Skehan (2005) and Tavakoli and Foster (2008). Both studies reported that task structure facilitated fluency of language performance: learners produced fewer repair measures and less silence in the more structured tasks. Interestingly, in both studies performance in structured tasks was also more accurate than that in the less structured tasks. Following from Tavakoli and Foster (2008), Ahmadian and Tavakoli (2012) examined the effects of loose and tight structure on performance of thirty Iranian language learners performing two video-based oral narrative tasks. The researchers were specifically interested in the effects of task design on learners' fluency in terms of their repair behaviour (indicating ongoing monitoring and focus on form). Their findings suggested that more structured tasks encouraged speakers to focus on grammatical or lexical repairs, whereas the task with a loose structure elicited more meaning-based and fluency focused repairs. Given the multilingual perspective to fluency adopted in this volume, it is necessary to acknowledge that these studies mainly represent an Anglophone perspective on understanding knowledge structures, and as such can be considered unidimensional. Although we have no hard evidence to argue for it, we are inclined to think that certain knowledge structures, e.g. problem–solution, maybe culturally more acceptable in one discourse community than in another. Further studies are needed to carefully examine the effect of knowledge structures on task performance in speakers of different language backgrounds.

A key conclusion to draw from the studies reported above is that task structure can help release some attentional resources that otherwise would have to be stretched to find the connection between different elements of a task. Levelt's model of speech production (see Chapter 1) becomes relevant here, as it suggests that the release of attentional resources would mean a lower processing load for the conceptualisation, hence a richer opportunity for preparing the preverbal message, and an easier job for the formulator which translates the preverbal message to language structures and lexis. The summary of the research findings provided above also reinforces the claim that task structure is a design feature that influences L2 performance in clear and predictable ways. We, therefore, consider structured tasks as pedagogically more suitable, especially for low proficiency learners, if learners' accurate and fluent performance is intended. As we have seen above, task structure mobilises fluency positively, and this is an important point that language professionals like material designers and language test writers, could embrace in their practises.

4.3.2 Amount of Information

Another feature of tasks that is also studied with its impact on fluency is the amount of information provided in a task. Research in this area suggests that either too much or too little information provided in a task makes it more demanding for L2 learners, which, in turn, affects both their perceptions of task difficulty and their actual task performance. In several studies, Tavakoli (2004, 2009a, 2009b) investigated learners' and teachers' perceptions of and criteria for task difficulty by collecting questionnaire and interview data from learners and teachers in different settings. Among others, the amount of information provided in a task was suggested as an important contributing factor to task difficulty. Teachers and learners in these studies reported that both an overload and a paucity of information available in a task

70   *Fluency in Second Language Task-Based Research*

could lead to higher cognitive demand, affecting learners' perceptions of task difficulty and having a damaging effect on their fluency, manifesting as a slower speech rate and more pauses.

The amount of information can be manipulated by increasing the number of elements in a task, or the number of steps required to be taken to complete the task. Brown, Anderson, Shillcock and Yule (1984) reported that fewer elements in their task were associated with more fluency, and more elements were linked with higher lexical variety. Robinson (2001) showed that adding more elements to a direction-giving map task increased the cognitive demands on the learners, leading speakers to produce less fluent language. Interestingly, in both studies lower fluency was associated with higher lexical variety, indicating that that the less-fluent performance might have resulted from the need to retrieve and use a larger number of lexical items.

4.3.3 Immediacy of Information

Another interesting aspect of task design is manipulating the immediacy of information provided in terms of whether the information is present to learners, or whether there is a need to refer to events happening elsewhere in time and place. The underlying assumption here is that performing a task with a degree of information displaced into the past is considered more demanding than performing a task that requires speaking about the present time and location with the stimuli available to the speaker. The immediacy of information (Robinson, 1995; Rahimpour, 1997), often operationalised along the +/− here-and-now dimension, requires learners to perform a story-retelling task under conditions where visual prompts are either available or unavailable. Removal of the visual prompts reduces *context-dependency*, i.e. the extent to which a communicative activity depends on the context of communication (Nunan, 1989), and as a result makes it more demanding on the speaker. Under this condition, learners are also prompted to perform the + here-and-now in present tense whereas the − here-and-now condition is to be narrated in the past. Consequently, the variable has been operationalised at two levels: availability of the visual prompts and narration of the story with either present or past grammatical structures. The underpinning principle stems from cognitive psychology, in which it is assumed that children's ability to talk about events happening in a displaced past time emerges after the ability to talk about here and now (Robinson, 2011). For L2 learners, SLA researchers consider the 'then-and-there' condition as more demanding, not only because of the pressure of using memory to remember the story but because of the linguistic demands of using the past tense, a structure that is acquired later than the present tense (Bardovi-Harlig, 1994).

Both Robinson (1995) and Rahimpour (1997) reported that when learners are asked to perform a narrative under the 'then-and-there' condition, i.e. when visual prompts are removed and the story had to be told in the past tense, learners slowed down and their overall fluency decreased. However, this finding was not replicated in studies by Gilabert (2007) and Gilabert, Barón and Levkina (2011). The latter group of researchers claims that the different results they achieved were since their learners belonged to a higher level of proficiency, and were arguably capable of maintaining their fluency when performing a more complex task. The conclusion to draw from the above discussion is that immediacy of information, in terms of availability of visual prompts, influences speech fluency, but interacts with other variables such as proficiency level. It is possible to argue that at higher levels of proficiency, when speech production is more automatic, removing the visual support might have a less debilitating effect on fluency. However, for lower proficiency learners the 'then-and-there' condition would have a damaging impact on the process of speech production because removing the visual and contextual support would impose more demands on the conceptualiser, and requiring learners to speak in the past tense would add pressure to the formulator, both with negative effects on fluency.

4.3.4 Reasoning Demands

Robinson (2007) proposed that fluency is decreased by the cognitive demands of complex reasoning about the intentions of others to encourage L2 learners to use language with higher syntactic complexity and lexical variety. He categorised reasoning into three kinds: (a) spatial reasoning, which requires navigating places and giving directions, (b) causal reasoning, which involves explaining why actions and events are happening, and (c) intentional reasoning, which includes understanding and explaining the reasons, motives and thoughts existing behind actions. The underlying assumption is that explaining the reasoning of others involves referring to their state of mind, which in the English language entails the use of specific language to show people's intentional and/or causal reasoning, such as 'she thinks', 'he wonders', 'they assume' and so on. Expressing this idea in English requires using complex structures like complement structures and subordinate clauses, thus resulting in language with a higher level of syntactic complexity. For a similar reason, describing how to move between places, i.e. spatial reasoning, requires the use of constructions for describing motion events, and therefore, promotes language with a wider range of verbs and lexical items.

It is plausible to claim that *reasoning* for oneself and/or for others, i.e. identifying the reasons and intentions for actions and justifying them, in a second language is a high-level cognitive activity, and especially so for L2 speakers of limited proficiency. In terms of its cognitive load, it has been proposed that performing a task that requires reasoning, whether intentional, causal or spatial, involves conceptual gaps that need to be filled with thoughts and inferences, hypothetical language about the intentions and desires of others, and expressions that go beyond the use of language when reasoning is not demanded. These attempts are considered more demanding for low-proficiency learners, whose attentional resources are already stretched when performing a task in their second language. However, there are two interrelated limitations to the above argument. Firstly, like many other task features, *reasoning* has not been clearly defined or systematically operationalised. Although it has been extensively researched in cognitive psychology, particularly concerning child development, reasoning has not been analysed or studied in an in-depth and thorough manner within SLA. Secondly, the existing conceptualisation of how reasoning affects language performance may work well with English language syntax, but we need a multilingual approach to examine reasoning to find out in what ways other languages present reasoning in their syntactic structures and other linguistic units.

Other studies investigating intentional reasoning, Ishikawa (2006, 2008) and Awwad (2017), and Awwad, Tavakoli and Wright (2017) have found positive effects of intentional reasoning on syntactic and lexical complexity and accuracy with either negative or neutral effects on fluency. The mixed results from studies on reasoning and its effects on fluency suggest that this is an area that deserves more investigation.

4.3.5 Prior Knowledge and Familiarity

Research in L2 acquisition has long maintained that prior knowledge and familiarity with the content/topic of a language activity can facilitate comprehension and production (Prabhu, 1987; Ellis, 1994). The basic assumption is that learning opportunities are promoted with familiar content because of the impact schematic knowledge (Rutherford, 1987) has on comprehension and production (Carrell, 1985). Familiarity with the task promotes fluency for two main reasons. Firstly, working with a familiar task involves procedures that are either well-known or predictable by the learner. For example, borrowing a book from a library is a familiar topic for most students, and therefore, the procedures for borrowing a book are well-known or largely predictable to most students. Such familiarity and/or predictability of the process would reduce the cognitive demands imposed on the speech production processes. Secondly, familiarity with the task often includes familiarity with the discourse genre as well, which Skehan (1998) defined as 'easifying macrostructures' (p. 100) readily available for use. In our library example, most speakers know that in a borrowing task a request has to be made and a confirmation is expected. This aspect of familiarity also makes the task less demanding and therefore, reduces the cognitive load of performing it. Such a reduction in the demands associated with a task is expected to enhance fluency.

Prabhu (1987) was one of the first researchers to report that his learners found it easier to perform tasks containing familiar information. Chang (1999) and Bui (2014) have also reported improvements in fluency when learners had prior knowledge of a task. Foster and Skehan (1996) looked into the familiarity of information in three different tasks: personal information exchange, narrative and decision-making, and examined their influence on learner's performance. They considered the information task as the easiest since it contained familiar and accessible information. Their decision-making task was viewed as the most difficult because it not only provided unfamiliar information but also involved making a decision based on moral values. The results showed that the personal information task allowed for the most fluent performance in terms of the number of pauses and total silence. The authors concluded that the language elicited by these different tasks presented such varied patterns of performance that they implied different mechanisms of language processing may be at work. The results of Foster and Skehan (1996), however, should be interpreted with caution, as the obtained results are related to the combined effects of familiarity of information and task type. A decision-making task, whether in L1 or L2, seems to be more demanding than a narrative, and as such it seems logical to expect an impact on fluency.

Research in task design features and their impact on L2 performance has been produced along the dimensions of organisation of information and some aspects of cognitive demands. However, there are several other features of task design, e.g. task types, various aspects of cognitive demands and task linguistic needs that need careful investigation. It is necessary for future research in SLA to examine such features, since an in-depth understanding of task design and its impact on fluency seems crucial in understanding, operationalising and measuring fluency.

4.4 Implementation Conditions

Implementation conditions refer to the characteristics of the performance setting under which the task is performed, e.g. whether there is some kind of communicative pressure on the learner in terms of time, and whether the task is performed individually or in collaboration with others. Previous research has examined only a limited number of implementation condition features, e.g. task modality and planning time, to see whether they influence L2 performance in a way different from task design features. Implementation conditions features are often related to the conditions under which the task is performed or to the purpose and context of communication, and they influence not only language performance elicited by the task but also the learning opportunities they promote. It seems intuitive that one can speak more comfortably when relaxed or when speaking to someone one knows well. While L1 disfluent speech is often associated with physical, mental or psychological problems, L2 disfluent speech can be attributed to a range of task-external factors that go beyond physical and psychological issues and include matters related to the communicative stress or the amount of time available.

Like design features, implementation condition features explain whether and in what ways fluency of L2 performance is affected. Unlike design features, however, implementation conditions are extended beyond the L2 processing and cognitive demands to highlight the role of the social environments, interactional demands and communicative pressure in shaping fluency, the social and contextual requirements of performing the task, and the cultural norms and expectations that encourage a particular fluency pattern. We consider the context of communication, e.g. speaking to a large audience at a conference compared to speaking to a counsellor in an individual counselling/therapy session, as a crucial variable that shapes speech fluency. There are two central components to our broader perspective on researching fluency: (a) the communicative purpose, i.e. why the speaker is performing the task, and (b) the pragmatic function(s) of the task, i.e. what is the most appropriate and effective way of conveying the intended message to a given listener/interlocutor, and the way they influence the speed and pausing patterns of speech. In the discussion on implementation condition features, we would include social, context-specific and communicative features of task performance as well as the speakers' ability to recognise and deploy the communicative requirements of the speaking task. We argue, e.g. that the communicative purpose (and therefore the pragmatic functions) of reporting an accident to the police is different from that of informing the relatives of a person involved in the accident: performance is supposedly slower and interrupted by pauses and repair measures when one is involved in the latter task. The status of the listener, their perceptions and expectations, can also influence the speaker's fluency (see Chapter 2 for a discussion of listeners' perceptions of fluency). Issues such as these are typically neither examined nor discussed in fluency research. It is necessary to emphasise that although there has been substantial research on social, contextual and pragmatic factors affecting language acquisition and interactional competence (Schegloff, 2000, 2001; Hall, Hellerman & Pekarek Doehler, 2011, among others), to our knowledge not much of this body of research has examined L2 fluency. We will come back to these important issues later on in this chapter. In the section that follows we discuss two implementation condition features, task mode and planning time that are frequently researched and have been shown to have consistent effects with fluency.

4.4.1 Task Mode: Monologic, Dialogic and Group Task

In real life, as well as in the classroom, language users engage in tasks of varying degrees of interactivity like monologues, dialogues and small and large group discussions. In L2 fluency research the majority of studies have focused on monologic task performance, with studies looking at its influence on fluency including oral narratives (Foster & Skehan, 1996; Tavakoli, 2011), short talks (de Jong & Perfetti, 2011) and answering-machine message leaving tasks (Mehnert, 1998; Gilabert et al., 2011). Research in speech fluency has predominantly drawn on monologic data primarily because of the degree of control associated with task performance, the predictability of the outcome of the performance and the clarity and ease of the procedures for measuring language produced in a monologic task. A key challenge in using dialogic and interactive tasks is that the learner's L2 ability can more easily be masked by other factors such as the proficiency level and personality of the interlocutors. However, such challenges should not prevent researchers from investigating the differential effects of task mode on speech fluency, since studying dialogic and interactive task performance allows researchers to look beyond the learner linguistic ability and evaluate their communicative and pragmatic abilities, which are often equally important in fostering fluent and successful interaction.

Three recent studies, Michel (2011), Witton-Davies (2014) and Tavakoli (2016) have investigated the differential effects of task mode, i.e. a monologue versus a dialogue, on fluency. These studies have

76 Fluency in Second Language Task-Based Research

reported that dialogic task performance is more fluent than that in a monologue in terms of speed, silence and repair measures, i.e. the same learners speak faster, and make fewer pauses, repetitions and hesitations when speaking in dialogue. About the number and location of pauses, however, Tavakoli (2016) reported that performances in the monologic and dialogic tasks were similar. This is an interesting finding because research suggests that pauses are central to the language processing capacity of the human brain (see Chapters 1 and 2) and that L2 learners need to pause when involved in the conceptualisation and formulation stages of language production (Levelt, 1989). These results contradict Skehan's (2001) hypothesis that interactive tasks would be associated with lower fluency. Skehan argued that the need to accommodate the unanticipated contribution of a partner and the need for more online planning are two important factors affecting fluency. However, as can be seen above, there is convincing research evidence that dialogues are faster and interrupted by fewer pauses.

This is where the social factors and communicative purposes associated with task performance can help explain the differences between fluency in the two modes. One way to interpret the benefits of dialogic performance for fluency is to argue that speakers find dialogic performance less demanding, in that they can use the interlocutor's turn to plan for their turn (Tavakoli, 2016). It is also possible to argue that the urgency of communicating the message with a partner encourages speakers to put more effort into the dialogue and convey their meaning more promptly and effectively. Alternatively, it is possible to link the more fluent performance in a dialogue with the fragmented nature of dialogic discourse (Cameron, 2000). Dialogues by nature involve shorter utterances, more interruptions and disruptions and encourage opportunities for clarification and confirmation requests; these, in turn, reduce opportunities for constructing elaborated utterances, which typically involve more L2 processing and hence put more pressure on the speech production process. Seemingly, this is an impact of the social context of communication on fluency, a feature that task-based studies have not carefully studied yet.

It is necessary to mention that all these studies have reported that dialogues offer opportunities for interaction and for developing skills in the negotiation of meaning (e.g. clarification requests and confirmation checks) and interactional skills (e.g. turn-taking and interruptions). For reasons of scope, the development of such skills and their relationship with fluency is not discussed in this chapter. While the evidence suggests that being engaged in dialogue is an effective way of promoting fluency and mediating L2 development, the importance of developing skills to produce and sustain talk over an extended period, i.e. a monologue, cannot be underestimated. After all, in real life, in educational and employment contexts and language proficiency tests, one's monologic ability to speak is often tested.

The aforementioned findings have clear and significant implications for the language testing profession. Given the differences between fluency patterns in monologic and dialogic tasks (and perhaps other interactive task types), language tests need to include a broad enough sample of candidates' performance to ensure a true and wide-ranging representation of their language ability has been elicited. Besides, it is important to ensure candidates' fluency is assessed according to the differences expected for fluency in these different modes (see a full discussion of fluency in language testing in Chapter 6). So far, language testing research has often focused on investigating monologic and oral interview tasks (Lazaraton, 1996), with more standardised tests aiming for examining a range of dialogic and interactive tasks. We argue that oral interviews, although not monologic, are different from dialogues in that they provide rich opportunities for the candidates to produce long turns and to speak for extended periods (compared with dialogues that often elicit fragmented pieces of discourse). As we will discuss in more detail in Chapter 6, language testing organisations will also need a clear set of descriptors for fluency in different modes of speech. Another limitation the language testing field has faced is that the language benchmarks (e.g. Council of Europe CEFR, Canadian Language Benchmarks, etc.) make very broad and general references to the concept of fluency without providing detailed definitions for different aspects of fluency, or indicating the differences language testers should expect to see between fluency patterns at each level of proficiency, for each task mode and different communicative tasks and purposes.

Highlighting the pragmatic and communicative needs of a dialogue, a recent study investigating fluency in monologic and dialogic tasks (Tavakoli, 2018) has reported that dialogues provide a richer opportunity for producing substantially more discourse markers than monologues. While this finding is not surprising, as the frequent use of discourse markers is explained in the light of the interactional needs of dialogue, what seems inspiring is the link between this use and fluency in dialogic tasks. Researchers argue that discourse markers 'facilitate the construction of a mental representation of the events described by the discourse' (Louwerse & Mitchell, 2003: 199), and lead to more successful interaction between the speaker and their interlocutor. Previous L2 research (e.g. Wood, 2010; Tavakoli, 2011) has also indicated that the production of formulaic chunks positively correlates

78   *Fluency in Second Language Task-Based Research*

with more fluent speech since L2 learners do not make long pauses in the middle of a chunk (see Chapter 4 for a detailed discussion). Given these two pieces of evidence and drawing on the discussions presented in Chapters 2 and 4, we argue that use of longer discourse markers (e.g. *first of all, as a matter of fact*) which are formulaic helps with the retrieval and processing demands of L2 production (Schmidt, 1990, 2001) and improves fluency.

4.4.2 Planning Time

Researching planning time and its impact on L2 fluency has been of interest to SLA and L2 education researchers for several reasons. From an SLA research perspective, planning time is particularly important since language production in principle is viewed as a complex process of planning, execution and articulation (Levelt, 1989). The planning phase plays a crucial role in the production process as it allows users to scan their linguistic repertoire and to select the linguistic items and rules needed to reach their communicative intents; the execution phase entails the production of the language that has been planned. Planning time is also of interest to SLA researchers as it has been reported to interact with cognitive processes such as attention and notice, which are central to L2 learning (Schmidt, 2001). Different studies have concluded that since the planning process involves the activation and retrieval of knowledge about linguistic forms and the corresponding meanings (Ortega, 2005; Mochizuki & Ortega, 2008), it can promote a focus on form and encourage learners to notice the gap between their existing L2 knowledge and what they would like to achieve when communicating meaning. Planning time has been of interest to L2 educators because it is identified as an effective pedagogic tool that helps teachers mediate and scaffold the process of L2 development. From a pedagogical perspective, planning time is a highly valuable instructional tool that can attract and direct learners' attention to specific aspects of the L2 form and meaning and offers them an opportunity to monitor, plan and practise L2.

Many of the planning time studies are informed by Levelt's (1989) model of speaking, in which the three processing components of conceptualiser, formulator and articulator work in parallel to produce language (see Chapter 1 for further details). While there are several differences between the language production process in L1 and L2, e.g. degree of automaticity and lexical retrieval, research so far has suggested that there are also many similarities (Kormos, 2006). Given that language production may not be an automatic process for many L2 users particularly at lower levels of proficiency, serial rather than parallel processing might be at work. Planning time, therefore, would be a 'breathing space' for lower-proficiency level L2 speakers who cannot cope with the demands of parallel processing. It is possible to argue that a key function of planning time in L2 production is to increase the attentional resources available to L2 speakers leading to more fluent speech.

Planning time can be divided into pre-task (or strategic as some may call it) and within-task types. Pre-task planning has been suggested to have beneficial effects on fluency (Mehnert, 1998; Tavakoli & Skehan, 2005; Mochizuki & Ortega, 2008). However, within-task planning time may not necessarily benefit fluency, as speakers use the time available to them to improve the accuracy and complexity of the forms they use. Previous research (e.g. Tavakoli & Skehan, 2005) has shown that planning time interacts with the level of proficiency: the effects of planning time are greater for learners at lower language proficiency levels. Planning can also be operationalised as guided or unguided, according to whether or not the learners receive instructions about how to plan their performance or what to focus on. Research in this area suggests that guided planning results in more fluency and complexity in learner performance, but unguided planning leads results in more accurate performance (Foster & Skehan, 1996; Mochizuki & Ortega, 2008).

Research on the effects of planning time on L2 performance has been distinguished by the fact that the findings, unlike those for several other task design features, have generally been consistent about its effects on fluency. Regardless of the differences in interest and focus, there is consensus among language researchers and educators that the presence of planning time helps learners produce the language of higher quality, and planners generally outperform non-planners with improvement in one or more aspects of their performance.

4.5 Expanding Task Design Features to Include an Interactional Perspective

As discussed in the previous sections of this chapter, studies investigating L2 speech fluency, its development and acquisition have contributed greatly to our understanding of how fluency is acquired as mental and cognitive ability, and how specific aspects of task design and implementation conditions can facilitate or inhibit the development of L2 fluency. However, with few exceptions little is known about how fluency develops with communicative purposes, discourse-level pragmatic requirements and social and interactional expectations, or how it is shaped through and in the interaction of

80   *Fluency in Second Language Task-Based Research*

these factors. In the next section, we introduce some factors that contribute to the development of a socio-pragmatic perspective to researching fluency.

4.5.1 Communicative Purpose

There is little disagreement in our field that a crucial factor in an act of communication is the purpose (or function) for which the speakers, whether in L1 or L2, engage in a task. Existing research evidence suggests (Donato, 2000; Yule, 2003) that speakers may perform the same task differently when they have different purposes for task completion. We expect to see different performances from the following speakers discussing their weekend: Speaker A is describing what happened to him/her at the weekend to a colleague to socialise; Speaker B is describing the same events to his/her boss to apologise for his late arrival and Speaker C is describing them to a classmate to practise his L2. Yule (2003) reports on several studies in which the L2 learners interpreted the tasks differently from both the L1 speakers and researchers, suggesting that task outcomes are inevitably a function of the participants' recognition of what they are expected to do. Although tasks are communicatively oriented and there is a need to fulfil their communication goal, for L2 speakers, tasks also provide an opportunity to demonstrate their L2 ability and to practise it. This purpose at times may encourage them to go beyond the communicative purpose of task performance to put their L2 ability on display, resulting in changes to different aspects of performance, including speed and lexical choices. Besides, the same task may be interpreted differently by different speakers. Mondada and Pekarek Doehler (2004: 515), e.g. argued that 'a task can be collectively interpreted and even transformed' during the preparation and performance stages. Donato (2000), among others, also reported that the individual learners in his study interpreted and reinterpreted tasks during task performance. If task performance is at least to some extent a function of task purpose, researchers in fluency studies need to explore the impact of task purpose on fluency.

4.5.2 Context of Communication

There is consensus in SLA research that the context of communication plays an important and influential impact on L2 performance and L2 acquisition. Foster (1998), e.g. demonstrated that when L2 learners' context of performance varied, e.g. in a language lab versus an actual classroom, their performance changed accordingly. Analysing data

4.5 Expanding Task Design Features 81

from school children, Peets (2009) also reported changes in students' performance in terms of productivity and complexity measures, fluency measures (including pauses, repetitions and self-corrections) and turn-taking patterns when the context of interaction changed. Despite this initial evidence, the impact of the context of communication on L2 speech fluency has yet to be fully investigated and established. We argue that fluency research can draw on findings from the fields of Interactional Competence and Conversation Analysis (e.g. Young, 2003, 2011; Hall et al., 2011; Pekarek Doehler & Berger, 2018) to highlight the importance of social norms and expectations and the context of communication in shaping and characterising fluency. Intriguingly, such disciplines have paid considerable attention to a range of L2 variables, e.g. turn-taking and acquisition of syntactic structures, with little attention to the acquisition and development of fluency. This is where multidisciplinary research can help to create an opportunity for developing a more in-depth understanding of the social factors that affect fluency.

Examining the context of communication also includes the role of the interlocutor(s) and the relationship among them. Research in language testing examining the effects of examiners and interlocutors on candidates' L2 performance suggests that familiarity with the interlocutor, their gender and L1 background, the power relationship and the size of the group in discussion tasks influence the test-takers' performance (Lazaraton, 1996; Nakatsuhara, 2011). However, this body of research has not explored the effects of interlocutor on the fluency of their speech. A detailed discussion of the implications of fluency research findings for language testing will be presented in the following chapter.

4.5.3 Pragmatic Considerations

Bardovi-Harlig (2013: 67) defines pragmatics as a branch of research that is predominantly interested in 'the study of how-to-say-what-to-whom-when', and L2 pragmatics as concerned with 'how learners come to know how-to-say-what-to-whom-when'. With these definitions in mind, it can be seen that L2 pragmatics is central in studying the development of different L2 skills and competencies. For this reason, L2 pragmatics research can potentially make a major contribution to understanding and researching L2 fluency. As we have already discussed the relationship between fluency and pragmatic competence in Chapter 2, our interest here is linked with the effects of pragmatic knowledge on fluency. Our reading of the literature suggests that L2 fluency and L2 pragmatic knowledge have been

82   *Fluency in Second Language Task-Based Research*

commonly investigated separately, with very few studies exploring the close relationship between the two. For this chapter, we will discuss the potential relationship between pragmatic knowledge and fluency and refer to some important areas that can help shed light on this relationship.

An important area to look at is the effects of type of speech acts on fluency. As mentioned earlier in this chapter, breaking bad news is often associated with a slower rate of speech. While this common knowledge is based on our cultural understanding of how this speech act works, there is little research to show the fluency profiles of different speech acts. Taguchi (2007) has shown that L2 speakers, but not L1 speakers, perform different speech acts differently. In her study, L2 learners were more fluent when the task involved a low profile of power difference, social distance and degree of imposition. Taguchi's studies collectively (2007, 2011) demonstrate that variations in fluency can be expected when speech acts vary. Cirillio Colón de Carvajal and Ticca (2016), examining the structure of apology speech acts, argue that among the many characteristics of this speech act, a small pause and some hesitation are some of the salient temporal features speakers use to perform an apology.

The second area in which L2 pragmatics and fluency studies can mutually benefit one another is the impact of fluency on pragmatic interpretations of the message. Research in SLA has provided robust evidence that speakers' manner of producing an utterance can affect listeners' interpretation of the message in several ways. A simple example, although from a phonological perspective, is that a change of intonation or pitch, or placing more stress on one word in an utterance, can have an impact on the interpretation of the message by the listener. Our interest here lies in the different pragmatic interpretations that a change in the speaker's fluency can cause. For example, fluency features such as dysfluency markers and filled pauses are used in lie-detection studies (e.g. Barr & Seyfeddinipur, 2010; Loy, Rohde & Corley, 2017) to identify uncertainty or untruthfulness. Research in this area has also suggested that assessment of lie detection by listening to the speaker and drawing on their fluency profile is a more reliable predictor of truthfulness than a visual assessment of their body gestures and facial expressions (Loy et al., 2017).

About mid-clause pausing, as discussed in Chapters 1, 2 and 3, in L2 studies this kind of pause is often linked to processing demands associated with the speech production process, e.g. searching for the right word or trying to understand the task. However, in L1 lie-detection studies, often conducted in the context of identifying a potentially dishonest speaker, mid-clause filled pauses or other dysfluency markers, although similarly considered as evidence of processing demand, have different pragmatic interpretations: 'the listener may interpret the dysfluency as a pragmatic cue to deception' (Loy et al., 2017: 1450).

4.6 Conclusions

In the discussion above, we have summarised research in task design features and the way they influence learners' fluency. A fundamental assumption underpinning this body of research is that the cognitive demands of a task affect language production processes, and when this happens fluency appears to be affected by those demands, especially during the earlier stages of L2 acquisition when L2 knowledge is not yet proceduralised and L2 production processes are not automatic. It is hypothesised that the human brain's information processing capacity is challenged when the cognitive demands of a task are elevated, and this challenge often results in variations in different aspects of fluency. For example, learners find it easier to focus on conveying meaning when the task provides familiar and concrete information, portrays adequate (but not too much) information, is structured, its topic is familiar and there is an opportunity to plan.

We have also observed that a range of performance condition features affects fluency; these include the conditions under which a task is performed, social norms and cultural expectations. A serious apology, e.g. in many cultures is expected to be slower, with silent pauses and hesitations to signal the person's reflection and regret. A more important observation we have made is that there is a need for examining this wider range of task external features. Without such knowledge, our understanding of fluency and awareness of the variables that contribute to its representation and development will remain restricted. To gain this knowledge, we have suggested a multi-disciplinary approach to investigating L2 fluency as a way forward.

5 Fluency in Second Language Pedagogy

5.1 Introduction

In previous chapters, we have discussed the importance of fluency from second language (L2) acquisition and psycholinguistic perspective and argued that although fluency is recognised as an increasingly important aspect of successful communication, the pedagogic aspects of fluency research and practice have not attracted the attention they deserve. We also argued that the practical implications of fluency research are not adequately translated to the relevant aspects of practice, for example curriculum design and teacher education. To highlight the significant implications of L2 fluency research for language teaching, this chapter is dedicated to four aspects of L2 teaching practice: L2 policy documents, L2 textbooks, classroom practice and teacher cognition. This chapter aims to provide an analysis of how fluency is represented in each of these four aspects, and in what ways fluency research can help practitioners in these areas with everyday practices. After presenting a background to the role of fluency in L2 pedagogy, examples of L2 policy documents, for example the UK curriculum for teaching Modern Foreign Languages will be evaluated. We then provide a summary of research examining fluency in L2 textbooks, and discuss teaching activities that are reported as central to promoting fluency in the L2 classroom. Teacher understanding of fluency and the impact it has on promoting fluency in the language classroom will also be discussed.

5.2 Fluency in Second Language Teaching

Becoming a fluent and competent speaker of L2 is a central goal of L2 learning for many learners. Helping learners to become fluent and competent speakers of an L2 is also a key pedagogic objective in many L2 teaching programmes. The learner and teacher interest in fluency is

5.2 Fluency in Second Language Teaching   85

further encouraged by the attention language testing organisations pay to the assessment of speaking: fluency is one of the key constructs of communicative speaking ability and has been assessed regularly by many language testing organisations since the 1970s (see Chapter 6 for a detailed discussion). With the spread of globalisation and the increasing need for having competent and fluent multilingual speakers who use their L2 for education, employment and business purposes, fluency has gained more currency in the field of L2 pedagogy. This importance is gradually being recognised by different stakeholders and the impact can be seen on educational policy documents and pedagogic research. The introduction of fluency as a pedagogic objective in teaching Modern Foreign Languages (MFL) within the UK National Subject Content (2014) is an example of such impact at a national policy level. In Canada, a recent federal evaluation of language instruction for newcomers to Canada programmes highlighted 'extremely limited improvements in speaking and listening skills' (Diepenbroek & Derwing, 2014); this has reiterated learners' need to develop more competent speaking skills. This pedagogic interest has led researchers to invest more time in investigating fluency in L2 teaching and learning contexts (e.g. Lennon, 1990; Freed, 2000; Derwing, Munro, Thomson & Rossiter, 2009; Segalowitz, 2010). Researching fluency in pedagogic contexts can further help develop an in-depth understanding of how it is conceptualised, understood and practised in instructional settings, what objectives can be set for classroom teaching and learning, and to what extent such objectives can be achieved in instructional settings (Lennon, 1990; Freed, 2000; Koponen & Riggenbach, 2000).

While L2 fluency is a common goal in L2 teaching and assessment, researching it in a focused way in these contexts is a more recent and less productive endeavour (Lennon, 1990; Freed, 2000; Tavakoli & Hunter, 2018), with some recent publications labelling it as a 'neglected area' in language teaching (Derwing et al., 2009). The existing evidence suggests that the implications of this body of research have so far had little impact on practice in L2 pedagogy (Derwing et al., 2009; Tavakoli & Hunter, 2018). Some researchers argue that the scarcity of fluency research in L2 pedagogy can be attributed to the fact that the complex and multi-faceted construct of fluency does not lend itself well to classroom research (Freed, 2000; Tavakoli & Hunter, 2018). Others argue that the limited interest in promoting fluency in the classroom context might be motivated by the commonly held assumption that fluency develops when general proficiency progresses, and therefore fluency should not be directly taught in the L2 classroom (Lennon, 1990; Chambers, 1997). In the rest of this chapter, we will review research in this area and summarise some

86   *Fluency in Second Language Pedagogy*

important pedagogical implications it has for professional practice in L2 teaching.

5.3 Fluency in Second Language Benchmarks and Curricula

As discussed above, although fluency has for a long time been a key objective in many language teaching and learning contexts, its emergence in language benchmarks and curricula is a relatively new development. It is known that the dominance of Communicative Language Teaching (CLT) in L2 pedagogy over the last three decades has encouraged L2 educators to pay more attention to speaking skills in general, and to the role of fluency in fostering oral communication in particular. Contrary to this early interest from teachers and learners, emergence of fluency in L2 pedagogic documents and materials has occurred rather late, with many policy documents referring to fluency in a rather restricted and inadequate way. In this section, we will evaluate three rather different documents in order to understand their representations of fluency in these different contexts and to compare them with the findings of L2 fluency research. The three L2 teaching and learning documents are: the Council of Europe's CEFR document (2001), the UK GCSE Modern Foreign Languages Subject Content (2014) and the Hong Kong English Language Curriculum (2017).

5.3.1 Common European Framework of Reference for Languages (CEFR)

The Common European Framework of Reference for Languages (CEFR) (2001) document is one of the most comprehensive language policy documents that highlights the importance of fluency as a key aspect of communicative speaking ability. One of the strengths of the CEFR document is that it discusses communicative language ability from teaching, learning and assessment perspectives by providing detailed and research-led discussions of L2 ability, its constructs, processes and components. The CEFR document defines L2 speaking ability in terms of its linguistic components such as range, accuracy, fluency, interaction and coherence. In this conceptualisation, *range* refers to the diversity and complexity of language and includes both structures and lexis; *accuracy* focuses on the correctness of the language used, and *fluency* is understood in relation to the ability to convey the intended meaning efficiently and smoothly. It is interesting to see that the CEFR makes several references to the concept of fluency and discusses it in relation to all three aspects of fluency, that is cognitive, utterance and perceived fluency.

5.3 Fluency in Second Language Benchmarks & Curricula   87

Fluency descriptors used in the CEFR document refer to several examples of utterance fluency including *pauses, hesitation, a natural colloquial flow, false starts* and *reformulation*. These concrete aspects of fluency are perhaps overemphasised in the CEFR as they are more easily noticed and understood by a range of different practitioners including less-experienced teachers. The document goes beyond presenting concrete descriptors to also highlight some of the underlying processes that cause pausing and repair. Examples provided in the document to show such processes include 'pausing for grammatical and lexical planning and repair' (p. 7), and 'much pausing to search for expressions' (p. 7). Interestingly, the updated CEFR (Council of Europe, 2018) document makes an explicit distinction between cognitive demands and linguistic demands that affect fluency by considering the former as content-related and the latter as language-related hesitations and repair by arguing that 'Only a conceptually difficult subject can hinder a natural, smooth flow of language' (p. 83). The CEFR document also makes several references to the concept of perceived fluency. To underscore its significance, it provides examples that analyse what impact fluency (or lack of fluency) could have on the listener, for example 'backtracking around any difficulty so smoothly that the interlocutor is hardly aware of it' (p. 28). The more recent version of the CEFR, The Companion (Council of Europe, 2018), makes references to the findings of SLA research to explain the concept of fluency.

Spoken fluency, as discussed above, has a broader, holistic meaning (=articulate speaker) and a narrower, technical and more psycholinguistic meaning (=accessing one's repertoire). The broader interpretation would include propositional precision, flexibility, and at least to some extent thematic development and coherence/cohesion. For this reason, the scale below focuses more on the narrower, more traditional view of fluency. (p. 144)

The excerpt above suggests that the CEFR document considers fluency in a reasonably well-developed manner, providing valuable references to the concept of fluency as a key construct of the L2 speaking ability, and drawing users' and practitioners' attention to how fluency affects communication with and perceptions of the interlocutors. The CEFR document also considers fluency from an interactional perspective as it makes references to how speaker fluency affects the interlocutor.

Although it is one of the most detailed L2 policy documents discussing and defining fluency, it faces two main limitations. First, it fails to provide an adequately detailed and elaborate account of L2 fluency that can equip teachers and professional practitioners with the knowledge and awareness required to work with fluency. For instance, it

88   *Fluency in Second Language Pedagogy*

frequently highlights the impact of pausing on the listener, but it does not indicate what kind and how much pausing can have a negative impact on the listener. While research in this area has provided us with ample evidence about the length of pause considered acceptable (de Jong et al., 2013) and the location and character of pauses that are supportive of real-time communication (Tavakoli, 2011; Hunter, 2017), the findings of this body of research are not included in the discussions. Another limitation of the CEFR document is a lack of clarity about fluency expectations at different levels of L2 learning. For example, *speaking fluently and spontaneously* is considered a characteristic of both C1 and C2 levels without demonstrating how these two can be distinguished. Table 5.1 demonstrates to what extent fluency described in the CEFR document represents the construct of fluency in relation to Segalowitz's (2010) model.

5.3.2 UK Modern Foreign Languages Subject Content for General Certificate in Secondary Education

The second example of L2 curricula we discuss here is the UK Modern Foreign Languages (MFL) subject content for General Certificate in Secondary Education (GCSE) (2015). Although the GCSE for MFL Subject Content in the UK (2015) is not a curriculum, it provides key concepts, principles and guidelines for this subject and 'sets out the knowledge, understanding and skills common to all GCSE specifications in a given subject' (p. 1). It also provides, along with the assessment objectives, the framework in which 'the awarding organisations create the detail of their specifications', to ensure progression from a higher secondary school education level (Key Stage 3) to a pre-university level of education (A-Level). The document was updated in 2014 to reflect the new perspective on L2 communicative ability, and to set the expectations and standards for MFL teaching and learning in UK high schools.

The document sets out to determine what 'ability and ambition' (p. 7) students need to develop in order to communicate with native speakers in speech and writing. While the document emphasises communication with native speakers as the end-goal in MFL teaching, it pays attention to both fluency and accuracy of the language output. The statement 'a variety of structures and vocabulary with increasing accuracy and fluency for new purposes' (p. 7) is an example of the document's interest in both accuracy and fluency. There are a number of examples of references the document makes to the importance of fluency in oral communication.

Table 5.1 Representations of fluency in second language teaching and learning documents

	Cognitive Fluency	Utterance Fluency	Perceived Fluency
CEFR	• Only a conceptually difficult subject can hinder a natural, smooth flow of language. • The student can be hesitant as he/she searches for patterns and expressions. • Pausing for grammatical and lexical repair is very evident. • There is much pausing to search for expressions, to articulate less familiar words, and to repair communication.	The student's utterances are: • with a natural colloquial flow • with a fairly even tempo • with noticeably long pauses • hesitant • with very evidentpauses, false starts and reformulations.	• The student is avoiding or backtracking around any difficulty so smoothly that the interlocutor is hardly aware of it.
UK MFL GCSE subject content	The student can: • express and develop ideas and thoughts spontaneously and fluently • convey information and narrate events coherently and confidently.	The student: • speaks spontaneously, sustaining communication by using rephrasing or repair strategies as appropriate • produces extended sequences of speech • uses accurate pronunciation and intonation.	The student: • communicates confidently and coherently with native speakers • has developed language strategies, especially for repair • uses accurate pronunciation and intonation such as to be understood by a native speaker.
Hong Kong Curriculum for English Language	• The student can present information, ideas and feelings clearly and coherently.		• The student can express ideas fluently in accordance with the audience.

90   *Fluency in Second Language Pedagogy*

- Develop their ability to communicate confidently and coherently with native speakers in speech and writing.
- Express and develop thoughts and ideas spontaneously and fluently.
- Listen and understand clearly articulated, standard speech at near normal speed.
- Develop language strategies, including repair strategies.

These examples demonstrate that the new MFLsubject content has considered fluency as an important aim in MFL teaching and learning in the United Kingdom, and has formally and explicitly included references to fluency in this important policy document. When discussing speaking skill more specifically, the document makes further references to the importance of fluency (p. 5):

- Convey information and narrate events coherently and confidently.
- Speak spontaneously, responding to unexpected questions, points of view or situations, sustaining communication by using rephrasing or repair strategies, as appropriate.

It is necessary to note that the document appears to demonstrate more interest in grammar by expecting students to develop and use knowledge and understanding of grammar progressively throughout their course, and by explicitly setting out a list of grammatical requirements for different languages to be taught at schools. It also considers accuracy as central to speaking ability as it emphasises 'accurate' pronunciation and intonation. This is in contrast to some recent research that recommends intelligible pronunciation and intonation (e.g. Jenkins, 2003, 2007; Saito, Trofimovich & Isaacs, 2017). Unlike the CEFR document, the GCSE Subject Content does not provide any description of what fluency means or what factors influence it. Concepts such as pausing, silence, repetition and interruption are rarely discussed or exemplified. Although the concept of perceived fluency is implicitly referred to once, this happens subtly and scarcely. Similar to the CEFR document, the UK MFL policy document provides a limited account of the construct of fluency with very little clarity in explaining how to distinguish fluent speech from less fluent speech across different levels of proficiency.

5.3.3 Hong Kong English Language Curriculum

The third L2 policy document we examine here is the Hong Kong English Language Education Key Learning Area Curriculum Guide (2017) for schools in both primary and secondary levels. This document is produced by the Hong Kong National Curriculum

5.3 Fluency in Second Language Benchmarks & Curricula   91

Development Council and advocates a new era in which curriculum development is expected to keep up with the latest developments in 'local, regional and global landscapes' (p. 2). Compared to the UK MFL subject content, this is a highly ambitious curriculum that aims to enhance students' English proficiency not only for education, employment and leisure purposes, but for personal and intellectual development and global competitiveness.

Although fluency is recognised as an aspect of language use in this document, it seems that accuracy is prioritised over fluency on several repetitions. The importance of fluency comes to attention mainly when it is contrasted with accuracy, for example 'Due acknowledgement is given to fluency and effective expression of ideas in students' performance in addition to accuracy' (p. 91). More commonly, fluency is discussed in relation to assessment of speaking ability. In terms of assessment, students' speaking is examined for a range of constructs such as *content, grammar, task requirements, organisation* and '*pronunciation and fluency*' (p. 91). The fact that fluency is grouped with pronunciation suggests that fluency is not perceived as an independent construct in communicative language ability. To assess '*pronunciation and fluency*', examiners are asked to look at five descriptors of *audibility, pace, correct pronunciation, intonation* and *stress*. While pace is the only component that can demonstrate fluency, the other four descriptors are only minimally related to fluency in the way it is understood and used within fluency research.

When discussing the descriptors of expected achievements across the curriculum, fluency is considered as a subcategory of language abilities and is claimed 'to generate numerous ideas promptly' (p. 187). The references made, although useful and valuable, have hardly explained what is meant by fluency or what characterises fluent L2 speech. Like the UK MFL subject content, the Hong Kong curriculum contains very little reference to concepts such as cognitive, utterance and perceived fluency. The document fails to demonstrate in explicit and comprehensible ways how fluency can be defined, examined or promoted in L2 teaching and learning. Table 5.1 demonstrates the extent to which these three documents represent fluency in terms of Segalowitz's triadic model (2010).

Based on the analysis provided above, it is possible to conclude that although fluency is one of the key teaching and learning objectives stated in many language policy and curricular documents, fluency as a concept is neither clearly defined nor carefully presented in such documents. Our analysis demonstrates that at best, fluency is represented as a quality of speech that L2 learners are expected to develop during their L2 learning process, and teachers are required to help

92   *Fluency in Second Language Pedagogy*

learners develop this quality. The documents reviewed above also seem limited in analysing the complex construct of fluency by failing to show its different aspects and characteristics, including the interactive nature of fluency and the impact it has on the listeners and interlocutors. None of the documents we have reviewed above determine how fluent and dysfluent speech can be objectively distinguished, or what characterises a fluent L2 speaker at each stage of language learning. The fact that fluency is explicitly mentioned in these documents should be considered a new and valuable development in the field of L2 pedagogy. However, without a careful description of fluency as a concept, a detailed analysis of fluency as a construct, and a clear discussion of the procedures involved in the development of fluency, such curricular documents will fail to prepare teachers for the significant task of helping students become fluent speakers of their L2s.

5.4 Fluency in Second Language Textbooks

In many L2 teaching contexts, while teachers normally use a range of different materials and resources to complement their teaching, textbooks are often considered as the backbone of L2 teaching. L2 learners often prefer having a textbook as a reference for their learning and as a source to rely on. Whether this preference is motivated by teachers' workload and confidence or learners' interest and interdependence on published materials, textbooks are widely used in many L2 teaching and learning contexts. Textbooks are also perceived as central to L2 teaching processes as they are used for a range of pedagogic reasons including curriculum design, lesson planning and classroom assessment (Diepenbroek & Derwing, 2013). With our interest in fluency and pedagogy in this chapter, we will present a review of studies investigating the extent to which textbooks help promote fluency. There are three studies that are closely relevant to our discussion.

Rossiter, Derwing, Manimtim, and Thomson (2010) examined twenty-eight textbooks and fourteen teacher manuals to determine whether and to what extent fluency activities were included in these books. They reported five types of activities that were designed to promote fluency: consciousness-raising activities, rehearsal or repetition activities, activities that promoted use of formulaic sequences and/or discourse markers, and free production activities (also known as 'general speaking activities'). Rossiter et al. (2010) reported that free production activities were the most popular in these textbooks, followed by formulaic sequences and rehearsal activities.

Consciousness-raising activities and discourse markers, on the other hand, were the least used types. Rossiter et al. concluded that the textbooks under investigation were unbalanced in terms of fluency-enhancing activities and did not pay adequate attention to promoting fluency in instructional settings.

Diepenbroek and Derwing (2013) examined several popular integrated skills textbooks used in Language Instruction for Newcomers to Canada (LINC) and English as a Second Language (ESL) programmes to examine to what extent textbooks focus on oral fluency, and what activities are commonly featured in these textbooks to help promote fluency. Adopting Rossiter et al.'s (2010) framework to analyse the books, they found very similar results. They concluded that fluency was not a major focus in the textbooks they examined, but argued that the general speaking activities can help enhance fluency development if used effectively.

Morrison (2018) examined Chilean high school textbooks to determine whether they promoted fluency in the Chilean EFL instructional settings. It is necessary to note that these textbooks are developed for national educational purposes and are mapped onto the CEFR levels of proficiency. For this reason, it was assumed that the textbooks benefitted from a reasonably well-developed interest in and attention to fluency. In order to analyse the activities, Morrison adopted Tavakoli and Hunter's (2018) framework, and adapted it to ensure applicability. The analysis framework included activities that had recently been recommended by the literature to promote fluency, for example awareness-raising activities, task rehearsal and repetition, and use of formulaic sequences. Morrison's findings (2018) suggested that fluency was not actively promoted in these textbooks, as they prioritised general-speaking to fluency-focused activities. Only a small percentage of the activities in the Chilean textbooks helped promote fluency, while a large proportion were aimed at developing general speaking skills, for example ordering food and making a request. These findings are in line with previous results from Rossiter et al. (2010) and Diepenbroek and Derwing (2013).

Morrison's findings imply that despite the significant role of fluency in L2 learning and teaching, the textbooks researched so far are not designed to focus on preparing learners for the fluent communication advocated in the policy documents we reviewed earlier on. It is interesting to see that the principles valued by widely recognised language benchmarks and policy documents like CEFR are not promoted in textbooks. The findings of Morrison (2018) highlight the inconsistency between objectives presented in the Chilean National Curriculum and the actual teaching practices Chilean textbooks utilise. Although it

Fluency in Second Language Pedagogy

is possible to assume that many teachers have the necessary tools and strategies for promoting fluency in their everyday practice, recent studies (e.g. Rossiter et al., 2010; Diepenbroek & Derwing, 2013) suggest that EFL/ESL textbooks do not contain activities that are aiming at the development of fluency in instructional settings. In a later section of this chapter, by reviewing studies investigating teachers' understanding of fluency and their classroom practice, we will identify the conceptual mismatch between what research in this area suggests, what the L2 documents and materials project, and what teachers understand and practise as a potentially challenging divide to fill. We will first examine classroom practices that are reported in promoting fluency.

5.5 Fluency and Second Language Classroom Practice

Gatbonton and Segalowitz (1988), aiming to bring fluency research and practice closer together, drew on the findings of their own fluency research and argued that a 'creative automatization process' is needed to enable L2 learners to 'develop the automaticity component of fluency in second language production in a classroom setting' (p. 473). In another study, Gatbonton and Segalowitz (2005) argued that despite the fact that fluency is a key component of automatic, smooth and rapid language use, 'there are no provisions in current communicative language teaching methodologies to promote language use to a high level of mastery through repetitive practice' (p. 327). The call for more fluency-focused classroom practice was justified by the argument that, although fluency is typically expected to develop hand-in-hand with proficiency as it progresses and is to a great extent aided by practice and exposure inside and outside instructional settings, certain kinds of communicative and interactive activities would effectively help develop fluency in instructional settings. Some researchers (e.g. Derwing et al., 2009; Tavakoli, Campbell & McCormack, 2016) argued that when it is not possible to use and practise the target language outside the classroom, teachers will have a more central role in the development of fluency, as classroom practice is expected to provide learners with worthwhile opportunities for developing fluent speaking ability during lessons.

Following from Gatbonton and Segalowitz's studies, other researchers (de Jong & Perfetti, 2011; Kahng, 2014; Tavakoli et al., 2016; Tavakoli & Hunter, 2018) have continued to examine fluency in instructional settings. One major aim of this body of research is to determine whether it is possible to improve instructional practices that help learners develop fluency in classroom. Some researchers

5.5 Fluency and Second Language Classroom Practice 95

(Tavakoli et al., 2016; Hunter, 2017; Tavakoli & Hunter, 2018) have provided a list of effective techniques, tasks and activities that can help with the development of fluency in L2 classrooms. We summarise the activities and practices that research in this area has shown to be successful in classroom settings.

5.5.1 Recommended Classroom Activities to Promote Fluency

5.5.1.1 FORMULAIC SEQUENCES

In L2 teaching, it is commonly believed that knowledge of formulaic sequences is crucial in promoting naturalness in speech. Formulaic sequences, a distinctive feature of native speakers' speech (Nattinger & DeCarrico, 1992; Wray, 2002), are ready-made chunks of language that form a major part of language in use. Pawley and Syder's (1983: 191) argument that 'fluent and idiomatic control of a language rests to a considerable extent on knowledge of a body of sentence stems which are institutionalised or lexicalised' implies that fluency to a great extent depends on the speaker's access to these fixed expressions and their ability to use them. From a psycholinguistic point of view, Pawley and Syder (1983) argued that processing formulaic sequences is less demanding than processing a sequence of non-formulaic words, and as such, use of formulaic sequences is an advantage in processing. Since formulaic sequences are stored in the long-term memory as single units and stored in the mental lexicon as ready-to use items, they can be retrieved and processed as inseparable wholes or with a minimal amount of pressure from the encoding processes. These qualities of storage and processing lead to a more fluent production of language since they ease off the pressure on the working memory and allow the speaker to focus on comprehending and conceptualizing what needs to be said. The research evidence in this area shows that learners incorporating formulaic sequences into their speech are generally perceived as more fluent (Boers et al., 2006; Wood, 2009; Tavakoli, 2011; Tavakoli & Uchihara, 2020). This fluency is reflected in a degree of naturalness in their language use and the smoothness associated with producing phonological units without hesitations or pauses in the middle. Tavakoli and Uchihara (2020) found a linear relationship between frequency and proportion of these lexical sequences on the one hand and level of L2 speakers' proficiency and fluency on the other, suggesting that more competent speakers certainly employ frequent lexical sequences (frequency), and use a lot of them (proportion). Several researchers (e.g. Wray, 2000, 2008; Wood,

96   *Fluency in Second Language Pedagogy*

2010, 2016) have argued that explicit instruction of formulaic sequences contributes to the development of L2 fluency, and therefore, implications of this body of research seem to be important for language teaching and teachers aiming to promote learners' oral fluency.

5.5.1.2 PLANNING TIME

As discussed in Chapter 4, since the 1980s, several studies have reported that language performance in general and fluency in particular improve when learners are given time to plan before they speak (e.g. Foster & Skehan, 1996; Mehnert, 1998; Tavakoli & Skehan, 2005). Research in this area has shown that learners improve their fluency (as measured by rate of speech, mean length of run, and number of repairs) after they have been given time to plan before or during their speech. As the effects of planning time on fluency are discussed in Chapter 4, here we provide a summary of the implications for classroom teaching.

Guided planning time, that is teachers guiding students on how to use their planning time or what aspect of their work to focus on, has been shown to have an impact on the language L2 learners produce. Foster and Skehan (1996) reported that learners improved fluency and complexity of their language when they were guided by the teacher, but the accuracy of their language improved more when they worked under unguided planning time on their own. Mochizuki and Ortega (2008) provided their learners with grammatically embedded guidance during the planning time and found that learners were able to perform better when the teachers guided their planning time. Research also suggests that group-led planning time is effective in developing fluency and producing more ideas (Truong & Storch, 2007).

5.5.1.3 TASK REPETITION

Another important L2 teaching activity commonly reported to help with the development of fluency is task repetition (Bygate, 2001). Task repetition, also known as task rehearsal, whether repeating the same task or repeating the same task procedures with different content, has been found to have positive effects on fluency (Lynch & Maclean, 2000; Ahmadian, 2011; Hunter, 2017). Gatbonton and Segalowitz (1988: 331) explain the impact of task repetition in the light of its communicative nature and the use of 'inherently repetitive and functionally formulaic' language when a task is repeated. They suggest that

5.5 Fluency and Second Language Classroom Practice 97

that task repetition (performing it once before performing it again) provides speakers with the opportunity to have a 'dry-run' practice and plan for a more effective way of conveying the intended message. Hunter (2017) examined the development of fluency in task repetition and task rehearsal among sixty-four ESL learners. The results of her study suggested that while fluency increased in both task repetition and procedure repetition groups, the results were more significant for the task repetition group. Other studies have reported that the effects of task repetition on fluency may not persist over a long period of time as learners move on to other task types (Lynch & Maclean, 2000; Hsu, 2019); however, Lambert, Kormos and Minn (2017) showed that repeating a communicative task once or more consistently helps increase fluency of oral performance.

5.5.1.4 THE 4/3/2 TECHNIQUE

The 4/3/2 (or 3/2/1) technique is a special kind of task repetition involving time pressure. This means that while learners are asked to repeat the same task three times, for each repetition they have less time to perform that task, that is for 4, then 3 and finally 2 minutes. Several studies (e.g. Nation, 1989; de Jong& Perfetti, 2011; Boers, 2014), have reported that the 4/3/2 technique has a positive impact on fluency. Similar to task repetition however, the effects may not simply persist over an extended period of time or when different tasks are performed.

5.5.1.5 STRATEGY TRAINING

A number of researchers have looked into the effects of strategy training on the development of fluency in L2 classrooms (Guillot, 1999; Rossiter, 2003; Tavakoli et al., 2016). These strategies often include use of empty fillers (e.g. 'er' and 'uhm'), lexical fillers (e.g. 'right', 'well'), formulaic chunks (e.g. 'let me think') and avoidance strategies (e.g. paraphrasing and avoiding unnecessary repetitions). Tavakoli et al. (2016) found that strategy training combined with awareness raising activities administered over a period of four weeks helped ESL learners to become more fluent in terms of their speech rate, articulation rate and mean length of run. The learners who received the training also produced fewer repairs in their speech as a result of this training. Although a very useful classroom activity, strategy training would have limited impact on learners of lower proficiency level, as production processes are slower in rate and more interruptive in nature.

98 Fluency in Second Language Pedagogy

5.5.1.6 AWARENESS-RAISING

Only a few studies have examined the effects of awareness-raising activities on fluency. Raising learner awareness about the importance of fluency and the impact dysfluent speech has on the listener has been shown to help learners develop a better understanding of fluency and to encourage them to develop strategies that are conducive to fluent communication (Seifoori & Vahidi, 2012; Tavakoli et al., 2016). Tavakoli et al. (2016) provided ESL learners with classroom opportunities that involved listening to both fluent and dysfluent speakers performing a picture-story retelling task. The primary aim of this activity was to identify those features of fluency that had an impact on the learners' perceptions as listeners (e.g. long undue pauses, hesitations, repetitions). Working with a transcript of the narrative retellings, the learners had several opportunities to analyse the speech samples with their partners and discuss what could be done to avoid some of the dysfluency features. This activity was later followed by the learners recording themselves performing the same picture retelling task and listening to their own performance to identify dysfluent features of their speech. The interactional nature of speaking and the impact fluency has on this interaction was discussed with the students during the activities in both monologic and interactive tasks. The awareness-raising activities appeared to have an impact on not only their understanding of the impact fluency has on the listener, but it also encouraged them to think of strategies that could help them come across as more fluent. The results of Tavakoli et al. (2016) suggested that awareness-raising activities, combined with strategy training, helped learners avoid unnecessary repetitions and hesitations and led to a more effective use of lexical fillers. As discussed above, for more successful outcomes, awareness-raising activities need to be complemented by other activities such as strategy training (Tavakoli et al., 2016).

5.6 Fluency, Teacher Cognition and Teacher Practice

The last section of this chapter focuses on teachers' understanding of fluency and the extent to which this understanding is related to how they promote fluency in their teaching. There is ample research evidence in the L2 teacher education literature (e.g. Borg, 2003, 2009; Burns & Richards, 2009) to suggest that teacher cognition and teacher professional practice are inherently inter-related, and therefore, it is as important to learn about teacher understanding of key educational concepts is it is to learn about what they do in their practice. Foster (2009) argued that SLA research should be complemented by feedback

5.6 Fluency, Teacher Cognition & Teacher Practice 99

and input from the teaching community and yet, despite the growing body of research on L2 fluency, we know very little about how teachers understand L2 fluency and in what ways their understanding of fluency interacts with their classroom practices. For the purpose of this chapter, we argue that it is necessary to gain insight into how teachers understand and define fluency, as this knowledge can help in complementing the research-led definitions and conceptualisations of fluency.

As discussed in previous chapters, research in perceived fluency, although rather recent, has carefully examined speakers' perceptions of fluency (Préfontaine, 2013, 2015; Kormos & Préfontaine, 2016). While focusing on native speakers' perceptions has given vital insights into the nature of fluency, there has not been an equivalent push to examine teachers' understanding of the concept. Here, we report on three studies that have specifically examined teacher perceptions and/or understanding of fluency.

Dore (2015) examined teachers' perceptions of fluency in two different contexts of EFL in Italy and ESL in the United Kingdom. The participants were forty-eight experienced teachers working at the university language centres in these two contexts. Using an online questionnaire, Dore collected both quantitative and qualitative data. First, the teachers had to listen to three L2 speakers to decide who sounded more fluent. Having rated the speakers' fluency, they were then asked to explain in what ways they justified their ratings, and what characteristics of the speakers' speech contributed to their perceptions of fluency. Analysis of the data suggested that the participants were in agreement over a cluster of variables that indicated cognitive processing, for example effortlessness and automaticity. The analysis also confirmed that the teachers linked this underlying cognitive processing to the more objectively evaluated evidence of pauses, hesitations and reformulation. Although they had reservations about speed measures such as speech rate, they commonly referred to the idea of 'chunking', which Dore (2015) interprets in terms of 'length of run' aspect of fluency. In addition, coherence seemed to be highly important, as it seemed to indicate the cognitive efficiency with which language was produced. Strikingly, while L2 fluency research has not specifically focused on suprasegmental aspects of phonology and their relationship to fluency, the teachers considered phonology, e.g. rhythm and intonation, as a central element of fluency, and suggested this had made a major contribution to their perceptions. Such clear differences between conceptualisations of fluency from research vs. teaching perspectives reflect the gap between the two and imply that teachers' perceptions are not yet included in research-based models of fluency. The data analysis also indicated that although the UK-based participants were generally less experienced in terms of years of teaching, they had received more specific training than the Italy-based teachers. The responses elicited from the UK group appeared to be more in line with the CEFR document, while the Italy-based teachers' understanding of fluency articulated a broader interpretation of the concept of fluency.

Examining teachers' understanding of fluency, Tavakoli and Hunter (2018) collected qualitative and quantitative data from eighty-four second language teachers teaching a range of different languages in England. In addition to questions examining teacher understanding, the questionnaire investigated teachers' classroom practices in promoting fluency. The teachers, from a range of different educational and experience backgrounds, completed the questionnaires before attending a workshop on fluency. The results of the study suggested that teachers defined fluency in what Lennon (1990) viewed as a 'broad sense' of the term, with many using fluency and speaking ability interchangeably. The findings were similar to those of Dore (2015) in relation to perceptions of fluency: they considered aspects of cognitive and utterance fluency related, they emphasised the role of phonology, and they referred to coherence as a key element of fluency. Interestingly, teachers' self-reported practice was also closely linked with their understanding of fluency, and therefore many of the activities they reported in the questionnaires were good examples of general speaking exercises rather than fluency-focused activities. Tavakoli and Hunter (2018) reported that in their data fluency was defined and understood at four different levels.

- A very broad perspective, in which fluency is used synonymously with proficiency or mastery of L2 ability.
- A broad perspective, in which fluency reflects L2 speaking ability, and as such includes elements of pronunciation, accuracy in speech and ability to hold a conversation.
- A narrow perspective, in which fluency represents ease, flow and continuity of speech and is in contrast with other aspects of speaking, e.g. grammatical complexity and accuracy.
- A very narrow perspective, in which fluency demonstrates objectively measurable features (utterance fluency), e.g. speed, silence and repair.

Reporting a gap between fluency research and L2 pedagogy, Tavakoli and Hunter (2018) argued that adopting a narrower understanding of fluency would be more suitable for professional practitioners as it facilitates understanding the complex and multi-faceted nature of

5.6 Fluency, Teacher Cognition & Teacher Practice   101

fluency and enables them to take a more active and practical approach to promoting fluency in the classroom. Tavakoli and Hunter (2018) also suggested that for teachers and researchers to communicate successfully they must use a shared language. The gap between teachers and researchers will narrow if they have shared understanding of concepts and constructs. They also suggest that if a more evidence-based approach to L2 teaching practice is expected, teacher training and education programmes should work closely with researchers in second language acquisition to agree on definitions of key terms and ideas.

Similarly to the two studies above, Morrison (2018) investigated teacher understanding of fluency through a questionnaire eliciting both quantitative and qualitative data. The questionnaires, completed by sixty Chilean teachers of English working at state and private high schools, examined teachers' understanding of fluency, the level of their confidence in promoting fluency, and examples of activities they carried out in class to promote fluency. The findings suggested that teachers prioritised general-speaking to fluency-focused activities, with little attention to and focus on promoting fluency in its narrow sense. The results also highlighted a degree of misinterpretation of fluency-focused activities for some teachers who considered fluency activities interchangeable to general speaking activities. Even though teachers reported high levels of confidence in their knowledge and skills for promoting fluency in classroom, they appeared to have limited knowledge of fluency, or what activities could be used to promote it. In sum, these findings are in line with the results of Tavakoli and Hunter (2018) and suggest that teachers often adopt a very broad or broad perspective to fluency.

Although there is evidence suggesting that L2 teacher education is interested in preparing teachers to help learners become fluent, there is little research evidence to indicate to what extent L2 teacher education has systematically integrated a focus on fluency in their training programmes. The evidence supporting teachers' interest in fluency comes from both language testing and learner needs. As you will see in Chapter 6, fluency has for a long time been one of the key components of speaking assessment in several leading international language tests. The washback effect from the tests inevitably invites teachers and learners to do things that help develop fluent speaking abilities. As we argued in Chapter 1, many learners come to the L2 teaching context with the aim of becoming fluent speakers of the language. These two areas of interest in fluency together makes it easy to hypothesise that L2 teacher education should have a substantial interest in fluency-focused training in their programmes. Indeed, some teaching training resources (e.g. Harmer, 2005), make a distinction

102 *Fluency in Second Language Pedagogy*

between speaking activities with a focus on 'accurate' or 'fluent' L2 speech (e.g. Scrivener, 1994; Harmer, 2005). However, our observations of the current practices in teacher training programmes suggest that the attention paid to fluency is limited and inadequate.

5.7 Conclusions

In this chapter, we have reviewed fluency research in some important aspects of L2 teaching by looking at the professional practices that are central to successful L2 pedagogy. The evidence provided in this chapter, although limited, implies that while fluency as a concept is nothing new to the profession, systematic attempts at conceptualising, defining and explaining L2 fluency are rather recent. The very first conclusion to make is that there is scope for further work on L2 fluency from a pedagogical perspective. The analysis of the L2 policy documents has shown that the attention paid to fluency is rather limited, and inadequate descriptions and analyses are provided in the documents. Textbooks that are reviewed for this purpose have often been reported as failing to meet the students' and teachers' intended objectives in terms of promoting fluency. Teachers' perceptions and understanding of fluency are hardly examined, and as such, research on fluency has not benefitted from teachers' wealth of knowledge and experience. While research has provided a list of useful classroom activities and techniques that can help students develop their fluency, teachers are often not very familiar with these activities and may not be prepared to help their students.

Drawing on the findings of the studies discussed above, it is fair to conclude that fluency, in the narrow sense of the term, is neither systematically defined nor discussed in language teaching materials, whether curricula, textbooks or teacher training programmes. The existing evidence suggests that teachers tend to focus on helping students develop their speaking ability, and that perhaps they expect fluency to be developed when they become proficient speakers of their L2s.

6 *Fluency in Second Language Testing*

Assessing fluency in a second language (L2) speaking test like International English Language Testing System (IELTS) or Test of English as a Foreign Language (TOEFL) is a crucial part of any test of speaking as it demonstrates whether the speaker is able to communicate the intended meaning successfully and coherently in real-time. Despite the central significance attributed to fluency in the assessment of L2 spoken ability, research examining how language testing organisations measure fluency, design their fluency rating scales and develop their fluency descriptors is limited. The existing research evidence suggests that examiners often find the fluency criterion difficult to assess (Brown, 2006b) and that fluency seems to be the feature most susceptible to task effect, i.e. fluency is easily affected by both raters' rating and the type of task used to elicit speech samples (Nakatsuhara, 2012). Therefore, the complexities involved in human rating of fluency are another reason to make the assessment of an already complex and multidimensional construct of fluency difficult. The current chapter has two prime aims. First, it aims to highlight the importance of assessing fluency objectively, accurately and consistently. We will argue that measuring fluency accurately, objectively and consistently leads to a more valid assessment of fluency. Second, the chapter argues that in order to achieve a more valid assessment of fluency, developing a research-evidenced approach to assessing fluency in L2 tests of speaking is indispensable.

The chapter starts by providing a historical background to the assessment of fluency in a second language over the past decades. After examining the existing fluency descriptors and rating scales in some international tests of speaking, the chapter will report on recent research investigating fluency across different levels of proficiency. It will also discuss in what ways a broader theoretical perspective to assessment of fluency, e.g. using Conversation Analysis techniques, should be considered when validating assessment of fluency. Effects of

104   *Fluency in Second Language Testing*

raters, rating scales and rating descriptors on judgements of fluency will also be discussed, and merits and limitations of automated assessment of fluency will be evaluated. The chapter's main argument is that the gap between fluency research and language testing should be bridged if a valid and accurate assessment of the fluency construct is expected. The chapter will demonstrate that the approach taken in assessment of fluency so far has underestimated the interactional nature of fluency, and as such assessment of a complex multidimensional construct (see Chapters 2 and 3) has remained rather unidimensional in that the assessment principles are mainly based on the dimension of perceived fluency. We will conclude the chapter by discussing the implications of these important developments for practice in language testing and future research.

6.1 Assessing Fluency in Validated International L2 Tests

The speaking exam of most standardised proficiency tests typically involves using one or more test tasks to elicit samples of the test-takers' performance, which is then assessed by trained raters before a score is agreed upon and some inferences are made about how the speaker would show her/his spoken ability beyond the test performance. The inferences are often, but not always, articulated in *can-do* statements that describe what the speaker can do with the language knowledge and skills she/he has, e.g. 'the speaker is able to speak about everyday topics in a reasonably coherent manner'. Although the use of computer rating is the way forward in future assessment of oral performance, speaking ability is still widely measured by means of human listeners (or as they are called raters) and their judgment of the speech samples. This involves trained raters working with a set of rating scales to evaluate the speech samples and to decide which proficiency level the speaker belongs to. Some language tests use holistic ratings, i.e. a scale that considers and assesses the different aspects of performance as a whole, whereas others use analytic scales in which different key constructs underlying spoken language ability are evaluated separately. When speaking is rated analytically, the raters are asked to rate different features of the speaking performance including its accuracy, fluency, range, delivery and interaction. The choice of features representing spoken language ability is more or less arbitrary, often predictably selected from a limited list of possible linguistic features, such as range, accuracy, fluency, coherence and language use. Fluency as a concept is usually one of the key features appearing on spoken language descriptors and in the corresponding rating scales; the term *fluency*, however, may not necessarily be used to denote the concept. In a later section of the chapter, we will discuss fluency rating scales and how they relate to levels of proficiency. In the following section, however, we will examine the history of assessment of fluency in standardised and high stakes tests of English to provide a background to how fluency has historically been conceptualised and assessed.

6.2 Fluency Scales and Fluency Descriptors

The earliest test of speaking on record seems to be the College Board's English Competence Examination developed and used in the 1930s by American universities in order to admit international students (Fulcher, 2010). The speaking section of the test included a conversation on different topics with one examiner who also rated the candidate's performance. Different criteria were used for assessment of the speaking ability including fluency, responsiveness, rapidity and enunciation (see Fulcher, 2010 for a detailed discussion). Table 6.1 shows an outline of how spoken performance was assessed in this test.

As indicated in Table 6.1, fluency was considered a separate criterion along with responsiveness, rapidity, articulation etc. It is interesting to see rapidity was seen as a different quality of speech than fluency when nowadays fluency is considered to include speed (rapidity). Dedicating two of the eight criteria for assessing the spoken ability in the first documented speaking test's rating scales suggests that fluency has historically been considered a dominant quality of proficient speech even in the earliest records of assessing L2 speaking ability. The rating scales allowed raters to place speakers at three levels of proficient, satisfactory and unsatisfactory; this is rather different from the common practice in language tests today where more levels (five to nine) are employed.

Table 6.1 The College Board's English Competence Examination

Assessment Criteria/Scale	Proficient	Satisfactory	Unsatisfactory
Fluency			
Responsiveness			
Rapidity			
Articulation			
Enunciation			
Command of construction			
Use of connectives			
Vocabulary and idioms			

106   *Fluency in Second Language Testing*

The next example of fluency representation in the rating criteria and rating scales of an international test of speaking is the Foreign Service Institute's (FSI) test of English. Unlike the College Board's English Competence Examination, FSI language tests were developed to assess the language competencies of military personnel in America during and after the Second World War. The first speaking paper of the FSI test was developed in order to measure the oral skills of personnel and their familiarity with foreign languages and cultures (Fulcher, 1993). The first FSI rating scales were holistic, but soon a new set of analytic scales were developed in 1956, in which the raters were required to assess the spoken performance against the criteria of accent, comprehension, fluency, grammar and vocabulary.

The FSI rating scales were based on a six-point scale ranging from 1, 'no familiarity with the language', to 6, 'native speaker proficiency' (see Chapters 1 and 2). The rating scales considered fluency as a key aspect of spoken proficiency and assessed it on the same 6-point scale ranging from *uneven* to *even* fluency (see the Appendix for further details). Although the FSI rating scales were initially used for military purposes in America, they soon gained popularity in other institutions and countries (see Fulcher, 1993 for further details). In the coming years, many language test providers and educational institutions started developing similar rating scales for the assessment of students' oral proficiency. Currently, several language tests, e.g. Test of Pearson English Academic (PTE Academic) and the British Council's Aptis test, include *fluency* as an independent criterion for assessing oral proficiency, whereas some other international tests combine fluency with other criteria, such as *delivery* in TOEFL iBT (the internet-based TOEFL) and *fluency and coherence* in IELTS. One major turning point in the design and development of rating scales over the past decades has been the emergence and development of the Common European Framework of Reference for Languages (CEFR). While this framework was initially developed as a set of benchmarks for second language teaching and learning in Europe, it has been increasingly cited and used as a point of reference in the design of rating scales and descriptors by many international tests of English and other languages including IELTS, Aptis and DELE (Diplomas de Español como Lengua Extranjera, a test of Spanish as a foreign language). CEFR descriptors have also gradually changed over time between 1996 when they were first published and 2018 when the companion document was provided. The change has been required to reflect the most up-to-date conceptualisation of language in teaching, learning and communication, and to reflect research findings that guide these concepts. The details of fluency descriptors in the CEFR document are presented in

6.2 Fluency Scales and Fluency Descriptors   107

the Appendix. For a detailed discussion of fluency representations, see Chapter 5 in this volume.

In the next section of this chapter, we evaluate some of the rating scales used by the international language testing organisations to see to what extent they correspond to fluency features identified in SLA research. Table 6.2 demonstrates the fluency rating scales and descriptors in four standardised and internationally recognised tests of English proficiency, i.e. Aptis, IELTS, PTE Academic and TOEFL iBT.

As shown in Table 6.2, TOEFL iBT has four, Aptis and PTE have five and IELTS has eight operational levels[1] on their scales, ranging from a speaker who is incomprehensible due to their limited fluency to proficient speakers who deliver a speech with ease and flow without undue hesitations or interruptions. As for the rating descriptors, PTE Academic[2] has the most detailed descriptors discussing speed, flow, rhythm, phrasing, hesitations and repair measures. IELTS and Aptis also provide detailed descriptors highlighting the importance of flow, hesitation, pausing and repair measures. Interestingly, they both pay particular attention to pausing and repair by emphasising hesitations, self-corrections and pauses across the scales. Compared to the others, TOEFL iBT has relatively short descriptors, underlining the importance of flow, intelligibility (see Chapters 1 and 2) and pausing.

In an attempt to map these descriptors against the recent findings of fluency research discussed in previous chapters, a few important points are worth highlighting. First, it is important to note that all the tests represent the three aspects of utterance fluency (speed, breakdown and repair; see Chapters 2 and 3); they refer to cognitive fluency or the difficulty that might have triggered the dysfluent speech (e.g. Aptis: 'maybe hesitant when searching for patterns of expressions'); and they highlight perceived fluency by indicating the impact speakers' fluency might have on the listener (e.g. TOEFL iBT: 'listener effort is needed because of … choppy rhythm/pace'). Another strength of the rating scales demonstrated above is that they draw raters' attention to the combined effects of the different aspects of fluency on performance (e.g. IELTS: 'usually maintains flow of speech but uses repetition, self-correction or hesitation'), implying that assessment of fluency should obtain an overall view of the speaker's fluency behaviour.

Despite these merits, there is scope for developing the descriptors to reflect the current research-driven understanding of the concept of L2

---

[1] The differences between number of levels relate to how language proficiency is conceptualised in these different tests.

[2] It should be noted that the speaking test of PTE Academic is machine-scored, and therefore, the descriptors are not used for human rating purposes.

Table 6.2 Fluency-related rating descriptors in selected standardised tests

Test	Aptis	IELTS	PTE Academic	TOEFL iBT
Rating category	Fluency	Fluency and coherence	Oral fluency	Delivery
Fluency-related descriptors	(5) Speech is fluent and spontaneous, with little or no sign of effort. (4) Speaker produces stretches of language with fairly even tempo; can be hesitant when searching for patterns and expressions with fairly long pauses possible. (3) Speaker keeps going comprehensibly; pausing for grammatical and lexical planning and repair is very evident in longer	(9) Speaks fluently with only rare repetition or self-correction; any hesitation is content-related rather than to find words or grammar. (8) Speaks fluently with only occasional repetition or self-correction; hesitation is usually content-related and only rarely to search for language. (7) Speaks at length without noticeable effort or . . .; may demonstrate language-related hesitation at times, or some repetition and/or self-correction	(5) Speech shows smooth rhythm and phrasing. There are no hesitations, repetitions, false starts of non-native phonological simplifications. (4) Speech has an acceptable rhythm with appropriate phrasing and word emphasis. There is no more than one hesitation, one repetition or a false start. There are no significant non-native phonological simplifications. (3) Speech is at an acceptable speed but may be uneven. There are few repetitions or false starts. There are no long pauses and speech does not sound staccato. (2) Speech may be uneven or staccato. Speech (if >=6 words) has at least one smooth three-	(4) Generally well-paced flow (fluid expression). (3) Speech is generally clear, with some fluidity of expression, though minor difficulties with . . . or pausing are noticeable. (2) Speech is basically intelligible, though listener effort is needed because of . . . or choppy rhythm/pace. (1) Delivery is choppy, fragmented or telegraphic; frequent pauses and hesitations.

stretches of production.

(2) Speaker constructs phrases on familiar topics despite very noticeable hesitation and false starts.

(1) Speaker manages very short, isolated utterances, with much pausing, to search for expressions, to articulate less familiar words, and to repair communication.

(0) No or incomprehensible or irrelevant answer given.

(6) Is willing to speak at length, though may lose coherence at times due to occasional repetition, self-correction or hesitation

(5) Usually maintains the flow of speech but uses repetition, self-correction or hesitation

(4) Cannot respond without noticeable pauses and may speak slowly, with frequent repetition and self-correction

(3) Speaks with long pauses

(2) Pauses lengthily before most words

word run and no more than two or three hesitations, repetitions or false starts. There may be one long pause, but not two or more.

(1) Speech has irregular phrasing or sentence rhythm. Poor phrasing, staccato or syllabic timing, and/or multiple hesitations, repetitions, and/or false starts make spoken performance notably uneven or discontinuous. Long utterances may have one or two long pauses and inappropriate sentence-level word emphasis.

(0) Speech is slow and laboured with little discernible phrase grouping, multiple hesitations, pauses, false starts, and/or major phonological simplifications. Most words are isolated, and there may be more than one long pause.

110   *Fluency in Second Language Testing*

oral fluency. The changes we suggest in these descriptors should address the following limitations. First, the use of language describing fluency in these descriptors is often unspecific and at times, and at least to some extent, opens to personal interpretation. For example, it is necessary to define what 'some' means in 'some fluidity', what a noticeable hesitation is, or how long a long pause is. Expressions such as 'noticeable hesitation', 'generally clear with some fluidity of expressions', and 'long pauses' can be interpreted differently by different raters if clear guidelines, operational definitions and ongoing rater training programmes are not provided.

The second limitation of many of the descriptors is that they are expressed in an unrealistic or confusing language. For example, the descriptor 'any hesitation is usually content-related' suggests that hesitations can be simply classified as content, concept or language related. Existing SLA research evidence (Levelt, 1983, 1989; Kormos & Dénes, 2004; Ahmadian, Abdolrezapour & Ketabi, 2012) suggests that both first language (L1) and L2 speakers monitor their language for a range of reasons including content, appropriacy, error detection and communicative impact. This body of research also concludes that in many cases it is difficult to determine what the source of hesitation or pausing is. In many cases the source may not be established unless an insight is gained through retrospective data, e.g. stimulated recall into why speakers pause, hesitate or repair their speech.

Next, the emphasis on breakdown and repair phenomena in these rating scales will need to take into account the findings of recent fluency research (Peltonen, 2018; Duran-Karaoz and Tavakoli, 2020) implying that L2 fluency behaviour can be predicted, at least to some extent, from L1 fluency behaviour. Some of the descriptors in Table 6.2 seem to suggest that hesitations or false starts are a visible indication of dysfluency, but may, in fact, reflect the L1 style. For example, in the PTE Academic descriptors for top band, the expression 'there are no hesitations, repetitions, false starts . . .' seems unrealistic since research evidence in this area (Bosker et al., 2012; Duran-Karaoz & Tavakoli, 2020) has shown that a personal style can predict, to a certain extent, how frequently speakers pause or repair their speech. This means in a second language test, speakers may be penalised for their speaking style, e.g. pausing more frequently than others. Penalising speakers for features of their speech that are not relevant to the L2 speaking construct under investigation would increase the validity threat of construct-irrelevant variance. In other words, an extraneous uncontrolled variable, i.e. personal style, is introduced to the assessment of fluency and could adversely affect the assessment outcomes. In addition, such descriptors may encourage raters to pay unnecessary attention to speakers' repetition and hesitation, regardless of the fact that they may well be the test-takers' personal style rather than their L2 fluency.

Another key point with the existing rating scales is that they are based on a presumption that a linear relationship may exist between levels of proficiency and features of fluency. Rating descriptors may generally assume that as proficiency develops, speed fluency increases and breakdown and repair features decrease in a linear manner. Research in other aspects of SLA has shown that a linear relationship may not exist across all levels of proficiency (Spada, 1986; Lantolf & Frawley, 1988), but this has only recently been examined in fluency research. As we will discuss in the following section, research in this area (Tavakoli, Nakatsuhara & Hunter, 2017) has indicated that a linear relationship does not exist between fluency and proficiency for all measures or across all levels of proficiency.

We note that what we have discussed above does not suggest that using longer and more detailed descriptors of fluency should solve these problems. Instead, we argue that it is crucial to provide raters with descriptors that are useful (e.g. Taylor & Galaczi, 2011), concise and succinct (Tavakoli et al., 2017). Raters would benefit from descriptors that provide them with necessary details that allow them to make an informed and evidence-based decision about how to judge fluency. We make the argument that 'test designers need to strike an optimal balance between construct coverage and rater-usability' (Tavakoli et al., 2017: 7) in the test rating descriptors and other training documents. In what follows, we provide examples of recent research that aimed at helping develop research-oriented evidence to be used when developing fluency rating descriptors.

6.3 Fluency across Assessed Levels of Proficiency in International Tests

What we have discussed so far does not imply that fluency descriptors and scales are not based on empirical research evidence. In fact, over the past two decades, there has been a surge of interest in language testing discipline to encourage testing professional bodies to adopt an evidence-based approach to designing and developing fluency rating scales (e.g. Brown, Iwashita & McNamara, 2005; Ginther, Dimova & Yang, 2010; Nakatsuhara, 2014; Tavakoli et al., 2017). This body of research has had two prime aims: (a) to find out what characteristics of fluent speech distinguish different assessed levels of proficiency usually in an international and validated test of English, and (b) to determine which of these features can be used as criteria features in rating

112 *Fluency in Second Language Testing*

descriptors used by these tests. Although there are several other studies looking into fluency across levels of proficiency, (e.g. Saito et al., 2018; Awwad & Tavakoli, 2019), here we will only report studies that examined fluency across assessed levels of proficiency in such international and validated tests. Five studies predominantly focusing on the assessment of fluency across different levels of proficiency are selected for this purpose. For each study, we provide a summary of the findings to show in what ways the results could be used to inform the development of fluency rating scales and rating descriptors.

Brown et al. (2005) used 198 speech samples from TOEFL test-takers at five levels of proficiency in order to conduct a large-scale validation study exploring which features of speech distinguish each level. Examining the test-takers' speech in terms of number of filled pauses, number of silent pauses, total pause time, number of repairs, speech rate and mean length of run, they found significant differences for total pause time, silent pauses and speech rate. This study offered the first important set of evidence concerning the contribution of fluency, among other linguistic features of speech, to the assessment of speaking in a high-stake international test. Unfortunately, Brown et al. (2005) did not examine fluency in the wide range of the measures nowadays recommended by fluency research (e.g. for pause location or articulation rate). As such, their findings are restricted in offering the field an insight into how mid and end-clause pausing patterns develop as proficiency increases, or which specific measure(s) can be used effectively in rating descriptors to show the criteria features of fluency (see Chapter 3 for further information on pause location).

Ginther et al. (2010) examined 150 speech samples from test-takers at a wide range of proficiency levels taking Oral English Proficiency Test (OEPT). Examining fluency in terms of speed, pausing and repair, their results suggested that the OEPT scores strongly correlated with measures of speech rate, articulation rate and mean length of run, but not with measures of pause or repairs. The authors interestingly argued that the high correlations between these speed features and OEPT scores 'might even lead some to mistakenly suggest that if examinees simply speak faster, they will get higher scores' (Ginther et al., 2010: 388). Based on the strength of the relationship between mean length of run and OEPT scores, they argued that longer runs may indicate 'greater well-formedness and greater complexity at the phrase level' that encourage raters to assign the speaker higher fluency scores. These findings are rather different from Brown et al.'s (2005) who found significant differences for some breakdown fluency measures, indicating pauses can distinguish different levels of proficiency.

6.3 *Fluency across Assessed Levels of Proficiency*   113

In a similar study investigating the rating scales of Test of English for Academic Purposes (TEAP), Nakatsuhara (2014) examined test-takers' speech samples across three proficiency levels. The test-takers are typically college and university level students who need to demonstrate a specific level of English proficiency to enter and/or complete their degree. The data were analysed in terms of the number of silent pauses, speech rate, articulation rate, and ratio of pause and of repair to AS-units. Given the small sample size of the study, however, inferential statistics were not run. The descriptive analyses of the data suggested that the three proficiency levels were different in all fluency measures, and these were appropriately inked with the test rating descriptors.

Addressing the limitations of the studies reported above, two more recent studies (Tavakoli et al., 2017; Tavakoli, Nakatsuhara & Hunter, 2020) were conducted to establish whether there is a linear relationship between fluency and assessed levels of proficiency. Both studies also investigated whether certain fluency features can be considered as criteria features of each proficiency level. Tavakoli et al. (2017) looked into a wide range of different aspects of fluency in speech samples from of takers taking the British Council's Aptis Speaking test (O'Sullivan & Dunlea, 2015) at four levels of proficiency. The authors examined fluency of 128 speech samples from 32 test-takers performing four different tasks at proficiency levels of A2 to C1 CEFR. Including A2 level speakers in the study was an advantage as this group is often not included in fluency research due to their limited fluency. The researchers expanded their focus and went beyond the two previous studies to examine fluency along a wider proficiency continuum and across different task types. This new design allowed them to see which measures best distinguished candidates at each proficiency level. The data were examined for a range of different fluency features including speech rate, articulation rate, phonation time ratio, mean length of run, frequency and length of filled and silent pauses in mid and end-clause positions, and several repair measures (see Tavakoli et al., 2020, for further details).

The results of the study indicated that speed measures consistently distinguish fluency across levels of proficiency from A2 to B1 and B2 level, but above this level speed would not increase, and therefore implying that at upper levels of proficiency, i.e. B2 level and above of the CEFR, speed does not distinguish candidates' fluency. The findings also suggested that frequency of mid-clause pauses differentiate between lower (A2, B1) and higher proficiency levels (B2, C1), whereas the length of the pause is a good measure to distinguish only low proficiency speaker (A2 level) from others. The findings of the study for repair measures revealed little consistency for the effects of proficiency on repair encouraging the authors to argue that perhaps 'a more complex process is at play' with repair measures (Tavakoli et al., 2017: 2). Surprisingly, the results failed to show any significant differences emerging from task type. They argued that the four tasks were not adequately different to have an impact on the speakers' performance or their fluency. While Tavakoli et al.'s (2017) study revealed interesting findings, two points imply that their findings should be interpreted cautiously. First, the Aptis Speaking paper is a computer-delivered test in which the test-takers interact with a computer rather than with a human being. In addition, they had a relatively small sample size of thirty-two participants across four levels. Given the relationship between L1 fluency behaviour and L2 fluency, in a small sample size of 8 at each level, one may not rule the effects of individual speaker's fluency behaviour on the results. Given these two reasons, one can argue that there is still scope for further research with larger sample sizes and under different test settings.

To address the two limitations mentioned above, Tavakoli, Kendon, Hunter and Slaght (forthcoming) replicated Tavakoli et al.'s (2017) study examining fluency in a sample of sixty test-takers from four different proficiency levels (Low B1 to C1 of the CEFR). It is worth noting that there were differences between the test tasks and testing context between the two studies. Tavakoli et al. (2020) examined the Test of English for Educational Purposes (TEEP), an EAP test used by some British universities to assess test-takers' proficiency before they start their university degree. A key difference between the two tests is in the amount of planning time they offer test-takers: thirty seconds in the Aptis test and four minutes in the TEEP test. Another important difference between the two is the test setting and mode of performance. While the Aptis Speaking test involves a computer-mediated mode of performance, in which the candidates listen to pre-recorded instructions before they speak to a computer, the TEEP Speaking test involves face-to-face interaction with the examiner, interlocutor and another candidate. As discussed in Chapter 4, planning time has been shown to affect fluency significantly with positive impacts on speed, breakdown and repair aspects of fluency (Tavakoli & Skehan, 2005). Additionally, as we will discuss later, research has provided robust evidence that the context and setting of test administration has an impact on multiple aspects of performance (Bachman, 1990; Brooks & Swain, 2014).

Tavakoli et al.'s (forthcoming) findings suggested that in the TEEP Speaking test, speed measures distinguish lower levels (A2 and B1) from higher levels (B2 and C1). Breakdown measures of silent pauses

6.3 *Fluency across Assessed Levels of Proficiency*

distinguish between the lowest level and higher levels of B2 and C1. Neither filled pauses nor repair measures distinguish across any of the levels. The results also suggested that none of the measures distinguishes between B2 and C1 proficiency levels. These results are in large similar to those obtained by Tavakoli et al. (2017), indicating that fluency descriptors do not sufficiently distinguish speakers at different levels of proficiency.

The results of the two studies show that speed fluency develops across proficiency levels up to a certain point (perhaps at B2 level of the CEFR) before it plateaus, frequency of pauses distinguishes lower from high levels of proficiency, length of the pause is a useful measure to distinguish the low proficiency level from the rest, and no regular pattern of relationship can be established between repair measures and proficiency level. Interestingly, the results also suggest that a linear relationship cannot be expected for all fluency measures or across all levels of proficiency. For filled pauses and repairs, none of the studies has shown a linear relationship between proficiency and repair fluency. More importantly, the results of the two studies summarised here clearly suggest that there are no statistically meaningful differences in any aspects of fluency between upper levels of proficiency, i.e. B2 and C1. From a language testing perspective, this implies that the distinctions made between these upper levels of proficiency are based not on the assessment of fluency, but perhaps other aspects of performance, e.g. lexis, complexity or accuracy (see the results of Nakatsuhara, Tavakoli & Awwad, 2019 below).

To sum up, fluency research in language testing has shown that speed and pausing measures highly correlate with the assessment of fluency in language testing, but may fail to distinguish adjacent levels of proficiency at upper levels of proficiency. It seems necessary to stress that although most studies have shown speed and some pausing measures as a reliable predictor of proficiency and as measures to distinguish some levels of proficiency (to a certain extent), speed and pausing are only the tip of the iceberg. We now know that speed of performance, for example, is a reflection of cognitive fluency, i.e. ease of access and retrieval of lexical and syntactic units. Speed of speech is also inter-related to speakers' ability to produce larger chunks of language in one go, e.g. producing phrases and multiword sequences without pausing or hesitations; this ability is in turn connected to having a larger repertoire of formulaic language. Speed can also be linked to communicative strategies speakers use e.g. using lexical fillers to buy time while planning their next utterance, or it could be a characteristic of personal style, e.g. some people respond to questions more quickly than others. Therefore, it is reasonable to argue that the

116   *Fluency in Second Language Testing*

high correlation between speed and raters' assessment of fluency should point our attention to a range of skills and abilities associated with the speed of performance, and not only to speed itself. As such, a high score allocated to a speedy performance may not be pure because of the speaker's speed, but because of these other qualities associated with a speed that seems important to raters. Future research will need to investigate these important issues.

6.4 Broadening Research Methodologies Examining Fluency in Language Tests

For a long time, researchers working in different areas of language testing have argued that in order to promote a better understanding of how language is assessed by language testing organisations and of their use of rating scales and rating descriptors, adopting a mixed-methods approach to researching oral performance, i.e. combining qualitative analysis with the existing quantitative approach, is fundamental to ensuring test validity (Lazaraton, 1998; Brown, 2006b; Seedhouse & Egbert, 2006; de Jong, 2018; Seedhouse & Nakatsuhara, 2018). This argument is also in line with a more recent critique of fluency research (McCarthy, 2010; Tavakoli, 2016; Michel, 2017) claiming that the current models of measuring fluency are based on monologic talk, with limited attention to the interactional aspects of fluency, e.g. turn-taking, overlap talk and inter-turn pausing.

One frequently used qualitative methodology in test validation over the past two decades has been Conversation Analysis (CA). Simply put, CA can be defined as an attempt to 'describe, analyse, and understand talk as a basic and constitutive feature of human social life' (Sidnell, 2010: 1). CA in language testing primarily aims for developing a more in-depth understanding of the use of institutional talk in the oral assessment of language proficiency; this is in turn expected to help improve assessment of oral proficiency in terms of validity, fairness and impact. The rationale for use of CA in language testing is based on an understanding that human talk is a complex and dynamic construct that is shaped through participant interaction, and as such, its assessment would not be complete without a careful analysis of what actually happens in the interaction.

Lazaraton (1998) was one of the first researchers using CA to compare the relationship between candidate talk and ratings of the oral performance in language testing. The findings of her study revealed a few important points: there are fewer instances of repair at higher levels of proficiency; test-takers receiving higher scores use a broader range of expressions to speculate and test-takers at higher

6.4 Broadening Research Methodologies   117

bands provide more appropriate responses and demonstrate better skills in conversational discourse. In a follow-up study, Lazaraton (2002), using CA techniques, reported that interview tests of speaking are a type of institutional interaction that share some of the properties of interviews, demonstrating their interactional asymmetry. The results highlighted the imbalanced power-relationship between participants in the talk at these language tests.

We now turn to studies that have specifically used CA to examine the fluency of oral performance in language tests. In a study that aimed to identify speaking features distinguishing proficiency levels of Bands 5, 6, 7 and 8 in the IELTS Speaking Test, Seedhouse and Nakatsuhara (2018) used a mixed-methods approach to analysing the relationship between scores and features of test-takers' speech. Combining quantitative analysis with CA methodology (Lazaraton, 2002; Seedhouse, 2004) to examine the key characteristics of speaking that distinguished assessment across these levels, they explored different aspects of performance from measures of fluency and lexical choice to the structure of the conversations and power relations. To assess fluency, they followed Foster and Skehan's focus on pausing (1996), i.e. length of any pause longer than 0.5 second per 100 words was measured and collated. They also examined the frequency of pauses and a total number of words per performance. The descriptive analysis of their study showed that (a) the total number of words per performance increased in direct proportion to the scores for each band, (b) the longest pauses belonged to level 5 and the shortest to Level 8, and (c) pause length per 100 words increased in direct proportion to the scores. The inferential statistics, however, failed to show any statistically meaningful differences between different bands for the measure of pause length. Pause frequency was statistically different only between Bands 5 and 8. For a total number of words, Bands 5 and 6 were different from others, but no differences were observed between levels 7 and 8. The findings of this study shed light on the complex nature of fluency, and showcase the necessity of combining different methodologies if a broader perspective to understanding fluency is required.

The CA analysis of the data examined speaking features in relation to (a) *inter-turn* features (responses to examiner questions), and (b) *intra-turn* features (the test-takers' performance within a turn). For the former category, the researchers looked into features such as *requesting repetition*, *dealing with trouble* in answering questions, and *repair strategy*. They also identified features of high-scoring speakers' performance. For the intra-turn category, features such as *functionless repetition*, *hesitation markers* and *lexical choice* were examined. The results of the CA analysis clearly demonstrated 'the complexities

118   *Fluency in Second Language Testing*

intrinsic in the relationship between speaking features and candidate scores' (Seedhouse & Nakatsuhara, 2018: 195), and revealed a number of patterns and trends that can help shed light on the relationship between test scores and features of the test-takers' speech. As relates to the assessment of fluency, the most important features reported to be linked with the assessment were *how well a candidate answers a question, hesitation markers, functionless repetition, incidence of trouble and repair* and *turn length*. These findings are significant as they emerge from a mixed-methods approach that examines performance both quantitatively and qualitatively. However, some of the findings open a new platform for further research. For example, we need to know the criteria for considering a kind of repetition as functionless, and to examine whether functionless repetition is another aspect of personal style speakers carry over from L1 to L2 fluency behaviour. As stated earlier, without retrospective data and L1 baseline data, making a definitive decision about the function of repetition might be difficult.

A final study using a mixed-methods approach to examining fluency across levels of proficiency to be reported here is Nakatsuhara et al. (2019). Following from the findings of previous fluency research (Tavakoli et al., 2017, 2020), which suggest the upper bands of proficiency cannot be distinguished in terms of their fluency, Nakatsuhara et al. (2019) conducted a study to examine what helps distinguish speakers at these upper proficiency levels. Examining samples of speech from sixteen test-takers of the Aptis Speaking test at B2 and C1 levels of the CEFR, their study aimed at exploring whether there were differences between the two groups' performance in terms of accuracy, syntactic and lexical complexity, and use of metadiscourse markers. Adopting a mixed-methods approach, the researchers further examined the data qualitatively to examine the emerging patterns of fluency in relation to pausing and repair. A range of inferential statistics was used to examine the relationship between the linguistic performance of these two groups, while a Discourse Analysis approach was adopted to examine the test-takers' pausing and repair behaviour.

The quantitative results implied that it is not fluency features that distinguish the two levels of B2 and C1 in this test; rather, the key features distinguishing the two levels are accuracy and lexical diversity of performance. The qualitative dimension of the analyses suggested that the pauses speakers made at these upper levels of proficiency occurred for a range of reasons including access and retrieval of lexical and syntactic units, reformulating the language already produced, and facilitating communicative effectiveness. The findings highlight the complexity and breadth of the factors affecting fluency ranging from cognitive demands associated with processing and producing L2 to communicative pressure and the need to attend to monitoring processes (see Chapter 2). A more important conclusion the authors drew from this study was that without a broader perspective to understanding fluency and its interaction with other aspects of language performance, especially when contextual factors potentially affect performance, our understanding of fluency will continue to remain unidimensional, as discussed earlier in the chapter.

The context in which language is used is another factor that has been reported to affect spoken performance. Brooks and Swain (2014), for example, examined the spoken performance of university-level students in the TOEFL test context, in a class during a lecture, and at the university outside their class. The results suggested that the performances in the three contexts were distinct for different aspects of performance including complexity, use of vocabulary and choice of structures. The authors did not examine the speakers' performances in terms of fluency. Our hypothesis is that their fluency might also have been different when performing in different contexts. See further discussions on the effect of context in Chapter 7.

To conclude, it is necessary to note the invaluable contribution of mixed-methods approaches to investigating fluency in language testing. The discussions above have clearly shown that understanding the depth and essence of fluency is only possible when it is looked at from these varying perspectives. We have only seen a few studies looking into the assessment of fluency in oral language tests from a qualitative perspective, but we would like to consider this as a successful beginning rather than the end. As we will argue in the final chapter, research in the area will need to open its perspective to include a broader understanding of fluency by combining its existing research practice with research in other disciplines and other paradigms (see Chapter 8 for a full discussion). We suggest this is the way to achieve a more in-depth and comprehensive understanding of fluency and its application in practice.

6.5 Human Raters, Machine Rating and Rating Fluency Features

For a long time, researchers have agreed that assessment of oral proficiency based on human ratings is subject to a degree of error of measurement for a range of different reasons including the effects raters can have on the assessment of L2 speaking ability (Brown et al., 2005; In'nami & Koizumi, 2016; Dijum, Schoonen & Hulstijn, 2018;

120   *Fluency in Second Language Testing*

Kang, Rubin & Kermad, 2019). Raters' influence on the assessment of speaking can be linked to several factors including their academic and professional background, their leniency, level of experience, and social attitudes (Kang et al., 2019). In'nami and Koizumi (2016), conducted a meta-analysis of the studies investigating the effects of task type and raters on spoken performance. The results suggested there were noticeable rater and rating scales' effects on the judgements of the test-takers' performance. They also reported that the effects were larger when considering the interaction between the candidate's L2 ability, task type and raters' judgments. This finding highlights the complexity of subjective ratings of proficiency as different variables (e.g. task effect, rater effect, rating scales etc.) interact with one another, potentially affecting the score assigned to the candidates' ability under examination.

While raters' judgment of speaking performance is known to introduce error to the assessment of speaking ability, judgments of fluency seem to be more susceptible to variation, because examiners and raters are reported to find fluency the most difficult aspect of spoken performance to assess (Nakatsuhara, 2012). This difficulty is perhaps linked to the complex and multifaceted nature of fluency (discussed in Chapters 1 and 2), to the abstract representations of fluency and to the confusing language used in definitions of fluency across different tests documentation (as discussed earlier in this chapter). In Section 6.2, we compared fluency rating descriptors and rating scales of four international language tests where the analysis showed how fluency is perceived and represented rather differently and ambiguously in some of the rating descriptors. Our personal anecdotal evidence emerging from our professional engagement activities, e.g. workshops with language test designers, raters and examiners, also suggests that many language testing professionals admit that a unified understanding of fluency is missing among language test task designers, examiners and raters.

Dijum et al. (2018) investigated raters' judgements of fluency and linguistic accuracy in an occupational language testing context. Working with two groups of professional and non-professional raters, they examined the extent to which raters' background had an impact on the rating of fluency and accuracy when assessing the test-takers' L2 speaking ability. The expert group were certified raters who had received linguistics training in their careers, whereas the non-expert group were human resources managers with no linguistics background or training. Both groups, however, had extensive previous contact with L2 speakers. The results of Dijum et al.'s (2018) study showed that the raters with linguistic experience and training background paid more attention to accuracy, while fluency appeared to be more important to the non-trained raters. This finding, i.e. expert raters prioritise

6.5 Human Raters, Machine Rating & Fluency Features   121

accuracy to fluency, should be considered in the light of Nakatsuhara et al.'s (2019) finding, that suggests at upper levels of proficiency speakers' fluency is not actually different from B2 to C1 level (the same speed and breakdown fluency patterns observed in Tavakoli et al., 2017 reported above). Rather, it was their accuracy and lexical complexity that encourages raters to place the speakers in either of the two bands. The finding of Dijum et al.'s (2018) study is only one example of how raters' knowledge, leniency, background and other characteristics can affect the way they evaluate L2 speakers' speech fluency. While providing raters' training and improving rating scales and rating descriptors can reduce raters' impact on the assessment of fluency, the use of automated rating of speaking has been suggested as a promising future solution to reduce raters' subjectivity.

For years, it has been argued that the objective nature of utterance fluency and the existing computer programmes operating on artificial intelligence can automatically measure some aspects of fluency, e.g. speed and pausing. One prime aim of an automated scoring system would be to determine a set of linguistic features, e.g. number of syllables per second, that can be employed to predict human raters' judgment of performance. Automated evaluation of speech, compared to human rating, is appealing to both researchers and language testing organisations, although for different reasons. From a research perspective, it is hoped that the automatic measurement of speech in general and of fluency, in particular, can increase the consistency of the scoring system and decrease errors of measurement, e.g. raters' effect, leading to a more valid assessment of oral proficiency. For language testing organisations, automated assessment of speech will be associated with cost reduction and more facilitated assessment procedures.

One of the important issues remaining to be resolved in the automated assessment of fluency is to determine which fluency features should be assessed. The findings of a number of studies examining the relationship between human holistic ratings of fluency and objective measures of utterance fluency have been fundamental in providing the basis for automated assessment of fluency (e.g. Cucchiarini, Strik & Boves, 2000, 2002; Ginther et al., 2010; Bosker et al., 2012). These studies have collectively reported strong positive correlations between holistic ratings and analytic assessment of fluency based on measures of utterance fluency. In particular, they have provided evidence for strong relationships between speed measures and human ratings. Silent pausing was also strongly correlated with holistic ratings in Ginther et al.'s (2010) study, but not in others. Similarly, Préfontaine, Kormos and Johnson (2016), examine raters' judgements of fluency in a test of French as a second language and found similar

122   *Fluency in Second Language Testing*

results: mean length of run and articulation rate were the best predictors of raters' perceptions of fluency. Taken together, the findings of these studies imply that several features of fluency can be used in its automated assessment. While measures of speed, i.e. speech rate, articulation rate, and mean length of run, are unanimously suggested to be of great potential for this purpose, there has been less consistency in findings for measures of silence and repair (see the discussion in Section 6.3).

Notwithstanding the benefits of automated assessment of fluency, the complex and multifaceted nature of fluency makes the task of automated scoring complicated. As discussed above, speed of performance, for example, can potentially be objectively measured by a computer, but this speed represents a range of skills and abilities that may remain obscure to a non-human rater. The language testing research conducted so far suggests that speed is associated with judgements of proficiency, but this research does not support the idea that speed is the main basis for judgements of fluency across proficiency level. As discussed earlier, raters' judgements can be based on other characteristics associated with the speed of performance, e.g. ease of access or having a larger repertoire of formulaic sequences. Another problem is that who is considered a fluent speaker may vary among raters from different backgrounds (Dijum et al., 2018). If computer rating is going to mirror human rating judgements, are we going to consider linguist raters, non-linguist raters with substantial experience of the L2 speaker, non-linguist raters with little or no experience of working with L2 speakers, or a combination of these as the baseline for making the judgements? Ginther et al. (2010) argued that automated assessment of speech may not be appropriate because after all the aim of assessing test-takers' language ability is to 'predict the success of examinees' oral communication with humans' (p. 394). Clearly, future research will need to respond to these important questions before the assessment of fluency is offered through automated systems.

6.6 Conclusions and Implications for Future Fluency Research in Language Testing

Assessment of oral proficiency with regard to measuring fluency has made some significant improvements over the past decades. We have learnt a lot about how different aspects of fluency interact with proficiency level, and what features of fluency characterise speech at different levels of proficiency. Our discussions in this chapter demonstrated that for a number of tests, speakers at upper levels of proficiency are

6.6 Conclusions & Implications for Fluency Research   123

not different in terms of speed, breakdown or repair fluency. We also learnt that it might be other aspects of their performance, e.g. lexical choices, accuracy and their communicative effectiveness, that influence raters' scoring of fluency. Examining what characteristics of speech distinguish these higher proficiency level speakers in terms of their fluency is certainly an attractive area for future research. It is also necessary to put this hypothesis on trial with different tests, task types and groups of raters. The contribution of non-expert raters to our understanding of fluency should not be underestimated when examining the judgements of fluency.

The chapter also argued that mixed-methods approaches to investigating fluency in oral performance will help develop a more in-depth understanding of the concept. Fluency in language testing should be understood as a dynamic construct that is shaped in the discourse shared among the participants (speaker, listener, interlocutor and examiner). A range of crucial factors including the context, purpose, power-relations and characteristics of the language test (which is institutional talk (Lazaraton, 2002), a specific kind of talk used in certain contexts) influence the speakers' fluency. Without researching these aspects qualitatively, our assessment of fluency may not be as valid as language testing organisations aim for. Although CA has made a considerable contribution to our understanding of fluency, there is still a large scope for other qualitative methodologies, e.g. Discourse Analysis and interaction analysis, to help us understand the construct of fluency in language tests.

It seems that automated assessment of fluency will soon be common practice in the field of language testing. The summary of studies reported here indicates the wide scope for more research in this area. While we argue that not all human judgements of fluency can be replaced with machine rating, there are several aspects of fluency that can be measured by the use of artificial intelligence and automated assessment programmes. The temporal aspects of fluency, e.g. speed and breakdown measures, seem to be potential candidates for automated ratings as machines can measure these consistently and accurately without being affected by variability inherent in the subjective judgements of a human rater. In order to get to the stage where such automated ratings are able to consistently rate performance and reliably distinguish different proficiency levels, we will need more research to show the criteria features of fluency at each proficiency level.

7 *Fluency in Different Contexts*

7.1 Introduction

This chapter takes a fresh direction to move away from norms for fluency research and practice based on L2 English; the chapter's main focus is on fluency research 'in the wild', particularly looking at the challenges of developing fluency during immersion in the target language setting, for example, during Study Abroad (SA). SA is typically expected to bring benefits to fluency development through authentic spontaneous communication outside the classroom (Freed, 1995; Segalowitz, 2010; Tullock & Ortega, 2017), yet may not always do so (Wright, 2018a). We also aim to emphasise the benefits of taking a more multilingual/intercultural view on considering appropriate targets for fluency, by looking cross-linguistically at how languages other than English construct fluency and interactional patterns of communication, which can shape learners' expectations. This emphasis also raises the importance of considering L2 learner norms, rather than prestige established native speaker norms (see Chapter 2), for example, by using L2-based ratings of perceptions of fluency (Magne et al., 2019). We argue such research would be useful in practice to broaden assumptions about targets for fluency development among learners, teachers and assessors. We also aim to illustrate the issue of linguistic insecurity often identified as a factor affecting willingness to take part in conversations, for example, interacting outside formal classroom settings (see e.g. MacIntyre, Clément, Dörnyei & Noels, 1998; Wright & Schartner, 2013; Magne et al., 2019), as this can often create challenges for learners' fluency development even during immersion. We thus situate this discussion by considering how different language contexts create specific challenges for learners in enabling fluency development, in an increasingly globalised world where fluency in varieties of English as well as other languages is required.

The chapter begins by looking at how research and practice can benefit by moving away from standard monolingual native-speaker norms, starting with findings emerging from work on English as a Lingua Franca (e.g. Seidlhofer, 2001; Jenkins, 2003) and the World Englishes paradigm (e.g. Kachru, 1985; Canagarajah, 1999). Such work has been valuable in identifying the need for a more varied range of what constitutes target-like standards for language learning, including fluency development. We see the impact of attitudes that certain versions of English may be seen as more prestigious than others, despite the reality of English around the world in which the majority of L2 speakers would never realistically encounter the supposed prestige varieties, but who function successfully using internationally comprehensible forms. We also refer to research in which L2 or multilingual raters are used as reference norms for evaluating fluency development, rather than monolingual native speakers, alongside work on communicative adequacy (e.g. Révész, Ekiert & Torgersen, 2016). However, as we have seen in previous chapters, the use of such sociolinguistically varied or multilingual target norms does not yet appear to have crossed robustly into informing teaching and assessment practices for fluency development. We also look at the emerging cross-linguistic work on fluency in languages other than English to identify similarities or differences with assumptions taken from English, which can impact on learners' expectations of what fluent speech may require in different settings. We include a brief look at how existing bodies of research into L2 speech development, captured in learner corpora across a variety of languages, may be useful to help develop more robust cross-linguistic theories, methods and evidence of fluency development from a wider perspective.

The final section explores these themes in the context of fluency development through residence abroad, even over short periods such as SA. We highlight why SA is assumed to foster both fluency in the broad and narrow senses, but may not always do so. Fresh evidence is presented from a recent case study of learners of Mandarin Chinese within a more nuanced view of specific task constraints, to pull all the themes of the chapter together and highlight the varied nature of fluency development.

7.2 Going beyond Standard Target Norms for Fluency in Perception and Production

We have noted in earlier chapters (e.g. Chapters 2, 3 and 6) that much of the existing research into models of fluency, or ways of measuring and assessing fluency, have often adopted native speaker norms for

126 *Fluency in Different Contexts*

comparing L2 fluency development. However, there is now a growing awareness of the value of taking multilingual speakers as the target for both social and linguistic reasons (Tullock & Ortega, 2017; Magne et al., 2019), though many speakers themselves may still feel a degree of linguistic insecurity believing that native speaker fluency levels remain the most desirable (Magne et al., 2019: 8).

Despite the explosion in second-language speakers of English for economic and educational purposes, in research we see that there remains a deeply-ingrained tension at the heart of research and practice between expectations of fluency in idealisation and in reality. On the one hand, speakers may be expected to meet some appropriate (if scaled-down and idealised) target norm (Leung, 2005: 127) defined by teachers and assessors (Gilmore, 2007). On the other hand, once outside the classroom or test centre, speakers may have to face a very different, sociolinguistically varied, reality (van Compernolle & McGregor, 2016). For example, different views of what count as authentic language norms (Leung, 2005) have been particularly contentious in relation to the decades-long debates over L2 English, both in terms of World Englishes and of English as a Lingua Franca or International Language. The spread of English as a global language is often seen in the context of work based on Kachru's Circles of World Englishes model (1985), acknowledging the historical colonial impact of English. Kachru's three-circle model distinguished between the privileged 'Inner Circle' version of English in countries, mainly monolingual, where it is the mother tongue (the United Kingdom, the United States, Australia, Canada), 'Outer Circle' countries where English has official often bilingual status (e.g. Singapore, India) and 'Expanding Circle' countries where English is on the rise (e.g. China, Russia, Vietnam). Most of these tensions within this area lie beyond the scope of this volume, but are worth bearing in mind to understand the value of moving away from an over-reliance on L2 English fluency research. To note just some examples, Canagarajah (e.g. 1999, 2013), Jenkins (e.g. 2003, 2015), Seidlhofer (e.g. 2001) and many others have been preeminent in challenging the potentially politicised notion that there can be a single 'norm' often based on what may be perceived to be a prestigious 'inner-circle' variety, particularly given the evidence of growing variation within even Inner Circle countries. But we need to know more about the implications of these in relation to expectations of L2 fluency development. Seidlhofer (2001: 133) has argued that 'very little empirical work has so far been done on the most extensive contemporary use of English worldwide', compared to extensive reference to an idealised so-called native speaker norm. We note that in the last fifteen years or so, more has been done to draw attention in

7.3 L2 Speaker Expectations: Reframing the Norm

research and teaching towards a more varied model of what makes for effective multilingualism (e.g. García & Sylvan, 2011). To the best of our knowledge, not much research to date has specifically looked at fluency development with the multilingual approach, but we note that there is growing interest in describing multilingual speech, including code-switching and translanguaging, acknowledging these as elements within a language user's repertoire of effective interaction (e.g. Canagarajah, 2013; García & Li, 2014). However, the prevalence of current research based on learners of English has, by implication, privileged the reference to English native speaker norms for the comparison point. We argue that it would help L2 learners in their own expectations of fluency development if teaching, learning and assessing can move away from an idealised English-centric focus, as suggested by Seidlhofer (2001).

7.3 L2 Speaker Expectations: Reframing the Norm

Research into the daily practices of multilingual speech and awareness of the extent of authentic sociolinguistic variation can be limited in application to standard language pedagogy teacher training curricula, whether for English as a second language (Alsagoff, McKay, Hu & Renandya, 2012: 4) or for other languages such as French (Williams, Mercer & Ryan, 2016). Multilingual speech is rarely included as authentic material for the classroom in general, let alone as a model for fluency development (Gilmore, 2007). We suggest, therefore, that there are three main limitations for framing expectations of fluency development in relation to learners' goals for speech production and in considering appropriate targets for perceptions of fluency. The first issue, that is, over-reliance on the so-called native speaker norm as a comparison point for instructed learners, can affect learners' goals for production. Studies have found that L2 learners, even after long immersion in the target language, may often be very self-critical of their potential to speak fluently, which, in interviews, seem to relate to a self-perception that they should be speaking at native-like levels (Wright & Schartner, 2013). We would argue, therefore, that if fluency targets were more clearly related to bilingual learners and taking a more interactional view of fluency, rather than a comparison against monolingual natives, this could transform L2 speakers' confidence and willingness to communicate (MacIntyre et al., 1998; Léger & Storch, 2009; de Jong et al., 2013).

Second, many current studies may often use native speaker perceptions as to whether learners are speaking fluently (e.g. Préfontaine & Kormos, 2016). Indeed, Kormos and Dénes (2004: 146) noted that

128   *Fluency in Different Contexts*

objective information based on non-native speakers' perceptions of fluency 'is completely lacking'. We would argue that greater inclusion of non-native speaker perceptions is vital particularly for fluency research, given the limitations many speakers feel in communicating, as noted above. Some studies, for example, in school settings, have examined the importance of combining dialogic interaction and communicative strategies to try and boost speakers' fluency. Peltonen (2017) compared fluency in various tasks at two levels of proficiency in school learners in Finland, using both quantitative and qualitative analysis to investigate potential interactions between collaborative aspects of managing the tasks (dialogue fluency), in addition to individual temporal fluency and strategic resources for maintaining fluency. One interesting finding was that possibly superficially disfluent strategies such as use of filled pauses (as 'stalling' for time – see Chapter 3) were in fact perceived by speakers as indicating skilful usage to keep turns going effectively.

Other studies have begun to explore the use of multilingual raters for ratings of learner speech, though not always for fluency alone (e.g. Rossiter, 2009; Winke & Gass, 2013; Saito et al., 2018; Magne et al., 2019). Such studies shed light on the complexity of how fluency is perceived, and indeed just how dynamic fluency development continues to be, even over prolonged exposure. Saito et al. (2018) suggest that longer immersion can lead to continued improvements in perceived fluency, even up to twenty years after arrival, though specific aspects of speech production (e.g. prosodic accuracy) may not be significantly dependent on the length of immersion. Studies also reveal contrasting experiences of rater severity, again underscoring the complexity of perceptions around appropriate target norms. Magne et al. (2019) specifically examined L2 raters of learner speech, to compare to native speaker ratings carried out in an earlier study (Saito et al., 2018). Magne et al. (2019) found that the L2 raters showed some similarities, noting pausing and speech rate as factors affecting fluency rating. However, unlike the native speaker raters (Saito et al., 2018), the L2 raters focused more on mid-clause pausing and also included many aspects of more global oral proficiency (grammatical accuracy, lexical richness, accent) and expectations of 'social factors' related to native speaker benchmarks for fluency.

Thirdly, it is clear that fluency is integrated within even the broadest sense of oral proficiency or interactive communicative adequacy (Pallotti, 2009; Tavakoli & Hunter, 2018). It is therefore important to be able to operationalise fluency as part of communicative adequacy in interaction (Isaacs & Trofimovich, 2012; Révész et al., 2016). Révész et al.'s (2016) study included the impact of fluency

7.4 Fluency in Different Languages

(as well as accuracy and complexity) on ratings of communicative adequacy. Their measures of fluency were speed (articulation rate), breakdown (filled and silent pauses) and repair (false starts). Their four-point definition of communicative adequacy included whether the speaker addressed and supported in sufficient detail the task-specific content points, was easy or difficult to understand, delivered the message clearly and effectively, and took account of the communicative situation (p. 834). They found that fluency emerged as a critical determinant of communicative adequacy (p. 843), particularly in significant links between hesitant speech (use of filled pauses) and ratings of low communicative adequacy.

These findings help provide a much richer understanding of the variety and range in performance than is currently perceived to be effective fluent L2 speech (van Compernolle & McGregor, 2016). Extending such studies with bilingual raters across a range of languages, with a specific focus on fluency, would therefore be a helpful indication of how fluency and communicative adequacy interact among multilingual speakers, rather than in relation to idealised native speaker norms. In turn, this area of research could give learners a more realistic view of what to expect and to aim for in fluency development while interacting in target language settings such as during SA.

7.4 Fluency in Different Languages

Another factor to take into account in our broader multilingual view of fluency is an understanding of potential cross-linguistic differences in fluency performance. Two main areas have typically been identified in cross-linguistic research to date, which are relevant to current models of fluency, particularly in the narrow temporal sense. The first is expectations about speech tempo, and the second about use of silent or filled pauses. As discussed in Chapters 2 and 3, these measures are themselves potentially difficult to operationalise systematically, due to the many factors affecting an individual's speech and pausing patterns. Also, speech tempo research looking at cross-linguistic differences is typically found in fairly technical analyses of speech which do not necessarily easily cross over to L2 fluency research, for example, analysing articulation of syllables (e.g. Quené, 2008), or in identifying language impairment (e.g. McLeod & Goldstein, 2012).

However, some key areas worth pursuing to help inform our expectations of appropriate norms for L2 fluency include speech rate, run length and pausing. It has been found that short CV-type syllabic speech, for example, produced in Japanese, can be uttered at a faster rate compared to other languages. Even within varieties of the same language, there can be speech rate differences – speakers of Dutch in Belgium have been found to have a slower speech rate compared to speakers of Dutch in the Netherlands (Verhoeven, de Pauw & Kloots, 2004). Run and pausing patterns may also differ – for example, Finnish speakers have been found to produce more pauses and more staccato short-run speech compared to Swedish speakers (Ringbom, 2007). In relation to filled pauses, it has long been observed that use of phatic elements in L1 speech (such as filled pauses) can in fact be considered as a strategy for competent fluent speech rather than a marker of disfluency (Goldman-Eisler, 1968; Pawley & Syder, 1983; Clark & Fox Tree, 2002), so care needs to be taken in applying these measures to assess disfluency in L2 speech (Liyanage & Gardner, 2013).

Another element to consider is how languages differ in the rate of encoding semantic information, that is, how much semantic information is typically conveyed per syllable (known as information density – Pellegrino, Coupé & Marsico, 2011). Languages with more articulatory complexity have a denser phonological or morphological structure and are argued to need more syllables to convey the same semantic content as syllables with less information density. Therefore, Mandarin and Spanish convey similar information using two opposite encoding strategies per syllable: slower, denser and more complex for Mandarin vs. faster, less dense and less complex for Spanish (Pellegrino et al., 2011).

Such differences in fluency patterns are also observed in different cultural contexts within the same language. For example, as discussed in Chapter 3, Tian, Maruyama and Ginzburg (2017) report that the use of filled pauses varies between British English and American English. Their cross-cultural investigation also highlights the differences between use of filled pauses between Chinese, Japanese and English (see Chapter 3 for a more detailed discussion). This is one of the few studies that has so far explored cross-cultural differences in different languages' norms for utterance fluency. Differences in cultural or pragmatic expectations can also be assumed to affect fluency development. Tannen (1984, 2012) highlights differences in cultural expectations of fluent discourse and turn taking, comparing societies of 'high involvement'-style speech, with a lot of overlapping turns and often short utterances, vs. more indirect 'high considerateness' styles, where silence between turns is a sign of respect. These pragmatic factors have also highlighted the differences between cultures of the value of silence and interruptions and other discourse patterns such as backchannelling (e.g. Gass & Varonis, 1994; Jaworski, 1997; Nakane, 2006; Wolf, 2008; Culpeper, Mackey & Taguchi, 2018). Learners' own use of L1 sociopragmatic techniques such as backchannelling can also lead to greater L2 fluency development even at lower

7.5 Use of Corpora for Cross-Linguistic Evidence   131

levels of proficiency, as found in Wolf's (2008) study of Japanese learners of English. Therefore, if an L2 speaker is more aware of how to adapt their own L1 expectations of discourse management, this could affect how successfully they can manage interactions to further develop their L2 fluency.

It seems clear, therefore, that in understanding how L1 patterns may affect L2 speech, models of fluency may need to consider many complex cross-linguistic issues such as speech tempo, length of run, use of pausing and information encoding. However, as yet there is a lack of extensive research across varieties of L1 speakers who are developing fluency in a variety of L2s, so we do not yet have robust cross-linguistic comparisons to see if these L1 patterns do systematically transfer to an L2. Further research is therefore needed to verify how far speech rate, length of run and use of fillers, among other markers of fluency, show reliable cross-linguistic similarities or differences, which could then in turn feed into our understanding of how to operationalise fluency without invoking an oversimplified or overly-standardised norm.

7.5 Use of Corpora for Cross-Linguistic Evidence of Fluency

As noted above, more evidence is needed of cross-linguistic differences in what is perceived as fluency across a range of different L1 listeners and discourse settings, including larger-scale studies and replicable methodologies. Therefore, the rise of technology-supported resources, such as learner corpora, is particularly welcomed to further help us understand how fluency functions in different contexts.

The growth of interlanguage datasets and cross-linguistic learner corpora (see e.g. Granger, Dagneaux & Meunier, 2002; Granger, Gilquin & Meunier, 2015) can, in principle, provide some rich sources of helpful research. However, to date, it appears not much has been published from such corpora related to fluency (Brezina & Flowerdew, 2017). There is therefore an opportunity to take forward questions investigating non-English fluency factors referring to a wider range of language pairings, even if such research is currently primarily based on the large number of Learner English corpora. For example, the Centre for English Corpus Linguistics (CECL, 2019) at Louvain lists over 160 corpora, of which nearly 100 are L2 English. Among the non-English learner corpora, to date, very few include oral data – one listed for Chinese and one for Korean only contain written data, and oral data is included in one of the two Arabic corpora, five of the ten French corpora, five of the twelve Spanish corpora, and one of the nine German corpora listed. Some of these have been producing valuable directions in analysing cross-linguistic speech behaviour, such as

132 *Fluency in Different Contexts*

pausing, repetition and phonetic production (e.g. Götz, 2013), though often focused on L2 English. Given our interest in this chapter in different language varieties, we welcome the emergence of Spanish as a growing specialised area for learner corpus research (Mitchell et al., 2008; Alonso-Ramos, 2016). As work on global varieties of Spanish increase, a template could be provided for comparing Latin American to European Spanish, though so far, it has not been possible to identify separate corpora to enable this distinction. There are also increasing numbers of learner corpora beyond CECL, which include Mandarin Chinese (e.g. the Guangdong/Lancaster joint Chinese Learner Corpus). However, to date very little fluency research has emerged from these or other Mandarin corpora (Smith, 2011), nor for other Chinese languages, such as Cantonese, so we urgently call for such corpora to be set up to allow systematic comparisons and investigations of specific cross-linguistic predictions with more familiar studies using L2 English or European languages.

Nevertheless, research is beginning to take an interest in using corpora for pedagogical applications and assessment comparisons in relation to learner speech and fluency, which offers several valuable directions to take our understanding of cross-linguistic fluency forward. Smith (2011), for example, drew on L1 Mandarin corpora (Chen & Huang, 2000; McEnery & Xiao, 2004) to create task-based lessons for using collocations and colligations in self-created interviews for interacting with class-peers. In his exploratory study, he trained students in using authentic Chinese speech samples from the corpus to learn and use appropriate phrases successfully. The WEBCEF project (Baten, Beaven, Osborne & van Maele, 2013) created an online collaboration tool for self-, peer- and expert assessment of oral proficiency in seven foreign languages across the CEFR. The goal of this project was to help language teachers and students to understand and apply the CEFR criteria through a mutually supportive virtual community of practice. By providing and listening to authentic samples of speech via the online tool, each contributor could listen to and reflect on what was perceived to be examples of good oral proficiency in Dutch, English, Finnish, French, German, Polish and Italian. However, no detailed cross-linguistic analyses have yet emerged in the published literature from this project, so we look forward to future studies from this project, which could inform both research and applications to practice.

7.6 Fluency in the Wild: Study Abroad

In thinking about fluency in wider contexts, particularly what may affect the learner once immersed in the target language setting, we

7.6 *Fluency in the Wild: Study Abroad* 133

have explored the importance of moving beyond native speaker norms (often taken from English), including multilingual benchmarks for L2 fluency and cross-linguistic variation in fluency in different languages. It is also critical to understand the effects that moving beyond the classroom has on the underlying processes affecting fluency development – from managing speech in a controlled setting to handling the messy and challenging reality of managing to speak appropriately in the target country 'in the wild' (Segalowitz, 2010; Sanz & Morales-Front, 2018).

Segalowitz's analysis of fluency development (discussed in Chapter 2) makes the point that immersion in the target language may well be necessary to building the underlying cognitive processes (proceduralisation and automaticity) that support fluent speech. Immersion may be available to learners through sojourn abroad (Freed, 1995; Wright & Schartner, 2013); such experience can be assumed to provide the richest environment to trigger language development, including fluency, given the expected opportunities for authentic input, interaction and output. There are of course a host of factors and a wide range of ways of tapping into the phenomenon of language development during SA. Given the focus of this book, we do not explore in detail issues of sociocultural adaptation and motivational factors that are known from other arenas of research to affect engagement with target language environments. Nor do we address at length questions regarding the sociolinguistic and pragmatic challenges of handling informal vs. formal language, but refer readers to useful research in these topics (Churchill & DuFon, 2006; Duff et al., 2013; Mitchell, Tracy-Ventura & McManus, 2015; van Compernolle & McGregor, 2016).

Given the focus of this chapter, we highlight three key issues in relation to SA effects on fluency development: psychosocial factors affecting individual variability, cultural contrasts limiting opportunities for interaction, and problems in current methodologies in establishing comparisons between SA research findings and applications for practice. To finish, findings from a longitudinal study of learners of Chinese are discussed to examine fluency development during SA across different tasks. The study is used as a way of using languages other than English to discuss in more nuanced ways the operationalisation of factors that can constrain or support fluency development during SA.

7.6.1 *Study Abroad: Benefits for Oral Proficiency*

In general, the rapidly burgeoning field of SA research (e.g. Freed, 1995; Perez Vidal, 2014; Tullock & Ortega, 2017; Sanz & Morales-Front,

134   *Fluency in Different Contexts*

2018) has highlighted the benefits of SA for oral proficiency (e.g. O'Brien, Segalowitz, Freed & Collentine, 2007; Llanes & Muñoz, 2009; Mora & Valls-Ferrer, 2012), compared to written development (Sasaki, 2011) or grammatical development (Isabelli-García, 2010). Indeed, SA is sometimes assumed to offer a uniquely valuable environment for language development (Kinginger, 2011). However, the results of many current SA studies question this assumption (see, among others, Wright, 2013, 2018a; Sanz, 2014; Mitchell, Tracy-Ventura & McManus, 2017; Huensch, Tracy-Ventura, Bridges & Cuesta Medina, 2019), as they reveal greater variability in SA outcomes than might be expected. Influencing factors on such variability include quantity of input (Du, 2013), quality of input (Moyer, 2013) and differences in levels of proficiency at the start of the SA period (Davidson, 2010).

Given the potentially huge range of individual variation across the SA experience, it is challenging to arrive at a more systematic understanding and analysis of fluency development that would apply across a range of L2 settings. The growing body of research is, however, beginning to provide a basis for sound cross-linguistic research designs that allow us to test hypotheses about how fluency may develop similarly in different language contexts.

One such recent study provides useful data from a highly methodical study of American learners of Russian, Mandarin and Spanish. Di Silvio, Diao and Donovan (2016) tracked improvements among seventy-five learners at varying levels of proficiency after one semester in the target country, using a range of tasks taken from the standardised ACFL Oral Proficiency Interview (OPI), including picture description, personal description and a comparison task between advantages and disadvantages of SA. Overall, they found that the Mandarin learners improved the most, in terms of length of run and speech rate, while the Russian learners showed the smallest change. They note language-specific factors may play a role here, since length of run can be affected by variation in morphology – Mandarin lacks much overt morphology in comparison to Spanish and Russian and is therefore perhaps easier to articulate. However, Di Silvio et al. (2016: 622) also highlight the difficulties others have identified in assessing fluency during SA based on the linguistic, cultural and programme variation among their learners. They further reiterate the challenges unique to specific target languages, and call for caution in assuming that SA is a magic key to unlock fluency development in general.

Another limitation on why SA benefits on fluency may seem so individually variable can be explored in the context of a range of what we call psycho-social differences – cognitive, pragmatic, affective and cultural factors which could be argued to impact on individual variation in response to the SA experience. In view of the assumption that immersion particularly benefits cognitive fluency within authentic spontaneous interactions (Segalowitz, 2010, 2016), we turn to this area of research, which can be seen as impacting on learners' engagement with the target language during SA, and which may thus potentially lead to very different evidence of fluency development.

7.6.2 Psycho-Social Factors and Fluency during SA

Cognitive factors such as working memory have been widely assumed to facilitate fluency development. To test this claim for SA settings, Towell and Dewaele (2005) carried out a long-term study including a period of SA for L2 adult learners of French doing a language degree, including a period in France, comparing L1 speech rate and changes in L2 speech rate. They observed a positive correlation between L1 and developing L2 speech rates throughout the study; however, they found slightly stronger correlations during the first or second year of study than specifically after the period of SA. Although L2 fluency, including speech rate, improved over time for these learners, Towell and Dewaele's hypothesis that differences in working memory would account for the variability in the rate of improvement was not confirmed. Nonetheless, students whose speaking rates remained slow after SA performed less well on a memory recall task in their L1, which suggests that working memory constraints, in terms of limited short-term knowledge storage, may have been a contributing factor to both L1 and L2 speech rate.

Other studies, however, have not found a clear role for cognitive factors in relation to improved fluency development during SA. Segalowitz and Freed (2004), looking at fluency gains in temporal speech rate and hesitations during SA, found a range of individual differences in relation to cognitive processing capacities, noting some individuals with higher cognitive capacities were in fact less fluent after SA than those with lower cognitive resources. They posited a potential cognitive threshold relating to ability to use SA effectively to boost fluency. O'Brien et al. (2007) found that greater working memory (tested as phonological short-term storage) affected L2 oral fluency for SA (but also for those with intensive Stay-at-Home experience). Sunderman and Kroll (2009) investigated the possibility of a cognitive 'internal threshold' in testing the role of working memory in oral production, hypothesising that those with a higher level of cognitive capacity would benefit more from SA than those below a certain threshold of cognitive capacity. They compared two groups of university-level English-speaking learners of Spanish with or without

SA experience and used a Reading Span measure to test working memory. Linguistic oral proficiency was tested using speed and accuracy of lexical retrieval rather than temporal measures of fluency in connected speech. Among the fourteen who had studied abroad, a statistically significant, though marginal effect of working memory was found for speed of lexical retrieval. There was a clear statistically significant negative effect on accuracy suggesting that for those at the lower range of working memory it was as if these individuals had not studied abroad (Sunderman & Kroll, 2009: 10). In other words, it is possible to argue that there is a potential working memory threshold above which working memory capacity could enhance the effect of SA on fluency and other aspects of linguistic improvement, but below which the SA experience could be limited. It seems logical therefore to call for further research to explore the likely interaction between internal cognitive and external experiential factors, given the growing evidence that speech fluency in social/interactional uses, such as during SA, may co-vary in line with Sunderman and Kroll's (2009) internal cognitive threshold claim discussed above.

One possible experiential factor worth more exploration within our broader perspective on fluency is the notion that performance in SA contexts may be variable depending on pragmatic constraints. In turn, learners' confidence in engaging in conversations in the L2 (i.e. not just the quantity but also quality of engagement with the target language) may thus lead to very different evidence of fluency development, as most of the literature observes. For example, in Wright's (2013) research on a group of Chinese L2 learners of English during a year's immersion (see also Chapter 2), it was found that L2 fluency in story telling improved more than L2 fluency in question-formation. This was hypothesised as relating in part to the more 'natural' practice of telling stories, rather than asking questions; the task was seen by some students as too much like a classroom drill and not something they felt comfortable doing outside the class. This finding highlights the importance of how internal psycholinguistic and external social demands interact. As most of this research has been done on English, French or Spanish, there is an urgent need to consider these questions across a range of other languages, to test for robust evidence that cognitively-constrained task-based fluency effects can be found cross-linguistically.

However, interacting fluently in the second language can remain very challenging linguistically and pragmatically even after many months' sojourn, and wide variation is found in the types of local social interactions seen as required to drive fluency development (Coleman & Chafer, 2011; Kinginger, 2011). Difficulties for learners

7.6 Fluency in the Wild: Study Abroad 137

in finding local people to interact with in many settings is well documented and can even take up to four years – Umino and Benson's (2016: 766) case study of an Indonesian student studying for four years in Japan, noted his sorrow that he was silent for nearly a year, even into his third year of study. Wright and Schartner (2013) carried out a longitudinal study of mixed-L1 international students' experiences of interaction and fluency development in an L2 English university setting. Using quantitative measures of typical daily interaction levels and qualitative data from interviews, they found that even highly proficient learners struggle to adjust to the reality of living abroad, where confidence of how to interact affected the degree to which they actively sought opportunities to do so. Wright and Schartner concluded that there existed a high 'sociocultural threshold' acting as an internal barrier for international students and limiting their ability to engage appropriately. Many of the participants mentioned being put off trying to improve their L2 speech, feeling even after a year that they were 'shy' and did not know how to talk fluently to 'the foreigner' (i.e. a UK home student or local resident).

There are other challenges for SA students going to countries which, linguistically and culturally, may present 'extreme contrast', or when students are exposed to language varieties, for example, as discussed by Coleman in relation to SA in Senegal (Coleman & Chafer, 2011). Coleman's studies of French learners in Senegal reveal the complexities for many language learners going beyond the typical language variety. In Senegal, for example, not only were learners experiencing a different version of French to the standard European variety previously studied, but Senegalese French was itself a lingua franca in a country where Wolof was the home/social language spoken by most people. Coleman's work identified many of the challenges learners find in searching for opportunities to develop fluency (in a broad sense) in the proposed target language while handling the realities of multiple languages needed to survive and enjoy their experiences (Bonomo, 2017). These included sociocultural gender limitations (also noted by Shiri, 2013; Trentman, 2013), where some of the female learners reported fewer chances to develop fluency (defined here as part of their wider communicative ability). Opportunities to find people in general to talk to were restricted, and within female-only conversation groups, topics seemed to be limited (typically weddings and domestic issues), leaving learners feeling less fluent in more complex topics such as politics.

Arabic immersion experiences can be particularly challenging (Shiri, 2013; Trentman, 2013) as students find that the Modern Standard Arabic they study is not the variety they will encounter in everyday situations in the highly diglossic Arab world (Trentman, 2013: 458). Cultural issues can also significantly impact on and limit opportunities for western learners to interact with local Arabic speakers (Bown, Dewey & Belnap, 2015; Trentman, 2013). Therefore, there may be sociocultural factors for certain target languages experienced 'in-situ', which may present specific challenges for developing fluency in authentic communicative contexts. These need to be taken into account by teachers and assessors in order to prepare learners to be able to communicate in such multilingual settings across potential cultural differences and expectations (Kramsch, 1998; García & Li, 2014).

Through this overview of SA research and fluency development, alongside many reasons for individual variability in fluency development, such as psycho-social and cultural barriers, we also find a wide range of studies and methodologies, which affect our ability to evaluate and compare evidence of L2 fluency in SA research. We turn now to how methodological issues remain a challenge in tracking fluency development during SA.

7.6.3 Methodological Issues in Fluency Development during SA

Tullock and Ortega's (2017) recent meta-analysis of fluency research in SA identifies the difficulty of claiming consistent gains across different languages and even within similar language contexts, noting that consistency of measurement is as important as the control of variables (p. 16) when testing for SA gains in fluency. Studies using generalised measures of proficiency such as the standardised OPI are difficult to compare with studies using temporal measures such as speech rate, pausing and length of speech run (e.g. as seen by comparing Freed, Segalowitz & Dewey, 2004 with Brecht et al., 1995). The role of quantity and quality of exposure in aiding development is also unclear: Du (2013) claimed that oral fluency is most influenced by time-on-task, that is, the amount of time that students use the target language every day. However, Moyer (2013) found that quality of L2 experience is more important than quantity, as measured in terms of significant context-specific interaction. Wright's (2013) study mentioned above found no significant effect on improvement associated with qualitative or quantitative differences in target language use by the study participants. The role of social interaction with a variety of native speakers has been strongly identified in a range of SA studies (Mitchell et al., 2015), though it seems that it has not always produced a measurable effect on fluency. However, it seems clear that the heterogeneity of student interactions during SA must be expected to impact on individual capacities to develop fluency during SA. Future SA research must make it crucial to establish a range of expectations about fluency development that will fit the variability that most SA students will experience.

Comparability across SA research findings is further constrained by methodological gaps or lack of clear operationalisation (Sanz, 2014; Tullock & Ortega, 2017). Many studies are not designed for longitudinal comparisons of individual development; study designs do not always control for differences in length of time spent abroad and level of exposure while abroad, or students' level of proficiency prior to SA. Studies often use a wide range of tasks to elicit speech data, making comparison difficult, and there is a growing awareness of the need to establish clear protocols for SA data collection (see Perez Vidal, 2014; Mitchell et al., 2015, 2017 for good examples of clarity). Studies also rarely compare different target languages, again making it hard to confirm how language pairings may impact on fluency development.

Tullock and Ortega's (2017) meta-analysis of quantitative studies of fluency development during SA also highlights the importance of accounting for the sociolinguistic variability of language experiences in the target setting, alluded to throughout this chapter. The authors observe that many learners are themselves multilingual, setting up a multiplicity of prior language experience effects 'present in diverse configurations and to varying degrees of visibility in the contexts for SA' (p. 17). It is thus important for SA research to be more systematic in methodological design to take account of potential local variability impacting interaction and fluency development.

7.7 New Insights from Chinese Study Abroad Research

One way to address these issues is to investigate fluency development in less commonly studied target languages such as Mandarin Chinese. This is vital, as Tullock and Ortega (2017) among others have claimed, to help SA and SLA research move away from the limitations of looking at inter-European language pairings where cultural and linguistic experiences may have a degree of commonality. For many non-European learners of English, despite its Lingua Franca status, we have noted that immersion in any context may create high sociolinguistic and sociocultural barriers limiting interactional opportunities. We turn now to research into developing fluency in Chinese to examine whether such barriers seem to exist in this setting.

Developing fluency in Mandarin raises a number of specific issues for the learner, whether in the classroom, or during SA (see e.g. Xing, 2006; Everson & Xiao, 2009; Zhao, 2011; Kim et al., 2015;

Wright, 2018a, 2019; Shei, Zikpi & Chao, 2019). Information structure, for example, encoding adverbial phrases for time and place reference, require specific word orders, so the utterance must be planned as a whole before starting to articulate. While there is little overt morphology for encoding, elements can be omitted in different contexts. For example, the copula verb *shi* must be dropped in simple noun + predicate sentences, but is required in other structures; subject and object pronouns are not required if the information is assumed to be already known. There is a huge amount of polysemy, since there are approximately 400 syllables in Mandarin Chinese, which account for about 2,500 of the most frequent words in Mandarin, making appropriate sound-meaning pairings potentially challenging (Zhou & Marslen-Wilson, 1994). Mandarin tone is essential to distinguish different meanings, and speech patterns are typically based on faster speech tempi than English. The written system of characters is largely unrelated to phonology, so written input cannot be easily used to scaffold language development in integrated communicative activities. Teachers may be impacted by traditional Chinese teaching methods, where Confucian memorisation approaches may be prioritised over modern western pedagogic expectations of communicative fluency (Zhang & Li, 2010; Jin & Cortazzi, 2011; Han, 2014). Given the linguistic and pragmatic issues of utterance planning, the value of drilling can be very useful for learners, though it can limit their ability to move away from their repertoire of learned phrases towards freer spontaneous interaction (Wright, 2019).

Alongside these challenges in developing fluency in Mandarin, there are also difficulties in measuring and assessing fluency in Chinese, particularly when using word-based analyses in transcripts of speech, since there is ongoing debate over what constitutes a word in Chinese (Chen, 2019). Many lexical items carrying meaning are one-syllable one-character morpheme pairings of sound, form and meaning, while other lexical items are multi-syllabic, creating potential ambiguity over how to segment the sound-meaning-form connections into words (Chen, 2019). Given these linguistic and methodological challenges, there remain as yet few studies looking specifically at fluency development in Mandarin, particularly during SA.

There has been a recent explosion of interest in studying Mandarin at home and in China through SA (see e.g. Han, 2014; Tao, 2016; Lu, 2017; Shei et al., 2019). However, despite the increased numbers of students going to China for SA programmes (Wright, 2018a), there are very few longitudinal studies which can serve to corroborate or challenge the claims of the benefits of SA on fluency in general, or on our understanding of how to measure fluency development in

7.7 New Insights from Chinese Study Abroad Research   141

interaction for Mandarin (Duff et al., 2013; Diao, Donovan & Malone, 2018). Linguistic analysis of Mandarin speech in L1 or L2 has recently become easier by reference to native speaker corpora such as the Lancaster Corpus of Mandarin Chinese (McEnery & Xiao, 2004), though such comparisons have not yet been widely used to support research into L2 Mandarin.

A few studies have emerged recently on patterns of development in L2 Mandarin speech, which we can use to see how generalisable standard models of fluency are when applied to non-European languages. Yang (2012) investigated a small group of L2 learners' pauses during SA, comparing them against those of native speakers, and showed that native speakers paused more between clauses, phrases and conjunctions than non-native speakers, while non-native speakers paused more at other points. The study supports other comparisons of native/non-native speaker speech and pause patterns (e.g. Tavakoli, 2011), although it lacks any longitudinal data to see whether SA triggered any change. Du (2013) looked at the development of fluency during the period of one study-abroad semester (approximately four months). The value of this study is the extent of data collected and the breadth of contexts – once a month, tracking twenty-nine students in different contexts on and off campus, using recordings of Chinese speaking classes for planned instructed output, and individual interviews about students' daily lives and experiences to elicit spontaneous output. This study showed significant fluency progress over time, measured in terms of monologic speech rate (two other measures related to general oral performance were total words spoken and length of longest turn, which are not specifically fluency measures). A recent study of L2 development during SA examined how quickly fluency can improve even for beginner learners (Wang, Na & Wright, 2018). Following a group of Anglophone learners of Chinese over a semester, the authors found significant longitudinal improvements in monologic speech rate in just five weeks. However, the study did not use a variety of tasks or wider battery of fluency measures, again making comparability difficult.

There have been some small-scale explorations of learner Mandarin speech fluency to try and address these gaps (Wright, 2018a, 2020). The specific focus of this work is to try and establish a reliable methodology to evaluate the potential impact of task type on fluency development (Tavakoli, Campbell & McCormack, 2016), comparing effects of rehearsal vs. spontaneous speech across monologic and dialogic tasks. Participants were a group of twenty-two university learners of Chinese from western language backgrounds (mostly English, but also Italian and French), though only ten completed all

142 *Fluency in Different Contexts*

tasks at both times as reported below. Fluency development during ten months of living/studying abroad in China was assessed using six measures: total number of words per performance, mean length of run (MLR), articulation rate, number and mean length of clause-internal pauses, and hesitancy (a composite repair measure of filled pauses and repeats/reformulations, used in Wright, 2013). The rehearsed monologic task was assumed to have the least task load (Pallotti, 2017) and most likely to be performed well, even if mainly through memorised recitation (Segalowitz, 2010). Our study examined how far such performance could scaffold the other tasks: a spontaneously-produced monologue (a picture description) and two dialogues (a rehearsed role-play and a spontaneous unprepared chat). The spontaneous tasks were assumed to have greater task load (Pallotti, 2017), and would therefore show poorer fluency compared to the prepared tasks. The monologic vs. dialogic mode was assumed to make a difference due to interactional task demands (Michel, 2011), but we made no prediction over whether performance would be better or worse, as dialogic tasks can sometimes be assumed to be easier (Michel, 2011; see also Chapter 3 in this volume). Results of the tasks at Time 1 and Time 2 are shown in Table 7.1.

The prepared monologue outperformed the other three tasks at all time, but all four tasks improved over time, significantly so ($p < .05$) on most measures, apart from number and mean length of pause. Significant differences between tasks at Time 1 prior to SA were generally not found at Time 2 after SA; the spontaneous monologue seemed to show the most change, suggesting immersion during SA had reduced any task load disadvantage on speech fluency. Some task-related differences remained between the monologues and the dialogues for MLR and mean length of pausing (MLP). The spontaneous monologue (description) task produced the longest MLR at both times, compared to other tasks, as well as the highest MLP at both times, compared to shorter and comparable MLR on the four other tasks. Comparing the monologic and dialogic performances from Time 1 to Time 2, we found that the spontaneous dialogue generally (though not always significantly) outperformed the rehearsed dialogue at both Time 1 and Time 2. We also noted fewer pauses on the dialogues (and slowest articulation rate on the prepared role-play).

These task-related changes are taken to indicate clear SA benefits for spontaneous speech fluency, but that different performance mode (monologue vs. dialogue) can override effects of SA. There was also no sign that fluency in the rehearsed tasks 'bootstrapped' fluency in the spontaneous tasks, suggesting that rehearsed fluency at the utterance level (performative competence, Wright, 2018a) develops differently

Table 7.1 Mean (and SD) fluency scores by task at Time 1 (T1) and Time 2 (T2)

	Topic (rehearsed monologue)		Description (spontaneous monologue)		Role-Play (rehearsed dialogue)		Chat (spontaneous dialogue)	
	Mean	(SD)	Mean	(SD)	Mean	(SD)	Mean	(SD)
Output T1	169.90	(44.20)	120.70	(39.71)	123.86	(55.24)	140.43	(45.24)
Output T2	290.60	(101.28)	174.40	(78.29)	162.00	(47.113)	305.00	(100.02)
Articulation Rate T1	2.85	(0.48)	2.15	(0.27)	1.67	(0.26)	1.90	(0.332)
Articulation Rate T2	3.09	(0.27)	2.70	(0.92)	2.45	(0.27)	2.77	(0.324)
Hesitation Rate T1	0.144	(0.59)	0.234	(0.11)	0.306	(0.13)	0.236	(0.06)
Hesitation Rate T2	0.132	(0.48)	0.148	(0.64)	0.137	(0.04)	0.132	(0.05)
Mean Length of Run T1	1.52	(0.65)	2.20	(0.44)	1.27	(0.54)	1.49	(0.70)
Mean Length of Run T2	1.87	(0.46)	2.69	(0.28)	1.61	(0.41)	1.69	(0.33)
Mean Length of Pause T1	0.672	(0.15)	0.887	(0.23)	0.709	(0.25)	0.628	(0.16)
Mean Length of Pause T2	0.612	(0.14)	0.803	(0.31)	0.623	(0.19)	0.516	(0.08)
Number of Pauses T1	38.9	(9.69)	44.80	(14.79)	25.0	(11.63)	22.14	(13.13)
Number of Pauses T2	51.2	(21.87)	35.40	(9.85)	12.14	(3.44)	24.29	(8.14)

Source: Adapted from Wright (2020).

144 *Fluency in Different Contexts*

to creative fluency in spontaneous speech, relying on greater underlying cognitive fluency (Segalowitz, 2010, 2016). The topic covered in the spontaneous dialogue (free conversation about life in China) related to a highly familiar topic, which can facilitate fluency (Michel, 2011). Therefore, the cognitive demand in this spontaneous speech task may not have been as great as expected.

As in many other studies (Wray, 2002; Myles, 2004; Wood, 2010; Myles & Cordier, 2017), there was reliance on pre-formed chunks or multi-word sequences at both Time 1 and more so at Time 2, though these were found across all tasks, not just in the prepared tasks. We suggest that reliance on multi-word sequences may be a favoured strategy in Mandarin, due to common reliance on classroom drilling techniques (Wright, 2019). Students were also unable to use any phonetic cues from written input to support their development of spoken speech, given the character-based script of the Chinese writing system. There has been a growing body of work looking at how learners use increasingly multi-modal varieties of visual and aural strategies to learn characters/words (see e.g. Kan, Owen & Bax, 2018). To the best of our knowledge, however, little research has been published on how learners of Mandarin build up such mixed-mode strategies to support fluent communicative speech (rather than retrieval of single words or phrases). This is another rich area of fluency research to pursue in the future, in relation to Chinese and other non-alphabetic languages such as Korean and Japanese.

7.8 Directions for Future Research

This chapter has pointed out how many of our current assumptions about fluency – how it develops, how it is measured and taught, and used in interaction – are often based on standards derived from instructed L2 English and are usually related to native speaker norms from prestige varieties. These assumptions therefore need to be tested in other languages, and across a range of varieties and contexts, to be more reliably and systematically understood. However, we still have many questions which we cannot yet answer about fluency development in languages beyond the most common and often Eurocentric pairings. We have identified that most of the research to date on non-English fluency is based on small-scale case studies and that we still lack a cross-linguistic understanding about building fluency at the discourse level.

In highlighting key issues and challenges in looking at fluency development in a more global context, we have identified an urgent need to rebalance the focus away from current English-centric fluency research, and from a stereotypical or idealised native norm based on standard expectations of privileged languages such as English. Using non-native multilingual speakers as models and norms is also crucial to help shape speaker expectations in ways that may be more authentic and relevant for today's heteroglossic world (García & Sylvan, 2011). Further research could extend to a broader range of authentic multilingual language settings, such as in Francophone Africa, or across global Spanish or Arabic varieties. By engaging with more longitudinal studies in very different linguistic and sociocultural contexts, such as during SA in China, we can gain also a richer insight into a more multilingual interactive view of fluency development.

New opportunities are opening up to take forward burgeoning cross-linguistic interest in fluency in interaction. Technological resources such as learner corpora can be used alongside more informed pedagogic and sociocultural priorities, to help researchers, practitioners and learners converge on creating a more varied view of fluency targets. These targets can then be further evaluated and operationalised to support research, teaching and assessment; in turn, our ability to understand fluency in interaction as a multifaceted construct will be enriched.

8 Conclusion

8.1 Introduction

Throughout this volume, we have repeatedly argued how much second-language (L2) fluency research and practice has benefited from an extraordinary expansion of interest over the last few decades. Globalisation and the increased amount of high-stakes contact among speakers of different languages have highlighted the importance of fluency in many sub-disciplines of applied linguistics, including second-language education, discourse and interactional analysis and language testing. This has led to a surge of interest among researchers, language professionals and language educators, which has deepened and extended our understanding of the complex nature of second-language fluency. But, as we have noted throughout, this expansion and specialisation of knowledge have also led to disconnects between different domains of research, which we believe has led to some limitations in our current operationalisations of fluency and to gaps between research and practice, which need bridging. Our aim in addressing these disconnects and gaps has thus been twofold.

First, we have aimed to bring together for the first time in a single volume in applied linguistics an overarching and detailed discussion of L2 fluency research and its theoretical and methodological advancements. We have, within our current understanding, shown how the findings of this body of research can be used in a range of different language-related professions like language testing and teacher education. Moreover, we have presented this research in an accessible, coherent and relevant way for both early-stage and experienced researchers and practitioners, including language testers and teacher educators.

Our aim has been to present L2 fluency research alongside implications for practitioners, particularly in the chapters on measurement, pedagogy and assessment, and we hope therefore that this volume will

146

8.1 Introduction   147

provide comprehensive tools for practitioners to have a better understanding of the concept of fluency. This should also help build their confidence in adopting the most effective application for their own practice, whether broadly, more akin to general proficiency, or more narrowly, e.g. for checking articulatory speed or breakdown patterns when appropriate.

We have tried to address the two dilemmas we highlighted from the start. First, we have noted the gap currently found between research and practice in relation to fluency. While fluency seems to be crucial in a range of different disciplines including psycholinguistics, language teaching and testing and speech therapy and criminology, these different disciplines do not seem to be conversing with one another or to be building on each other's research. Even more difficult to interpret is the fact that professional practice, e.g. language testing, does not seem to be benefitting from research in this area (see a detailed discussion in Chapter 6). The conversation between research and practice, we argue, is a two-way street with benefits for both parties. Based on this assumption, we argue that it is both researchers' and practitioners' responsibility to work on bridging the gap between fluency research and practice. One way to do so is to carry out collaborative research projects (e.g. Tavakoli, Campbell & McCormack, 2016; Wright, 2019), in which researchers and practitioners work on areas of mutual interest to develop a better understanding of the construct of fluency.

Second, we have noted that current research has predominantly adopted a cognitive approach often based on information-processing, speaker-internal variables, leading to an overly narrow view of fluency, with little attention being paid to how external interactional factors affect fluency. While the dominant approaches to examining fluency do not discredit the importance of external factors such as context and purpose of communication, the narrow focus on speaker-internal factors has overshadowed the significance of speaker-external and interactional factors. Moreover, the emphasis on speaker-internal factors can sometimes lead to an over-idealised or overly-native-speaker-based description of fluency: 'normal' speed, no disruption or undue hesitation, fluid, continuous. However, our discussions in this book have suggested that the ideal sense of fluency may not work in authentic real-world situations. We have also argued that under certain conditions, speakers may choose to be slower, more repetitive and showing more breakdown in their speech. Clearly, for specific tasks and functions, e.g. apologising, slowing down and pausing are signs of reflection in many cultural contexts (Cirillo, Colón de Carvajal & Ticca, 2016). Therefore, 'normal speed' varies among individuals, contexts, tasks and cultural norms. Furthermore, this

148   *Conclusion*

narrow perspective has primarily relied on a monologic model of fluency built on psycholinguistic approaches and disregards a range of other important factors that affect fluency, like the role of the interlocutor. This is what Foster (2020) calls 'Susceptibility to a variety of internal and external influences' (Foster, 2020: 1).

The research presented here on different aspects of fluency represents invaluable work done on extending the theoretical and empirical understanding of fluency, leading to a more in-depth conceptualisation of fluency as called for by Koponen and Riggenbach (2000). But it has also been shown throughout the volume that such research has not, so far, offered consistent insights into how aspects of L2 fluency are represented in different contexts, e.g. in conversations, in less-frequently researched languages and for the differing demands on communicative effectiveness arising in formal and informal situations. This brings us back to the second disconnect that we have been high-lighting in our volume: the disconnect between different L2 disciplines interested in fluency. In this case, for example, Conversation Analysis and Discourse Analysis are areas that can have a major contribution to fluency research if collaborative studies are carried out. We referred to a recent study by Nakatsuhara, Tavakoli and Awwad (2019), which examines fluency in test-takers' performance from both a psycholinguistic and discourse-analytic perspective. Studies of this kind will introduce a broader sociocognitive perspective on understanding fluency and provide a new direction that allows for multidisciplinary insights to develop. Thus, to the best of our knowledge, this book is the first volume to present the case for a broad multidisciplinary perspective on defining, understanding and researching L2 fluency by considering fluency as a dynamic variable in language performance that interacts with cognitive factors as well as with external factors.

In this concluding chapter, the main themes from throughout the volume are synthesised to evaluate our current insights into fluency across cognitive, interactional, pedagogic and assessment domains. We finish by identifying remaining gaps in our understanding of how fluency relates to issues of real-life second language communication.

8.2 Developing Fluency

Whatever definition of fluency is used, clearly the concept must combine some element of fluidity, ease in speaking (and, usually, ease in being comprehended by the listener) and, more technically, a degree of automaticity in speech production. However, we have seen that the constructs of fluidity and ease can be subjective and difficult to operationalise, making it hard for practitioners to know how to develop these abilities in their learners. Automaticity in the speech production process, by contrast, has been relatively widely researched, e.g. in relation to observable temporal changes across the usual framework of speed, breakdown and repair. We have argued throughout that simply assuming fluency is the product of greater learner-internal automaticity and taking a unidimensional temporal or cognitive perspective is not enough to understand the many contextual factors affecting fluency and fluency development. We recap now how we see key different factors playing a role in how fluency develops in a more multidimensional perspective, with implications for how practitioners may have a more nuanced view of what is involved in fluency development.

8.3 Fluency Development and Automaticity

We can safely assume that fluency does, in many aspects, rely on greater automaticity in the speech production process. But first, we need to know more on how to identify and differentiate automaticity at different stages of the speech production process (conceptualisation, formulation, articulation), e.g. through the location of pausing (mid-clause vs. end pause). It is currently believed that in a narrow, temporal sense, mid-clause pausing and repair is one of the most accepted indicators of disfluency, as it usually indicates a problem in automatically formulating the form of the utterance. However, how to reduce such pausing remains tricky to understand – does such disfluency relate to cognitive or utterance fluency (Segalowitz, 2010), and reflect problems just at the formulation stage, or may it be affected by issues at the conceptualisation or articulation stages? While we know that L2 pausing behaviour and repair are at least to some extent affected by L1 fluency behaviour, we do not have clear evidence of how utterance fluency changes with different L1 backgrounds, proficiency levels and individual learner characteristics. Similarly, we do not yet know how mid-clause pausing and repair may be affected by different situations, or in talking to different listeners for different purposes. We can see that certain task contexts, such as task familiarity and straightforward repetition activities, can build automaticity in some ways, but we do not know whether these skills and the underlying automaticity are transferable to other tasks, contexts and communicative purposes. Therefore, we need more research and evidence from practice on how to foster greater automaticity across the speech production process to understand fluency development across more varied settings.

Additionally, and in relation to this last point, we suggest we need to look more closely at how to reframe automaticity within the contextual demands of interactional discourse. This will have a bearing on how to

150 *Conclusion*

understand the impact of variation in fluency patterns, e.g. in terms of filled pausing, appropriacy of different repair strategies, or remaining silent for pragmatic, discoursal and potential cultural variation in relation to who the interlocutors are. As discussed above, using filled pauses to hold one's turn in a conversation, or slowing down to give bad news, are not signs of disfluency; rather, they are appropriate strategies which L1 speakers adopt to ensure successful communication. In L1 automatised speech production, the use of such strategies is not considered as a sign of disfluency; but for L2 speakers, whose interlanguage system is still developing, the same strategies are often considered indicators of disfluency. Whether speakers' fluency behaviours are affected by the variations in L1 and L2 processing demands, or whether they simply are L2 speakers' communicative strategies that promote speech processing, are some of the complex questions that need unpacking in future L2 fluency research.

8.4 Fluency Development and CALF

In fluent speech performance, ease in formulating and articulating speech is closely linked to effective retrieval of underlying linguistic knowledge (syntax, lexis, phonology), demonstrated through increasing levels of complexity and accuracy, as measured in the now well-established CALF framework. However, there remain gaps in understanding the relationship between fluency and other aspects of performance measured via the CALF framework, not least in relation to dialogic and interactional contexts. Much effort has gone into examining how fluency as a general measure of performance may relate to complexity, accuracy and lexis in the L2, though the precise operationalisations and conclusions remain debated, particularly in relation to task demands. Research still has some gaps in understanding whether fluency in performance is hindered or fostered by demands of greater accuracy or greater complexity, which will have to be filled before we can apply such research in practice.

Moreover, we do not yet have a comprehensive understanding of fluency development in relation to CALF – e.g. does growing ability to produce longer utterances (greater complexity) precede or result from greater fluency in managing to conceptualise more complex ideas and articulate more complex formulations more easily? We note that even less research has been done in relation to lexis, particularly on L2 multiword sequences (Tavakoli & Uchihara, 2020). Therefore, we are not yet clear about how fluency development may relate to processes of retrieving lexical and syntactic information, e.g. in using chunks or developing more complex speech (i.e. how the speech processing stages work with underlying linguistic knowledge). We have seen how effective the use of multi-word chunks can improve speed and reduce repair, and that use of more frequent words and chunks can foster fluent speech. We also assume that more complex speech (e.g. using longer richer utterances) may impact fluency. However, we do not yet fully understand the connections between CALF in different interactional settings, which may require more creative adaptability to produce a fluent spontaneous speech to suit the context (Segalowitz, 2016; Pallotti, 2017). We are only beginning to explore how fluency development relates to such contextual demands on fluency and how they can be fostered in teaching or task practice. Therefore, further research will be useful in finding clearer ways to operationalise fluency development across the CALF paradigm more fully.

8.5 Fluency Development and Variation

We have argued that it is valuable for practitioners to understand why fluency, both in performance and as a developing skill, is variable along a wide continuum and does not easily suit a binary fluent/ disfluent distinction. First, it is essential to move away from an idealised sense of fluency based on a native speaker model. Recall Fillmore's definition of the highly fluent monolingual native speaker, cited in Chapter 1, as someone who has:

... the ability to talk at length with few pauses; the ability to fill time with talk; the ability to talk in coherent and semantically dense sentences; the ability to have appropriate things to say in a wide range of contexts; and the ability to be creative and imaginative in the language use.

Fillmore (1979: 51)

It is evident that this kind of standard is hard to reach in daily life, even for many L1 speakers. It seems therefore rather unrealistic to take it as a standard for L2 speakers. However, using the native-speaker norm, and using native speaker raters for assessments of fluency, remain prevalent practices in the research. We argue instead that future fluency research must take bilingual speakers as their norm, at least in assessments for comparing production, in order to allow for greater validation. It is also important to take account of the gaps in research into variation in fluency rating as speech recognition and assessment become more automated. Even in the press it has been noted how popular speech recognition software fails to consider variation in L1 speech in terms of accents (e.g. Harwell, 2018); therefore, bilingual and learner varieties of speech fluency need to be incorporated in emerging assessment technology too.

152   Conclusion

Second, research has investigated individual differences that can affect fluency, but as can be seen in Chapter 2, this body of research is rather limited. Two key factors seem to us relevant to explore in further research, but also of potential benefit for practitioners. First, we highlight the need to factor in the impact on L2 speech of L1 speaking patterns, both cross-linguistically and individually. For example, someone from a Finnish background whose L1 speech patterns may typically be slower than a speaker of Spanish or Chinese, may neither even think it is appropriate to try to match the L2 patterns, nor be able to. Similar cross-linguistic issues have been seen to impact on what is seen as appropriate conversational fluency (Morales-Lopez, 2000), such as turn-taking, overlaps and backchannelling. Then, there is the impact of a speaker's own speech habits (e.g. de Jong, Groenhout, Schoonen & Hulstijn, 2015) – someone who tends to pause a lot in their L1 is more likely to pause a lot in their L2. Assessment of fluency, therefore, should not solely depend on the speaker's speed or pausing as isolated phenomena. However, greater awareness of ranges of typical speech patterns is needed for assessment purposes as they provide greater cross-linguistic evidence about what is acceptable from speakers at different stages of their interlanguage development.

We also note the role of individual psychosocial factors such as working memory, levels of motivation (in terms of willingness to communicate) and stance (in terms of being a 'safe' speaker, unwilling to take the kind of initiative to practice speaking which is required to build fluency). Yet we have seen how little research in these areas has specifically focused on fluency, and it remains somewhat unclear what impact such variables have. It is also necessary to understand how these factors may co-occur in trying to understand why one speaker may seem to develop fluency relatively easily compared to another from the same L1, with the same amount of exposure, and the same opportunity for interaction. From a practitioner's perspective, allowing for a degree of variability among a class, or in a particular test, would help learners feel more confident as they develop L2 fluency and to avoid the sense of linguistic insecurity (Magne et al., 2019), in which anything less than native speaker speed and repair-free delivery could be seen as a failure to be fluent (Wright & Schartner, 2013).

More research is needed, therefore, on developing both subjective and objective ways of measuring fluency across a dynamic continuum, which can be valued as communicatively adequate but which does not have to equate to native speaker/monolingual patterns. Going right back to the earliest days of SLA, we note the value to the field of

8.7 Fluency Development and Pedagogy   153

Selinker's (1972) concept of interlanguage (systematic errors along the journey of acquisition of morpho-syntax) and suggest that a concept of 'interfluency' could be helpful in creating a more positive view of fluency development.

8.6 Fluency Development and Task Characteristics

Turning now to fluency development in different contexts, it is essential to understand the importance of task characteristics and task design on fluency development, which we see as particularly relevant for practitioners. Here, extensive research has helped identify the different aspects of fluency that are affected by task design, cognitive load and familiarity. We highlighted the impact of task design, particularly task structure, information organization and performance conditions. Amount of information and immediacy (e.g. with prompts) could also affect speakers. Some aspects of tasks may encourage specific linguistic behaviour in their communicative requirements (e.g. reasoning demand) and this can promote or prohibit fluency. Given the wide range of task-based factors impacting on fluency performance, we suggest there is scope to extend research into task effects on fluency development. Many task design features have not been investigated so far (e.g. the type of cognitive processes required for task completion). Gaps remain in how we understand performance conditions which directly affect everyday communication (e.g. at home vs. at work); research in such situations would help inform our understanding of how to foster real-world interactive fluency.

8.7 Fluency Development and Pedagogy

What do teachers think fluency is? Can fluency be taught? These have been key questions driving our whole approach to this volume. Current research, however, shows that teachers' expectations of fluency development in the classroom have been rather poorly researched. This is a problem for the field, given the many issues affecting fluency raised earlier. Nevertheless, we believe that our proposed dynamic multidimensional approach to fluency development should be helpful to teachers and learners alike and can be a useful way to connect research and practice.

Research in relation to teachers' perceptions of fluency, unlike raters' perceptions, seems to be an area about which more work needs to be done. We suggest our four-way continuum framework of fluency, from very broad to very narrow (Tavakoli & Hunter, 2018)

154   *Conclusion*

should be helpful for teachers in developing their own more nuanced understanding of fluency. Research into teachers' own understanding of fluency targets could shed light on inherent assumptions of a native speaker norm, and to help teachers taking a more variable view of bilingual 'interfluency' development. Such insights will be necessary for shifting expectations and helping reduce learners' linguistic insecurity.

Similarly, we have not yet established, in either research or practice, a clearly identifiable framework of how teachers can easily use activities to specifically promote fluency (whether broad or narrow), despite the decades of work on communicative language teaching. We note that here it is important to distinguish speaking activities and communicative tasks in a general sense from activities that specifically promote fluency either in monologic or interactional ways. It has been established that there can be benefits of providing scaffolded structures in interactive communicative activities to build automaticity (e.g. Gatbonton & Segalowitz's 2005 ACCESS model) and of using speeded task repetition to build ease of articulation (e.g. de Jong & Perfetti, 2011). Other teaching-based techniques include building strategic awareness of how to increase fluency (Tavakoli et al., 2016), or of using task familiarity and planning time (Skehan, 2014) to reduce cognitive load. In these senses, teaching can foster fluency development. But it would be helpful to have clearer evidence of how teachers could take account of the potential impact of the wide range of task characteristics that we have identified, relating e.g. to task design and structure (see Chapter 5). Also, we need a better understanding of how trade-offs against complexity or accuracy affect fluency development in the classroom over time, or what kind of fluency is expected by teachers and learners at different levels.

As more work starts to be done on teacher perceptions and practices (as well as learner expectations and goals), the benefits will spread to wider applications for practitioners, such as designing effective fluency-building activities by textbook designers. Further, we envisage fluency-related training being incorporated on typical teacher training programs, where so far little has been specifically done on fluency development as the focus has been on communicative practices in general.

8.8 Fluency Development and Assessment

In reviewing the existing research on fluency in assessment, we have seen that many challenges remain, especially to separate speaking proficiency from fluency and with little yet embedded in relation to

8.9 Fluency Development 'In the Wild'   155

discourse and task demands in assessing fluency. We have seen how fluency can sometimes overlap with other aspects of performance in assessments. High-proficiency scores usually entail high levels of fluency, but at a certain point of proficiency, objective measures of speed and pausing seem to hit a ceiling. Therefore, differentiating advanced level speakers as more or less fluent may not, in fact, be based on temporal measures, but more based on their range of lexical choice, prosody or sophistication of expression – and usually taken against a native-speaker norm. Research in this area has also suggested that those other factors, e.g. sophistication of expression, more competent use of lexical chunks, and more accuracy, may be internally perceived by raters as aspects of fluency. Future research will need to investigate perceived fluency from both experts (e.g. trained raters and language specialists) and non-expert (professionals in non-language areas) perspectives to see what is perceived central to the construct of fluency from these two equally important points of view.

Given the high-stakes impact of assessment, we accept that the need to shift from a unidimensional rating of fluency performance to a more dynamic variable notion of fluency in interaction, at different stages of development, and based on bilingual speaker norms, is potentially very hard to operationalise, particularly as oral assessments become more automated. However, we note that there is emerging research on discourse-based elements in newer, more interactive speaking assessments such as the Oxford Test of English. This test has an automated four-task test of spoken English, which seems to include interactive elements (Frost, Clothier, Huisman & Wigglesworth, 2019). Ensuring good quality research into how fluency is operationalised and rated in such assessments should help research and practitioners converge on appropriate features of fluency development in interactive settings.

8.9 Fluency Development 'In the Wild'

As well as considering fluency development in instructed settings (classroom or assessment) from a more variable interactional perspective, research and practice must also keep firmly rooted in how fluency develops as a key element in successful real-world communication, as the ultimate goal for most learners. Here it is vital to retain a view of fluency development against multilingual, intercultural norms for fluency development. We have seen that the chance to study or reside abroad may not be possible for all learners, but in a more interconnected world, technological opportunities can be found to speak with other target-language speakers. We have seen how Study Abroad research has given many valuable insights into fluency development, within broad and narrow senses. Yet we have also seen how variable fluency development can be during Study Abroad (if measured separately from other linguistic and sociocultural factors affecting communication). Such variability once again highlights the need to find a better way to operationalise multidimensional measures of fluency and fluency development, particularly in interactional settings. We have also seen that most research has been done on L2 English and suggest that wider research, both cross-linguistically and into more language pairings, needs to be done, so we can validate current measures for fluency development across different contexts.

8.10 Conclusion

Since early days of research on fluency (e.g. Dechert's work in the 1980s), through Riggenbach's (2000) seminal collection of perspectives on fluency, we can see that both research on fluency and our understanding of applications to practice have moved on tremendously, particularly in clarifying and operationalising fluency across many different domains of language use. As Koponen and Riggenbach noted (2000: 6), definitions of different types of fluency need to be unambiguous 'for there to be consistency among those implementing the definitions'. However, we have also seen that the drive for defining fluency in different ways has led to separations between different research agendas that have different priorities. While in scientific terms this is understandable – to gain precise understanding of specific constructs – we regret that, in other ways, there have also been some gaps in connecting the main value of the different research paradigms. Meanwhile, research has not always managed to bridge the gap to practice. Therefore, for professionals, and most of all for learners, fluency can remain a fuzzy, unteachable, unattainable goal. Such barriers risk creating significant demotivation and anxiety in learners, blocking their capacity to interact even when chances are available (Wright & Schartner, 2013). Furthermore, fluency remains poorly defined for practical applications such as bilingual language development or forensic analysis of speech.

We have aimed throughout this volume to clarify some of the fuzziness of fluency as a goal, to affirm that fluency can be teachable and applicable beyond a standard language classroom or assessment setting. Most of all, we have tried to find ways to address the two dilemmas noted at the start, of the gaps between research agendas, and between research and practice. First, we have argued that fluency is a variable skill that develops in many ways, that emerges differently across tasks and interactional settings. Second, we have reviewed

8.10 Conclusion 157

existing research for its benefits for practice, but also argued in favour of taking a richer, more socially-contextualised multidimensional perspective on fluency in professional and practice-based settings. We have further argued that whether in daily classroom settings, in assessments or for research purposes, it is time to move away from the assumption of using the model of a highly competent L1 speaker as the target for fluency development, in which deviation from that norm is deemed to be disfluent. Rather, we would argue it is essential to base our understanding of fluency development on multilingual norms, both in research and practice. It will be challenging to put this into practice, particularly for assessment that becomes increasingly automated, but given the pace of technological change, it may be achievable sooner than we think.

To conclude, fluency remains a complex and multidimensional construct, and we cannot and should not try to find a single or simplified definition for it. It remains imperative, as Riggenbach (2000) noted, to investigate 'how different aspects of language-using skills are integrated into learners' performances ... conscious of the complexity of language, speech, interaction and communication' (p. 20). We believe in this volume we have gone some way to address that challenge, and to present our more updated understandings from research in easily accessible ways for researchers and language professionals, so that research can benefit practice and vice versa. Still, we reiterate Riggenbach's challenge as we look ahead to the next few decades, calling for second-language fluency research and practice to seek further questions and answers together, as we face increasingly fast-moving real-world demands in how to communicate fluently in a digital, globalised, multilingual world.

Appendix: Fluency Descriptors across Time

A.1 FSI Fluency Ratings (1958, Cited in Fulcher, 1987)

Fluency (ranging from 1, *no familiarity* with the language to 6, *native speaker proficiency*)

1. Speech is so halting and fragmentary that conversation is virtually impossible.
2. Speech is very slow and uneven except for short or routine sentences.
3. Speech is frequently hesitant and jerky; sentences may be left uncompleted.
4. Speech is occasionally hesitant, with some unevenness caused by rephrasing and groping for words.
5. Speech is effortless and smooth, but perceptibly non-native in speed and evenness.
6. Speech on all professional and general topics as effortless and as smooth as a native speaker's.

The FSI (1958) band descriptors for the lowest and highest proficiency levels are given here as examples. References to fluency are in bold.

Level 1: Elementary Proficiency.

Able to satisfy routine travel needs and minimum courtesy requirements. Can ask and answer questions on topics very familiar to him: within the scope of his very limited language experience can understand simple questions and statements, **allowing for slowed speech, repetition or paraphrase**; speaking vocabulary inadequate to express anything but the most elementary needs: errors in pronunciation and grammar are frequent, but can be understood by a native speaker used to dealing with foreigners attempting to speak his language: while topics which are 'very familiar' and elementary needs vary considerably from individual to individual, any person at Level 1 should be able to order a simple meal, ask for shelter or lodging, ask and give simple directions, make purchases, and tell time.

Level 5: Native or Bilingual proficiency. Speaking proficiency equivalent to that of an educated native speaker.

Has **complete fluency in the language** such that his speech on all levels is fully accepted by educated native speakers in all its features,

158

Appendix: Fluency Descriptors across Time   159

including breadth of vocabulary and idiom, colloquialisms, and pertinent cultural references.

A.2 CEFR (Council of Europe, 1996) Fluency Scale

C2: Can express him/herself at length with a natural, effortless, unhesitating flow. Pauses only to reflect on precisely the right words to express his/her thoughts or to find an appropriate example or explanation.

C1: Can express him/herself fluently and spontaneously, almost effortlessly. Only a conceptually difficult subject can hinder a natural, smooth flow of language.

B2: Can communicate spontaneously, often showing remarkable fluency and ease of expression in even longer complex stretches of speech. Can produce stretches of language with a fairly even tempo; although he/she can be hesitant as he/she searches for patterns and expressions, there are few noticeably long pauses. Can interact with a degree of fluency and spontaneity that makes regular interaction with native speakers quite possible without imposing strain on either party.

B1: Can express him/herself with relative ease. Despite some problems with formulation resulting in pauses and 'cul-de-sacs', he/she can keep going effectively without help. Can keep going comprehensibly, even though pausing for grammatical and lexical planning and repair is very evident, especially in longer stretches of free production.

A2: Can make him/herself understood in short contributions, even though pauses, false starts and reformulation are very evident. Can construct phrases on familiar topics with sufficient ease to handle short exchanges, despite very noticeable hesitation and false starts.

A1: Can manage very short, isolated, mainly pre-packaged utterances, with much pausing to search for expressions, to articulate less familiar words, and to repair communication.

A.3 CEFR (Council of Europe, 2009b) Fluency Scale

C2: Can express him/herself spontaneously at length with a natural colloquial flow, avoiding or backtracking around any difficulty so smoothly that the interlocutor is hardly aware of it.

C1: Can express him/herself fluently and spontaneously, almost effortlessly. Only a conceptually difficult subject can hinder a natural, smooth flow of language.

160   *Appendix: Fluency Descriptors across Time*

B2: Can adjust to the changes of direction, style and emphasis normally found in conversation. Can produce stretches of language with a fairly even tempo; although he/she can be hesitant as he or she searches for patterns and expressions, there are few noticeably long pauses.

B1: Can exploit a wide range of simple language flexibly to express much of what he/she wants. Can keep going comprehensibly, even though pausing for grammatical and lexical planning and repair is very evident, especially in longer stretches of free production.

A2: Can make him/herself understood in very short utterances, even though pauses, false starts and reformulation are very evident. Can expand learned phrases through simple recombinations of their elements.

A1: Can manage very short, isolated, mainly pre-packaged utterances, with much pausing to search for expressions, to articulate less familiar words, and to repair communication.

A.4 Council of Europe (2018) Companion: Fluency Scale

Spoken fluency, as discussed above, has a broader, holistic meaning (=articulate speaker) and a narrower, technical and more psycholinguistic meaning (=accessing one's repertoire). The broader interpretation would include: Propositional precision, Flexibility, and at least to some extent Thematic development and Coherence/cohesion. For this reason, the scale below focuses more on the narrower, more traditional view of fluency. Key concepts operationalized in the scale include the following:

- ability to construct utterances, despite hesitations and pauses (lower levels);
- ability to maintain a lengthy production or conversation;
- ease and spontaneity of expression." (p. 144)

A.4.1 Spoken Fluency

C2: Can express him/herself at length with a natural, effortless, unhesitating flow. Pauses only to reflect on precisely the right words to express his/her thoughts or to find an appropriate example or explanation.

C1: Can express him/herself fluently and spontaneously, almost effortlessly. Only a conceptually difficult subject can hinder a natural, smooth flow of language.

B2: Can communicate spontaneously, often showing remarkable fluency and ease of expression in even longer complex stretches of speech. Can produce stretches of language with a fairly even tempo; although he/she can be hesitant as he/she searches for patterns and expressions, there are few noticeably long pauses. Can interact with a degree of fluency and

Appendix: Fluency Descriptors across Time   161

spontaneity that makes regular interaction with speakers of the target language quite possible without imposing strain on either party.

B1: Can express him/herself with relative ease. Despite some problems with formulation resulting in pauses and 'cul-de-sacs', he/she can keep going effectively without help. Can keep going comprehensibly, even though pausing for grammatical and lexical planning and repair is very evident, especially in longer stretches of free production.

A2: Can make him/herself understood in short contributions, even though pauses, false starts and reformulation are very evident. Can construct phrases on familiar topics with sufficient ease to handle short exchanges, despite very noticeable hesitation and false starts.

A1: Can manage very short, isolated, mainly pre-packaged utterances, with much pausing to search for expressions, to articulate less familiar words, and to repair communication.

Pre-A1: Can manage very short, isolated, rehearsed, utterances using gesture and signalled requests for help when necessary

For copyright email: publishing@coe.int.

References

Ahmadian, M. (2011). The effect of 'massed' task repetitions on complexity, accuracy and fluency: Does it transfer to a new task? *The Language Learning Journal*, 39, 269–280.

Ahmadian, M., Abdolrezapour, P. and Ketabi, S. (2012). Task difficulty and self-repair behaviour in second language oral production. *International Journal of Applied Linguistics*, 22(3), 310–330.

Ahmadian, M, J. and Tavakoli, M. (2011). The effects of simultaneous use of careful online planning and task repetition on accuracy, complexity, and fluency in EFL learners' oral production. *Language Teaching Research*, 15(1), 35–59.

Alonso-Ramos, M. (Ed.) (2016). *Spanish Learner Corpus Research: Current Trends and Future Perspectives*. Amsterdam: Benjamins.

Alsagoff, L., McKay, S., Hu, G. and Renandya, W. (Eds.) (2012). *Principles and Practices for Teaching English as an International Language*. New York/ London: Routledge.

Anderson, J. (1983). *The Architecture of Cognition*. Mahwah, NJ: Lawrence Erlbaum.

Anderson, J. (1993). *Rules of the Mind*. Hillsdale, NJ: Lawrence Erlbaum.

Arnold, J., Fagnano, M. and Tanenhaus, M. (2003). Disfluencies signal theee, um, new information. *Journal of Psycholinguistic Research*, 32(1), 25–36.

Awwad, A. (2017). The effects of task complexity manipulated by intentional reasoning demands on second language learners' speech performance: Interaction with language proficiency and working memory. Unpublished PhD thesis, University of Reading.

Awwad, A. and Tavakoli, P. (2019). Task complexity, language proficiency and working memory: Interaction effects on second language speech performance. *International Review of Applied Linguistics in Language Teaching* (published online ahead of print). doi: https://doi.org/10.1515/iral-2018-0378.

Awwad, A., Tavakoli, P. and Wright, C. (2017). 'I think that's what he's doing': Effects of intentional reasoning on second language (L2) speech performance. *System*, 67, 158–169.

Bachman, L. (1990). *Fundamental Considerations in Language Testing*. Oxford: Oxford University Press.

Baddeley, A. (2007). *Working Memory, Thought and Action*. Oxford: Oxford University Press.

Bardovi-Harlig, K. (1994). Reverse-order reports and the acquisition of tense: Beyond the principle of chronological order. *Language Learning*, 44, 243–282.

Bardovi-Harlig, K. (2013). Developing L2 pragmatics. *Language Learning*, 63(1), 68–86.

References   163

Barr, D. and Seyfeddinipur, M. (2010). The role of fillers in listener attributions for speaker disfluency. *Language and Cognitive Processes*, 25(4), 441–455.

Baten, L., Beaven, A., Osborne, J. and van Maele, J. (2013). WebCEF: An online collaboration tool for assessing foreign language proficiency. In P. Pumilia-Gnarini, E. Favaron, E. Pacetti, J. Bishop and L. Guerra (Eds.), *Handbook of Research on Didactic Strategies and Technologies for Education: Incorporating Advancements* (pp. 559–570). IGI Global. http://doi:10.4018/978-1-4666-2122-0.ch048

Bavelas, J., Gerwing, J., Sutton, C. and Prevost, D. (2008). Gesturing on the telephone: Independent effects of dialogue and visibility. *Journal of Memory and Language*, 58, 495–520.

Berger, J. (2014). Word of mouth and interpersonal communication: A review and directions for future research. *Journal of Consumer Psychology*, 24(4), 586–607.

Blake, C. (2009). Potential of text-based internet chats for improving oral fluency in a second language. *The Modern Language Journal*, 93(2), 227–240.

Board, T. and Tinsley, K. (2017). *Languages for the Future*. London: British Council. Available at: www.britishcouncil.org/sites/default/files/languages_for_the_future_2017.pdf [Accessed 4 September 2019].

Bock, K. and Levelt, W. (1994). Language production: Grammatical encoding. In M. Gernsbacher (Ed.), *Handbook of Psycholinguistics* (pp. 945–984). San Diego, CA: Academic Press.

Boers, F. (2014). A reappraisal of the 4/3/2 activity. *RELC Journal*, 45(3), 221–235.

Boers, F., Eyckmans, J., Kappel, J., Stengers, H. and Demecheleer, M. (2006). Formulaic sequences and perceived oral proficiency: Putting a Lexical Approach to the test. *Language Teaching Research*, 10(3), 245–261.

Boersma, P. and Weenink, D. (2013). *Praat: Doing Phonetics by Computer*. Version 5.3.51. Available at: www.praat.org/ [Accessed 3 September 2019].

Bonomo, A. (2017). *World English(es) and the Multilingual Turn: Frameworks of Complex Phenomena*. Newcastle: Cambridge Scholars Publishing.

Borg, S. (2003). Teacher cognition in language teaching: A review of research on what language teachers think, know, believe, and do. *Language Teaching*, 36, 81–109.

Borg, S. (2009). English language teachers' conceptions of research. *Applied Linguistics*, 30, 358–388.

Bortfeld, H., Leon, S., Bloom, J., Schober, M. and Brenan, S. (2001). Disfluency rates in conversation: Effects of age, relationship, topic, role and gender. *Language and Speech*, 44(2), 123–147.

Bosker, H., Pinget, A.-F., Quené, H., Sanders, T. and de Jong, N. H. (2012). What makes speech sound fluent? The contributions of pauses, speed and repairs. *Language Testing*, 30(2), 159–175.

de Bot, K. (1992). A bilingual production model: Levelt's 'speaking' model adapted. *Applied Linguistics*, 13, 1–24.

de Bot, K. and Jaensch, C. (2015). What is special about L3 processing? *Bilingualism: Language and Cognition*, 18(2), 130–144.

164   References

Bown, J., Dewey, D. and Belnap, K. (2015). Student interactions during study abroad in Jordan. In R. Mitchell, N. Tracy-Ventura and K. McManus (Eds.), *Social Interaction, Identity and Language Learning During Residence Abroad* (pp. 199–221). Amsterdam: EuroSLA Monograph Series.

Brecht, R. D., Davidson, D. E. and Ginsberg, R. B. (1995). Predictors of foreign language gain during study abroad. In B. F. Freed (Ed.), *Second Language Acquisition in a Study Abroad Context* (pp. 37–66). Philadelphia: John Benjamins.

Brezina, V. and Flowerdew, L. (Eds.) (2017). *Learner Corpus Research: New Perspectives and Applications*. London: Bloomsbury.

British Council (2019). *Teaching Speaking: Unit 9*. Available at: www.teachingenglish.org.uk/article/teaching-speaking-unit-9-fluency [Accessed 29 October 2019].

Brooks, L. and Swain, M. (2014) Contextualizing performances: comparing performances during TOEFL iBTTM and real-life academic speaking activities. *Language Assessment Quarterly*, 11(4), 353–373.

Brown, A. (2006a). An examination of the rating process in the revised IELTS speaking test. In P. McGovern and S. Walsh (Eds.), *IELTS Research Report* (pp. 41–70). Canberra: IELTS Australia and British Council.

Brown, A. (2006b). Candidate discourse in the revised IELTS Speaking Test. In P. McGovern and S. Walsh (Eds.), *IELTS Research Report* (pp. 71–89). Canberra and Manchester: IELTS Australia and British Council.

Brown, A., Iwashita, N. and McNamara, T. (2005). *An Examination of Rater Orientations and Test-Taker Performance on English for Academic Purposes Speaking Tasks*, TOEFL Monograph Series MS-29. Princeton, NJ: Educational Testing Service.

Brown, G., Anderson, A., Shillcock, R. and Yule, G. (1984). *Teaching Talk: Strategies for Production and Assessment*. Cambridge: Cambridge University Press.

Brumfit, C. (1984). *Communicative Methodology in Language Teaching: The Roles of Fluency and Accuracy*. Cambridge: Cambridge University Press.

Bui, G. (2014). Task readiness: Theoretical framework and empirical evidence from topic familiarity, strategic planning, and proficiency levels. In P. Skehan (Ed.), *Processing Perspectives on Task Performance* (pp. 63–93). Amsterdam: John Benjamins.

Burns, A. and Richards. J. (2009). *The Cambridge Guide to Second Language Teacher Education*. New York: Cambridge University Press.

Bygate, M. (2001). Effects of task repetition on the structure and control of language. In M. Bygate, P. Skehan and M. Swain (Eds.), *Researching Pedagogic Tasks, Second Language Learning, Teaching and Testing* (pp. 23–48). Harlow, Essex: Longman.

Cameron, D. (2001). *Working with Spoken Discourse*. London: Sage.

Canagarajah, A. (1999). *Resisting Linguistic Imperialism in English Language Teaching*. Oxford: Oxford University Press.

Canagarajah, S. (2013). *Translingual Practice: Global Englishes and Cosmopolitan Relations*. London/New York: Routledge.

References   165

Canale, M. and Swain, M. (1980). Theoretical bases of communicative approaches to second language teaching and testing. *Applied Linguistics*, 1, 1–47.

Centre for English Corpus Linguistics (CECL) (2019). *Learner Corpora around the World. Louvain-la-Neuve: Université Catholique de Louvain.* Available at: https://uclouvain.be/en/research-institutes/ilc/cecl/learner-corpora-around-the-world.html [Accessed 26 October 2019].

Chambers, F. (1997). What do we mean by fluency? *System*, 25, 535–544.

Chang, Y. F. (1999). Discourse topics and interlanguage variation. In P. Robinson (Ed.), *Representation and Process: Proceedings of the 3rd Pacific Second Language Research Forum*, 1 (pp. 235–241). Tokyo: PacSLRF.

Chen, T. (2019). Joint contributions of multilevel linguistic knowledge to character meaning retention in L2 Chinese. *Journal of Psycholinguistic Research*, 48(1), 129–143.

Chen, K. and Huang, C. (2000). *Sinica Corpus: Academia Sinica Balanced Corpus for Mandarin Chinese.* Available at: www.sinica.edu.tw/SinicaCorpus [Accessed 27 October 2019].

Churchill, E. and DuFon, M. (Eds.) (2006). *Language Learners in Study Abroad Contexts.* Clevedon: Multilingual Matters.

Cirillo, L., Colón de Carvajal, I. and Ticca, A. (2016). 'I'm sorry + naming the offense': A format for apologizing. *Discourse Processes*, 53, 83–96.

Clark, H. and Fox Tree, J. (2002). Using *uh* and *um* in spontaneous speaking. *Cognition*, 84, 73–111.

Cohen, A. and Macaro, E. (Eds.) (2007). *Language Learner Strategies: Thirty Years of Research and Practice.* Oxford: Oxford University Press.

Coleman, J. and Chafer, T. (2011). The experience and long-term impact of study abroad by Europeans in an African context. In F. Dervin (Ed.), *Analysing the Consequences of Academic Mobility and Migration* (pp. 67–96). Newcastle: Cambridge Scholars Publishing.

van Compernolle, R. and McGregor, J. (Eds.). (2016). *Authenticity, Language and Interaction in Second Language Contexts.* Bristol: Multilingual Matters.

Cook, V. (Ed.) (2002). *Portraits of the L2 User.* Clevedon: Multilingual Matters.

Cordier, C. (2013). The presence, nature and role of formulaic sequences in English advanced learners of French: A longitudinal study. Unpublished PhD thesis, Newcastle University.

Costa, A. (2005). Lexical access in bilingual production. In J. Kroll and A. de Groot (Eds.), *Handbook of Bilingualism* (pp. 308–325). New York: Oxford University Press.

Council of Europe (2001). *The Common European Framework of Reference for Languages: Learning, Teaching, Assessment.* Available at: https://rm.coe.int/1680459f97 [Accessed 22 June 2020].

Council of Europe (2009a). *A Common European Framework for Language Learning and Teaching: Draft 1 of a Framework Proposal.* Strasbourg: Council of Europe. www.coe.int/lang.

Council of Europe (2009b). *Relating Language Examinations to the Common European Framework of Reference for Languages: Learning, Teaching,*

166   *References*

Assessment (CEFR). A Manual. Language Policy Division, Strasbourg: Council of Europe. www.coe.int/lang.

Council of Europe (2011). The *Common European Framework of Reference for Languages: Learning, Teaching, Assessment.* Strasbourg: Council of Europe. Available at: https://rm.coe.int/16802fc1bf [Accessed 26 October 2019].

Council of Europe (2018). *The Common European Framework of Reference for Languages: Learning, Teaching and Assessment Companion Volume with New Descriptors.* Strasbourg: Language Policy Division, Council of Europe. Available at: www.coe.int/lang-cefr [Accessed 26 October 2019].

Cucchiarini, C., Strik, H. and Boves, L. (2000). Quantitative assessment of second language learners' fluency by means of automatic speech recognition technology. *Journal of the Acoustical Society of America*, 107(2), 989–999.

Cucchiarini, C., Strik, H. and Boves, L. (2002). Quantitative assessment of second language learners' fluency: Comparisons between read and spontaneous speech. *Journal of the Acoustical Society of America*, 111(6), 2862–2873.

Culpeper, J., Mackey, A. and Taguchi, N. (2018). *Second Language Pragmatics: From Theory to Research.* New York: Routledge.

Daneman, M. (1991). Working memory as a predictor of verbal fluency. *Journal of Psycholinguistic Research*, 20(6), 445–464.

Daneman, M. and Green, I. (1986). Individual differences in comprehending and producing words in context. *Journal of Memory and Language*, 25, 1–18.

Davidson, D. (2010). Study abroad: When, how long, and with what results? New data from the Russian front. *Foreign Language Annals*, 43(1), 6–26.

Dechert, H. (1980). Pauses and intonation as indicators of verbal planning in second language speech productions. In H. Dechert and M. Raupach (Eds.), *Temporal Variables in Speech* (pp. 271–285). The Hague: Mouton.

DeKeyser, R. (2001). Automaticity and automatisation. In P. Robinson (Ed.), *Cognition and Second Language Instruction* (pp. 125–151). Cambridge: Cambridge University Press.

DeKeyser, R. (Ed.) (2007). *Practice in A Second Language: Perspectives from Applied Linguistics and Cognitive Psychology.* Cambridge: Cambridge University Press.

Derwing, T., Munro, M. and Thomson, R. (2008). A longitudinal study of ESL learners' fluency and comprehensibility development. *Applied Linguistics*, 29(3), 359–380.

Derwing, T., Munro, M., Thomson, R. and Rossiter, M. (2009). The relationship between L1 fluency and L2 fluency development. *Studies in Second Language Acquisition*, 31(4), 533–557.

Derwing, T., Rossiter, M., Munro, M. and Thomson, R. (2004). Second language fluency: Judgments on different tasks. *Language Learning*, 54, 655–679.

Dewaele, J.-M. (1996). How to measure formality of speech? A Model of Synchronic Variation. In K. Sajavaara and C. Fairweather (Eds.), *Approaches to Second Language Acquisition, Jyväskylä Cross-Language Studies, No. 17* (pp. 119–133). Jyväskylä: University of Jyväskylä.

References   167

Dewaele, J.-M. and Furnham, A. (2000). Personality and speech production: A pilot study of second language learners. *Personality and Individual Differences*, 28, 355–365.

Diao, W., Donovan, A. and Malone, M. (2018). Oral language development among Mandarin learners in Chinese homestays. *Study Abroad Research in Second Language Acquisition and International Education*, 3(1), 33–58.

Diepenbroek, L. and Derwing, T. (2014). To what extent do popular ESL textbooks incorporate oral fluency and pragmatic development. *TESL Canada Journal*, 30, 1–20.

Dijum, K., Schoonen, R. and Hulstijn, J. (2018). Professional and non-professional raters' responsiveness to fluency and accuracy in L2 speech: An experimental approach. *Language Testing*, 35(4), 501–527.

Di Silvio, F., Diao, W. and Donovan, A. (2016). The development of L2 fluency during study abroad: A cross-language study. *Modern Language Journal*, 100(3), 610–624.

Donato, R. (2000). Sociocultural contributions to understanding the foreign and second language classroom. In J. Lantolf (Ed.), *Sociocultural Theory and Second Language Learning* (pp. 27–50). Oxford: Oxford University Press.

Dore, C. (2015). *Perceptions of Fluency*. London: British Council. Available at: https://englishagenda.britishcouncil.org/sites/default/files/attachments/dissertation_design_for_publication_2016_reading_university_cecilia_dore.pdf [Accessed 30 October 2019).

Dörnyei, Z. and Kormos, J. (1998). Problem-solving mechanisms in L2 communication. *Studies in Second Language Acquisition*, 20, 349–385.

Dörnyei, Z. and Ushioda, E. (2013). *Teaching and Researching Motivation*. Abingdon: Routledge.

Du, H. (2013). The development of Chinese fluency during study abroad in China. *The Modern Language Journal*, 97(1), 131–143.

Duff, P., Anderson, T., Ilnyckyj, R., Van Gaya, E., Wang, R. and Yates, E. (2013). *Learning Chinese: Linguistic, Sociocultural, and Narrative Perspectives*. Berlin/Boston: DeGruyter.

Duran-Karaoz, Z. and Tavakoli, P. (2020). Predicting L2 fluency from L1 fluency behaviour: The case of L1 Turkish and L2 English speakers. *Studies in Second Language Acquisition*, 1–25.

Edwards, J. (2008). The transcription of discourse. In D. Schiffrin, D. Tannen and H. Hamilton (Eds.), *The Handbook of Discourse Analysis* (pp. 321–348). London: Routledge.

Ejzenberg, R. (2000). The juggling act of oral fluency: A psycho-sociolinguistic metaphor. In H. Riggenbach (Ed.), *Perspectives on Fluency* (pp. 287–313). Ann Arbor: University of Michigan Press.

Ellis, R. (1994). *The Study of Second Language Acquisition*. Oxford: Oxford University Press.

Ellis, R. (2003). *Task-Based Language Learning and Teaching*. Oxford: Oxford University Press.

168 *References*

Ellis, R. (2005). Planning and task-based performance: Theory and research. In R. Ellis (Ed.), *Planning and Task Performance in a Second Language* (pp. 3–36). Amsterdam: John Benjamins.

Ellis, R. (2009). The differential effects of three types of task planning on the fluency, complexity and accuracy in L2 oral production. *Applied Linguistics*, 30(4), 474–509.

Ellis, R. and Shintani, N. (2014). *Exploring Language Pedagogy Through Second Language Acquisition Research*. London: Routledge.

Everson, M. and Xiao, Y. (Eds.) (2009). *Teaching Chinese as a Foreign Language*. Boston: Cheng & Tsui.

Faerch, C., Haastrup, K. and Phillipson, R. (1984). *Learner Language and Language Learning*. Clevedon: Multilingual Matters.

Faulkner, D., Littleton, K. and Woodhead, M. (2013). *Learning Relationships in the Classroom*. London: Routledge.

Felker, E., Klockmann, H. and de Jong, N. H. (2019). How conceptualizing influences fluency in first and second language speech production. *Applied Psycholinguistics*, 40, 111–136.

Fillmore, C. J. (1979). On fluency. In C. J. Fillmore, D. Kempler and W. Wang (Eds.), *Individual Differences in Language Ability and Language Behavior* (pp. 85–101). New York: Academic Press.

Finlayson, I. and Corley, M. (2008). Disfluency in dialogue: An intentional sign from the speaker. *Psychonomic Bulletin and Review*, 19(5), 921–928.

Fortkamp, M. (1999). Working memory capacity and aspects of L2 speech production. *Communication and Cognition*, 32(3–4), 259–295.

Foster, P. (1998). A classroom perspective on the negotiation of meaning. *Applied Linguistics*, 19(1), 1–23.

Foster, P. (2009). Task-based language learning research: Expecting too much or too little? *International Journal of Applied Linguistics*, 19, 247–263.

Foster, P. (2013). Fluency. In C. Chapelle (Ed.), *The Encyclopaedia of Applied Linguistics*. London: Wiley-Blackwell. doi: https://doi.org/10.1002/9781405198431.wbeal0417.

Foster, P. (2020). Oral fluency in a second language: A research agenda for the next ten years. *Language Teaching*, Early view, June 2020.

Foster, P. and Skehan, P. (1996). The influence of planning and task type on second language performance. *Studies in Second Language Acquisition*, 18, 299–323.

Foster, P. and Tavakoli, P. (2009). Native speakers and task performance: Comparing effects on complexity, fluency and lexical diversity. *Language Learning*, 59, 866–896.

Foster, P., Tonkyn, A. and Wigglesworth, G. (2000). Measuring spoken language: A unit for all reasons. *Applied Linguistics*, 21, 354–375.

Freed, B. (Ed.) (1995). *Second Language Acquisition in a Study Abroad Context*. Amsterdam: John Benjamins.

Freed, B. (2000). Is fluency, like beauty, in the eyes (and ears) of the beholder? In H. Riggenbach (Ed.), *Perspectives on Fluency* (pp. 243–265). Ann Arbor: University of Michigan Press.

Freed, B., Segalowitz, N. and Dewey, D. (2004). Context of learning and second language fluency in French: Comparing regular classroom, study abroad, and intensive domestic immersion programs. *Studies in Second Language Acquisition*, 26(2), 275–301.

Frost, K., Clothier, J., Huisman, A. and Wigglesworth, G. (2019). Responding to a TOEFL iBT integrated speaking task: Mapping task demands and test takers' use of stimulus content. *Language Testing*. doi: 10.1177/0265532219860750.

Fulcher, G. (1987). Tests of oral performance: the need for databased criteria. *English Language Teaching Journal*, 41(4), 287–291.

Fulcher, G. (1993). The construction and validation of rating scales for oral tests in English as a foreign language. Unpublished PhD thesis, University of Lancaster.

Fulcher, G. (2010). *Practical Language Testing*. London: Hodder Education.

Fusaroli, R. and Tylen, K. (2016). Investigating conversational dynamics: Interactive alignment, interpersonal synergy and collective task performance. *Cognitive Science*, 40(1), 145–171.

García, O. and Li, W. (2014). *Translanguaging: Language, Bilingualism and Education*. Basingstoke: Palgrave Macmillan.

García, O. and Sylvan, C. (2011). Pedagogies and practices in multilingual classrooms: Singularities in pluralities. *The Modern Language Journal*, 95(3), 385–400.

Gass, S. and Varonis, E. (1994). Input, interaction, and second language production. *Studies in Second Language Acquisition*, 16(3), 283–302.

Gatbonton, E. and Segalowitz, N. (1988). Creative automatization: Principles for promoting fluency within a communicative framework. *TESOL Quarterly*, 22, 473–492.

Gatbonton, E. and Segalowitz, N. (2005). Rethinking communicative language teaching: A focus on access to fluency. *The Canadian Modern Language Review*, 61(3), 325–353.

GCSE Subject Content for Modern Foreign Languages (2014). Department of Education, UK. Available at: www.gov.uk/government/publications/gcse-modern-foreign-languages [Accessed 29 October 2019].

Gilabert, R. (2007). Effects of manipulating task complexity on self-repairs during L2 oral production. *International Review of Applied Linguistics*, 45, 214–240.

Gilabert, R., Barón, J. and Levkina, M. (2011). Manipulating task complexity across task types and modes. In P. Robinson (Ed.), *Second Language Task Complexity: Researching the Cognition Hypothesis of Language Learning and Performance* (pp. 105–138). Amsterdam: John Benjamins.

Gilmore, A. (2007). Authentic materials and authenticity in foreign language learning. *Language Teaching*, 40, 97–118.

Ginther, A., Dimova, S. and Yang, R. (2010). Conceptual and empirical relationships between temporal measures of fluency and oral English proficiency with implications for automated scoring. *Language Testing*, 27(3), 379–399.

Goldman-Eisler, F. (1951). The measurement of time sequences in conversational behaviour. *British Journal of Psychology*, 42, 355–362.

170   References

Goldman-Eisler, F. (1968). *Psycholinguistics: Experiments in Spontaneous Speech*. London/New York: Academic Press.

Götz, S. (2013). *Fluency in Native and Nonnative English Speech*. Amsterdam: John Benjamins.

Granger, S., Dagneaux, E. and Meunier, F. (2002). *The International Corpus of Learner English*. Louvain-la-Neuve: Presses Universitaires de Louvain.

Granger, S., Gilquin, G. and Meunier, F. (Eds.) (2015). *The Cambridge Handbook of Learner Corpus Research*. Cambridge: Cambridge University Press.

Green, D. (1998). Mental control of the bilingual lexico-semantic system. *Bilingualism: Language and Cognition*, 1, 67–81.

Gregg, K. (1996). The logical and developmental problems of second language acquisition. In W. Ritchie and T. Bhatia (Eds.), *Handbook of Second Language Acquisition* (pp. 50–84). San Diego, CA: Academic Press.

Grosjean, F. (1982). *Life with Two Languages: An Introduction to Bilingualism*. Cambridge, MA: Harvard University Press.

Grosjean, F. (2008). *Studying Bilinguals*. Oxford: Oxford University Press.

Guillot, M. (1999). *Fluency and Its Teaching*. Clevedon: Multilingual Matters.

Hall, J., Hellerman, J. and Pekarek Doehler, S. (2011). *L2 Interactional Competence and Development*. Bristol: Multilingual Matters.

Han, Z.-H. (Ed.) (2014). *Studies in Second Language Acquisition of Chinese*. Clevedon: Multilingual Matters.

Harmer, J. (2005). *The Practice of English language Teaching*. London: Longman.

Harwell, D. (2018). *The Accent Gap*. Available at: www.washingtonpost.com/graphics/2018/business/alexa-does-not-understand-your-accent/ [Accessed 20 October 2019].

Hoey, M. (1983). *On the Surface of Discourse*. London: Allen & Unwin.

Hong Kong English Language Education Key Learning Area Curriculum Guide (2017). Available at: www.edb.gov.hk/attachment/en/curriculum-development/renewal/ELE/ELE_KLACG_eng_draft_2017_05.pdf [Accessed 29 October 2019].

Horwitz, E., Horwitz, M. and Cope, J. (1986). Foreign language classroom anxiety. *Modern Language Journal*, 70, 125–132.

House, J. (1996). Developing pragmatic fluency in English as a foreign language: Routines and metapragmatic awareness. *Studies in Second Language Acquisition*, 18, 225–252.

Housen, A. and Kuiken, F. (2009). Complexity, accuracy and fluency in second language acquisition. *Applied Linguistics*, 30(4), 461–473.

Housen, A., Kuiken, F. and Vedder, I. (2012). *Dimensions of L2 Performance and Proficiency*. Amsterdam: John Benjamins.

Hsu, H. C. (2019). The combined effect of task repetition and post-task transcribing on L2 speaking complexity, accuracy, and fluency. *The Language Learning Journal*, 47(2), 172–187.

Huensch, A. and Tracy-Ventura, N. (2017). L2 utterance fluency development before, during, and after residence abroad: A multidimensional investigation. *The Modern Language Journal*, 101, 275–293.

References 171

Huensch, A., Tracy-Ventura, N., Bridges, J. and Cuesta Medina, J. (2019). Variables affecting the maintenance of L2 proficiency and fluency four years post-study abroad. *Study Abroad Research in Second Language Acquisition and International Education*, 4(1), 96–125.

Huifen, L. (2015). Computer-mediated communication (CMC) in L2 oral proficiency development: A meta-analysis. *ReCALL*, 27(3), 261–287.

Hunt, K. (1965). Grammatical structures written at three grade levels. NCTE Research report No. 3. Champaign, IL: NCTE.

Hunter, A.-M. (2017). Fluency development in the ESL classroom: The impact of immediate task repetition and procedural repetition on learners' oral fluency. Unpublished PhD thesis, University of Surrey, Guildford.

IELTS (2018). *IELTS Speaking Band Descriptors*. Available at: www.ielts.org/-/media/pdfs/speaking-band-descriptors.ashx?la=en [Accessed 28 March 2018].

In'nami, Y. and Koizumi, R. (2016). Task and rater effects in L2 speaking and writing: A synthesis of generalizability studies. *Language Testing*, 33(3), 341–366.

Isaacs, T. and Trofimovich, P. (2012). Deconstructing comprehensibility: identifying the linguistic influences on listeners' L2 comprehensibility ratings. *Studies in Second Language Acquisition*, 34(3), 475–505.

Isabelli-García, C. (2010). Acquisition of Spanish gender agreement in two learning contexts: Study abroad and at home. *Foreign Language Annals*, 43(2), 289–303.

Ishikawa, T. (2006). The effect of task complexity and language proficiency on task-based language performance. *The Journal of AsiaTEFL*, 3(4), 193–225.

Ishikawa, T. (2008). The effect of task demands of intentional reasoning on L2 speech performance. *The Journal of Asia TEFL*, 5(1), 29–63.

Jaworski, A. (Ed.) (1997). *Silence: Interdisciplinary Perspectives*. Berlin: Mouton de Gruyter.

Jenkins, J. (2003). *World Englishes: A Resource Book for Students*. London: Routledge.

Jenkins, J. (2007). *English as a Lingua Franca: Attitude and Identity*. Oxford: Oxford University Press.

Jenkins, J. (2015). Repositioning English and multilingualism in English as a Lingua Franca. *Englishes in Practice*, 2(3), 49–85.

Jin, L. and Cortazzi, M. (Eds.) (2011). *Researching Chinese Learners' Skills, Perceptions and Intercultural Adaptations*. London: Palgrave MacMillan.

de Jong, N. and Perfetti, C. (2011). Fluency training in the ESL classroom: An experimental study of fluency development and proceduralisation. *Language Learning*, 61(2), 533–568.

de Jong, N. H. (2016). Predicting pauses in L1 and L2 speech: The effects of utterance boundaries and word frequency. *International Review of Applied Linguistics in Language Teaching*, 54(2), 113–132.

de Jong, N. H. (2018). Fluency in second language testing: Insights from different disciplines. *Language Assessment Quarterly*, 15(3), 237–254.

de Jong, N. H. and Bosker, H. (2013). Choosing a threshold for silent pauses to measure second language fluency. In R. Eklund (Ed.), *Proceedings of the 6th*

172 References

Workshop on Disfluency in Spontaneous Speech (DiSS) (pp. 17–20). Stockholm: Royal Institute of Technology (KTH).

de Jong, N. H., Groenhout, R., Schoonen, R. and Hulstijn, J. (2015). Second language fluency: Speaking style or proficiency? Correcting measures of second language fluency for first language behavior. *Applied Psycholinguistics*, 36, 223–243.

de Jong, N. H., Steinel, M., Florijn, A., Schoonen, R. and Hulstijn, J. (2013). Linguistic skills and speaking fluency in a second language. *Applied Psycholinguistics*, 34(5), 893–916.

de Jong, N. H. and Vercellotti, M. (2015). Similar prompts may not be similar in the performance they elicit: Examining fluency, complexity, accuracy, and lexis in narratives from five picture prompts. *Language Teaching Research*, 20(3), 387–404.

Kachru, B. (1985). Standard, codification and sociolinguistic realism: The English language in the Outer Circle. In R. Quirk and H. Widdowson (Eds.), *English in the World: Teaching and Learning the Language and Literatures* (pp. 11–30). Cambridge: Cambridge University Press.

Kahng, J. (2014). Exploring utterance and cognitive fluency of L1 and L2 English speakers: Temporal measures and stimulated recall. *Language Learning*, 64(4), 809–854.

Kan, Q., Owen, N. and Bax, S. (2018). Researching mobile-assisted Chinese-character learning strategies among adult distance learners. *Innovation in Language Learning and Teaching*, 12(1), 56–71.

Kang, O. and Johnson, D. (2018). Contribution of suprasegmental to English speaking proficiency: Human rater and automated scoring system. *Language Assessment Quarterly*, 15(2), 150–168.

Kang, O., Rubin, D. and Kermad, A. (2019). The effects of training and rater differences on oral proficiency assessment. *Language Testing*, 36(4), 481–504.

Kasper, G. and Kellerman, E. (Eds.) (1997). *Communication Strategies: Psycholinguistic and Sociolinguistic Perspectives*. London: Longman.

Kim, J., Dewey, D., Baker-Smemoe, W., Ring, S., Westover, A. and Eggett, D. (2015). L2 development during study abroad in China. *System*, 55, 123–133.

Kinginger, C. (2011). Enhancing language learning in study abroad. *Annual Review of Applied Linguistics*, 31, 58–73.

Koponen, M. and Riggenbach, H. (2000). Overview: Varying perspectives on fluency. In H. Riggenbach (Ed.), *Perspectives on Fluency* (pp. 5–24). Ann Arbor: University of Michigan Press.

Kormos, J. (1999). Monitoring and self-repair in L2. *Language Learning*, 49, 303–342.

Kormos, J. (2006). *Speech Production and Second Language Acquisition*. Mahwah, NJ: Lawrence Erlbaum.

Kormos, J. and Dénes, M. (2004). Exploring measures and perceptions of fluency in the speech of second language learners. *System*, 32, 145–164.

Kramsch, C. (1998). *Language and Culture*. Oxford: Oxford University Press.

Kroll, J. and Bialystok, E. (2013). Understanding the consequences of bilingualism for language processing and cognition. *Journal of Cognitive Psychology*, 25, 497–514.

References 173

Kroll, J., Bobb, S. and Hoshino, N. (2014). Two languages in mind: Bilingualism as a tool to investigate language, cognition, and the brain. *Current Directions in Psychological Science*, 23(3), 159–163.

Kuhl, J. (1994). A theory of action and state orientations. In J. Kuhl and J. Beckmann (Eds.), *Volition and Personality* (pp. 9–46). Gottingen: Hogrefe & Huber Publishers.

Lambert, C., Kormos, J. and Minn, D. (2017). Task repetition and second language speech processing. *Studies in Second Language Acquisition*, 39(1), 167–196.

Lantolf, J. and Frawley, W. (1988). Proficiency. Understanding the construct. *Studies in Second Language Acquisition*, 10(1), 181–195.

Lazaraton, A. (1996). Interlocutor support in oral proficiency interviews: the case of CASE. *Language Testing*, 13(2), 151–172.

Lazaraton, A. (1998). An analysis of differences in linguistics features of candidates at different levels of the IELTS speaking test. Report prepared for the EFL division, University of Cambridge Local Examinations Syndicate, Cambridge, UK.

Lazaraton, A. (2002). *Studies in Language Testing, No. 14: A Qualitative Approach to the Validation of Oral Language Tests*. Cambridge, UK: UCLES/Cambridge University Press.

Leeson, R. (1975). *Fluency and Language Teaching*. London: Longman.

Léger, D. and Storch, N. (2009). Learners' perceptions and attitudes: Implications for willingness to communicate in an L2 classroom. *System*, 37, 269–285.

Lehtonen, J. (1978). On the problems of measuring fluency. In M. Leiwo and A. Räsänen (Eds.), *AFinLA Yearbook 1978* (pp. 53–68). Jyväskylä: Jyväskylän yliopisto.

Lennon, P. (1990). Investigating fluency in EFL: A quantitative approach. *Language Learning*, 40(3), 387–417.

Lennon, P. (2000). The lexical element in spoken second language fluency. In H. Riggenbach (Ed.), *Perspectives on Fluency* (pp. 25–42). Ann Arbor: University of Michigan Press.

Leung, C. (2005). Convivial communication: Recontextualising communicative competence. *International Journal of Applied Linguistics*, 15(2), 119–144.

Levelt, W. (1983). Monitoring and self-repair in speech. *Cognition*, 41, 41–104.

Levelt, W. (1989). *Speaking: From Intention to Articulation*. Cambridge, MA: MIT Press.

Levelt, W. (1999). Language production: a blueprint of the speaker. In C. Brown and P. Hagoort (Eds.), *Neurocognition of Language* (pp. 83–122). Oxford: Oxford University Press.

Lewis, M. (1997). *Implementing the Lexical Approach: Putting Theory into Practice*. Hove, England: Language Teaching Publications.

Lin, H. (2014). Establishing an empirical link between computer-mediated communication and SLA: A meta-analysis. *Language Learning Technology*, 18(3), 120–147.

Liyanage, I. and Gardner, R. (2013). Assessing fluency: Are the criteria fair? *Classroom Discourse*, 41(1), 27–41.

174 *References*

Llanes, À. and Muñoz, C. (2009). A short stay abroad: Does it make a difference? *System*, 37(3), 353–365.

Long, M. (2015). *Second Language Acquisition and Task-Based Language Teaching*. Oxford: Wiley-Blackwell.

Long, M. and Crookes, G. (1992). Three approaches to task-based syllabus design. *TESOL Quarterly*, 26, 27–56.

Louwerse, M. and Mitchell, H. (2003). Toward a taxonomy of a set of discourse markers in dialog: A theoretical and computational linguistic account. *Discourse Processes*, 35(3), 199–239.

Loy, J., Rohde, H. and Corley, M. (2017). Effects of disfluency in online interpretation of deception. *Cognitive Science*, 41, 1434–1456.

Lu, Y. (Ed.) (2017). *Teaching and Learning Chinese in Higher Education*. London: Routledge.

Lynch, T. and Maclean, J. (2000). Exploring the benefits of task repetition and recycling for classroom language learning. *Language Teaching Research*, 4, 221–250.

MacIntyre, P., Clément, R., Dörnyei, Z. and Noels, K. (1998). Conceptualising willingness to communicate in an L2: A situational model of L2 confidence and affiliation. *Modern Language Journal*, 82(4), 545–562.

MacIntyre, P. and Doucette, J. (2010). Willingness to communicate and action control. *System*, 38, 161–171.

Magne, V., Suzuki, S., Suzukida, Y., Ilkan, M., Tran, M. and Saito, K. (2019). Exploring the dynamic nature of second language listeners' perceived fluency: A mixed-methods approach. *TESOL Quarterly*, 53(4), 1139–1150.

Marshall, R. (2000). Speech fluency and aphasia. In H. Riggenbach (Ed.), *Perspectives on Fluency* (pp. 220–240). Ann Arbor: University of Michigan Press.

McCarthy, M. (2010). Spoken fluency revisited. *English Profile Journal*, 1, 1–15.

McEnery, T. and Xiao, R. (2004). The Lancaster Corpus of Mandarin Chinese: A corpus for monolingual and contrastive language study. In M. Lino, M. Xavier, F. Ferreire, R. Costa and R. Silva (Eds.), *Proceedings of the Fourth International Conference on Language Resources and Evaluation* (pp. 1175–1178). Cambridge: Cambridge University Press.

McFarland, D. (2001). Respiratory markers of conversational interaction. *Journal of Speech, Language and Hearing Research*, 44, 128–143.

McLeod, S. and Goldstein, B. (2012). *Multilingual Aspects of Speech Sound Disorders in Children*. Bristol: Multilingual Matters.

Mehnert, U. (1998). The effects of different lengths of time for planning on second language performance. *Studies in Second Language Acquisition*, 20, 83–108.

MFL subject content for General Certificate in Secondary Education (GCSE) (2015). Department for Education in England. https://assets.publishing .service.gov.uk/government/uploads/system/uploads/attachment_data/file/ 485567/GCSE_subject_content_modern_foreign_langs.pdf.

Michel, M. (2011). Effects of task complexity and interaction on L2 performance. In P. Robinson (Ed.), *Second Language Task Complexity: Researching the Cognition Hypothesis of Language Learning and Performance* (pp. 141–174). Amsterdam: John Benjamins.

References 175

Michel, M. (2017). Complexity, accuracy, and fluency in L2 production. In S. Loewen and M. Sato (Eds.), *The Routledge Handbook of Instructed Second Language Acquisition* (pp. 66–84). New York: Routledge.

Mitchell, R., Dominguez, L., Arche, M., Myles, F. and Marsden, E. (2008). SPLLOC: A new database for Spanish second language acquisition research. *EuroSLA Yearbook*, 8(1), 287–304.

Mitchell, R., Tracy-Ventura, N. and McManus, K. (2015). *Social Interaction, Identity and Language Learning during Residence Abroad*. EuroSLA Monograph Series, 4. Amsterdam: The European Second Language Association.

Mitchell, R., Tracy-Ventura, T. and McManus, K. (2017). *Anglophone Students Abroad: Identity, Social Relationships, and Language Learning*. London: Routledge.

Mizera, G. (2006). Working memory and L2 oral fluency. Unpublished PhD thesis, University of Pittsburgh.

Mochizuki, N. and Ortega, L. (2008). Balancing communication and grammar in beginning-level foreign language classrooms: A study of guided planning and relativization. *Language Teaching Research*, 12(1), 11–37.

Mohan, B. (1991). LEP students and the integration of language and content: Knowledge structures and tasks. In A. Stein (Ed.), *Proceedings of the First Research Symposium on Limited English Proficient Students' Issues* (pp. 113–160). Washington, DC: U.S. Department of Education, Office of Bilingual Education Research and Evaluation.

Möhle, D. (1984). A comparison of the second language speech production of different native speakers. In H.W. Dechert, D. Möhle and M. Raupach (Eds.), *Second Language Productions* (pp. 26–49). Tübingen: Gunter Narr Verlag.

Mondada, L. and Doehler, S.P. (2004), Second language acquisition as situated practice: task accomplishment in the French second language classroom. *The Modern Language Journal*, 88, 501–518.

Mora, J. M. and Valls-Ferrer, M. (2012). Oral fluency, accuracy and complexity in formal instruction and study abroad learning contexts. *TESOL Quarterly*, 46(4), 610–641.

Morales-Lopez, E. (2000). Fluency levels and the organization of conversation in non-native Spanish speakers' speech. In H. Riggenbach (Ed.), *Perspectives on Fluency* (pp. 266–286). Ann Arbor: University of Michigan Press.

Morrison, A. (2018). *Fluency in the Chilean Classroom*. London: British Council. Available at: https://englishagenda.britishcouncil.org/sites/default/files/attach ments/astrid_morrison_university_of_reading_dissertation.pdf [Accessed 29 October 2019].

Moyer, A. (2004). *Age, Accent and Experience in Second Language Acquisition*. Clevedon: Multilingual Matters.

Moyer, A. (2013). An investigation of experience in L2 phonology: Does quality matter more than quantity? *Canadian Modern Language Review*, 67(2), 191–216.

Myles, F. (2004). From data to theory: The over-representation of linguistic knowledge in SLA. *Transactions of the Philological Society*, 102(2), 139–168.

176 References

Myles, F. and Cordier, C. (2017). Formulaic sequence (FS) cannot be an umbrella term in SLA: Focusing on psycholinguistic FSs and their identification. *Studies in Second Language Acquisition*, 39(1), 3–28.

Nakane, I. (2006). Silence and politeness in intercultural communication in university seminars. *Journal of Pragmatics*, 38(11), 1811–1835.

Nakatani, Y. (2006). Developing an oral communication strategy inventory. *Modern Language Journal*, 90(2), 151–168.

Nakatsuhara, F. (2011). Effects of the number of participants on group oral test performance, *Language Testing*, 28(4), 483–508.

Nakatsuhara, F. (2012). The relationship between test-takers' listening proficiency and their performance on the IELTS Speaking Test. In L. Taylor and C. Weir (Eds.), *IELTS Collected Papers 2: Research in Reading and Listening Assessment* (pp. 519–573). Cambridge, UK: UCLES/Cambridge University Press.

Nakatsuhara, F. (2014). *A Research Report on the Development of the Test of English for Academic Purposes (TEAP) Speaking Test for Japanese University Entrants – Study 1 and Study 2*. Available online at: www.eiken.or.jp/teap/group/pdf/teap_speaking_report1.pdf [Accessed 29 October 2019].

Nakatsuhara, F., Tavakoli, P. and Awwad, A. (2019). Towards a model of multi-dimensional performance of C1 level speakers assessed in the Aptis Speaking Test. ARAGs Research Report Online. London: British Council.

Nation, I. (1989). Improving speaking fluency. *System*, 17(3), 377–384.

Nattinger, J. and DeCarrico, J. (1992). *Lexical Phrases and Language Teaching*. Oxford: Oxford University Press.

Nitta, R. and Nakatsuhara, F. (2014). A multifaceted approach to investigating pre-task planning effects on paired oral test performance. *Language Testing*, 31(2), 147–175.

Norris, J. and Ortega, L. (2009). Towards an organic approach to investigating CAF in instructed SLA: The case of complexity. *Applied Linguistics*, 30, 555–578.

Norton, B. (2013). *Identity and Language Learning: Extending the Conversation*. Bristol: Multilingual Matters.

Nunan, D. (1989). *Designing Tasks for the Communicative Classroom*. Cambridge: Cambridge University Press.

O'Brien, I., Segalowitz, N., Freed, B. and Collentine, J. (2007). Phonological memory predicts second language oral fluency gains in adults. *Studies in Second Language Acquisition*, 29, 557–581.

O'Sullivan, B. and Dunlea, J. (2015). *Aptis Genearal Technical Manual Ver 1.0 TR/2015/005*. Available at: www.britishcouncil.org/sites/default/files/aptis_general_technical_manual_v-1.0.pdf [Accessed 29 October 2019].

Oppenheim, N. (2000). The importance of recurrent sequences for non-native speaker fluency and cognition. In H. Riggenbach (Ed.), *Perspectives on Fluency* (pp. 220–240). Ann Arbor: University of Michigan Press.

Ortega, L. (2005). What do learners plan? Learner-driven attention to form during pre-task planning. In R. Ellis (Ed.), *Planning and Task Performance in a Second Language* (pp. 77–110). Amsterdam: John Benjamins.

References   177

Osaka, M. and Osaka, N. (1992). Language-independent working memory as measured by Japanese and English reading span tests. *Bulletin of the Psychonomic Society*, 30(4), 287–289.

Oxford, R. (1990). *Language Learning Strategies: What Every Teacher Should Know*. New York: Newbury House.

Pallotti, G. (2009). CAF: Defining, refining and differentiating constructs. *Applied Linguistics*, 30, 590–601.

Pallotti, G. (2017). Assessing tasks: The case of interactional difficulty. *Applied Linguistics*, 40(1), 176–197.

Pawley, A. and Syder, F. (1983). Two puzzles for linguistic theory: nativelike selection and nativelike fluency. In J. Richards and R. Schmidt (Eds.), *Language and Communication* (pp. 191–226). New York: Longman.

Pawley, A. and Syder, F. (2000). The one-clause-at-a-time hypothesis. In H. Riggenbach (Ed.), *Perspectives on Fluency* (pp. 163–199). Ann Arbor: University of Michigan Press.

Payne, J. and Whitney, P. (2002). Developing L2 oral proficiency through synchronous CMC: Output, working memory and interlanguage development. *CALICO Journal*, 20(1), 7–32.

Peets. K. (2009). The effects of context on the classroom discourse skills of children with language impairment. *Language, Speech, and Hearing Services in Schools*, 40(1), 5–16.

Pekarek Doehler, S. and Berger, S. (2018). L2 interactional competence as increased ability for context-sensitive conduct: A longitudinal study of story-openings. *Applied Linguistics*, 39(4), 555–578.

Pellegrino, F., Coupé, C. and Marsico, E. (2011). A cross-language perspective on speech information rate. *Language*, 87, 539–558.

Peltonen, P. (2017). Temporal fluency and problem-solving in interaction: An exploratory study of fluency resources in L2 dialogue. *System*, 70, 1–13.

Peltonen, P. (2018). Exploring connections between first and second language fluency: A mixed methods approach. *The Modern Language Journal*, 102, 676–692.

Perez Vidal, C. (Ed.) (2014). *Language Acquisition in Study Abroad and Formal Instruction Contexts*. Amsterdam: John Benjamins.

Pope, B., Blass, T., Siegman, A. and Raher, J. (1970). Anxiety and depression in speech. *Journal of Consulting and Clinical Psychology*, 35(1), 128–145.

Prabhu, N. (1987). *Second Language Pedagogy*. Oxford: Oxford University Press.

Préfontaine, Y. (2013). Perceptions of French fluency in second language speech production. *Canadian Modern Language Review*, 69(3), 324–348.

Préfontaine, Y. (2015). Perceptions of French fluency in second language speech production. *Canadian Modern Language Review*, 69(3), 324.

Préfontaine, Y. and Kormos, J. (2016). A qualitative analysis of perceptions of fluency in second language French. *International Review of Applied Linguistics in Language Teaching*, 54(2), 151–169.

Préfontaine, Y., Kormos, J. and Johnson, D. (2016). How do utterance measures predict raters' perceptions of fluency in French as a second language? *Language Testing*, 33(1), 53–73.

178 References

Prins, R., Snow, C. and Wagenaar, E. (1978). Recovery from aphasia: Spontaneous speech versus language comprehension. *Brain and Language*, 6(1), 192–211.

Quené, H. (2008). Multilevel modeling of between-speaker and within-speaker variation in spontaneous speech tempo. *Journal of the Acoustical Society of America*, 123, 1104–1113.

Rahimpour, M. (1997). *Task Complexity, Task Condition, and Variation in L2 Oral Discourse*. Unpublished PhD thesis, University of Queensland, Australia.

Raupach, M. (1980). Cross-linguistic descriptions of speech performance as a contribution to contrastive psycholinguistics. In H. Dechert and M. Raupach (Eds.), *Towards a Cross-Linguistic Assessment of Speech Production* (pp. 9–22). Frankfurt: Lang.

Razagifard, P. (2013). The impact of text-based CMC on improving L2 oral fluency. *Journal of Computer Assisted Learning*, 29(30), 270–279.

Révész, A., Ekiert, M. and Torgersen, E. (2016). The effects of complexity, accuracy, and fluency on communicative adequacy in oral task performance. *Applied Linguistics*, 37, 828–848.

Riazantseva, A. (2001). Second language proficiency and pausing: A study of Russian speakers of English. *Studies in Second Language Acquisition*, 23, 497–526.

Riggenbach, H. (Ed.) (2000). *Perspectives on Fluency*. Ann Arbor: University of Michigan Press.

Ringbom, H. (2007). *Cross-Linguistic Similarity in Foreign Language Learning*. Clevedon: Multilingual Matters.

Robinson, P. (1995). Task complexity and second language narrative discourse. *Language Learning*, 45(1), 99–140.

Robinson, P. (2001). Task complexity, task difficulty, and task production: Exploring interactions in a componential framework. *Applied Linguistics*, 22(1), 27–57.

Robinson, P. (2003). The Cognition Hypothesis, task design, and adult task-based language learning. *Second Language Studies*, 21(2), 45–105.

Robinson, P. (2005). Cognitive complexity and task sequencing: Studies in a componential framework for second language task design. *International Review of Applied Linguistics in Language Teaching*, 43(1), 1–32.

Robinson, P. (2007). Task complexity, theory of mind, and intentional reasoning: Effects on L2 speech production, interaction, uptake and perceptions of task difficulty. *International Review of Applied Linguistics in Language Teaching*, 45(3), 193–213.

Robinson, P. (Ed.) (2011). *Second Language Task Complexity: Researching the Cognition Hypothesis of Language Learning and Performance*. Amsterdam: John Benjamins.

Robinson, P. (2015). The Cognition Hypothesis, second language task demands, and the SSARC model of pedagogic task sequencing. In M. Bygate (Ed.), *Domains and Directions in the Development of TBLT* (pp. 87–121). Amsterdam: John Benjamins.

Rodriguez, L. and Torres, M. (2006). Spontaneous speech events in two speech databases of human-computer and human-human dialogs in Spanish. *Language and Speech*, 49(3), 333–366.

Rossiter, M. J. (2003). The effects of affective strategy instruction in the ESL classroom. In special issue: strategy research and training (N. J. Anderson, Ed.). *TESL-EJ*, 7 (2), 1–20.

Rossiter, M. (2009). Perceptions of L2 fluency by native and non-native speakers of English. *Canadian Modern Language Review*, 65, 395–412.

Rossiter, M., Derwing, T., Manimtim, L. G. and Thomson, R. I. (2010). Oral fluency: The neglected component in the communicative language classroom. *Canadian Modern Language Review*, 66, 583–606.

Saito, K., Ilkan, M., Magne, V., Tran, M. and Suzuki, S. (2018). Acoustic characteristics and learner profiles of low, mid and high-level second language fluency. *Applied Psycholinguistics*, 39, 593–617.

Saito, K., Trofimovich, P. and Isaacs, T. (2017). Using listener judgements to investigate linguistic influences on L2 comprehensibility and accentedness: A validation and generalization study. *Applied Linguistics*, 38, 439–462.

Samuda, V. and Bygate, M. (2008). *Tasks in Second Language Learning*. Basingstoke: Palgrave.

Sanz, C. (2014). Contributions of study abroad research to our understanding of SLA processes and outcomes: The Sala project. In C. Perez Vidal (Ed.), *Language Acquisition in Study Abroad and Formal Instruction Contexts* (pp. 1–13). Amsterdam: John Benjamins.

Sanz, C. and Morales-Front, A. (Eds.) (2018). *The Routledge Handbook of Study Abroad Research and Practice*. Abingdon: Routledge.

Sasaki, M. (2011). Effects of varying lengths of study abroad experiences on Japanese EFL students' L2 writing ability and motivation: A longitudinal study. *TESOL Quarterly*, 45(1), 81–105.

Savignon, S. (1972). *Communicative Competence: An Experiment in Foreign Language Teaching*. Philadelphia: The Centre for Curriculum Development.

Savignon, S. (2007). Beyond communicative language teaching: What's ahead? *Journal of Pragmatics*, 39, 207–220.

Schegloff, E. (2000). Overlapping talk and the organization of turn-taking for conversation. *Language in Society*, 29(1), 1–63.

Schegloff, E. (2001). Accounts of conduct in interaction: Interruption, overlap and turn-taking. In J. Turner (Ed.), *Handbook of Sociological Theory* (pp. 287–321). New York: Kluwer Academic.

Schmidt, M. and Fägersten, K. B. (2010). Disfluency markers in L1 attrition. *Language Learning*, 60, 753–791.

Schmidt, R. (1992). Psychological mechanisms underlying second language fluency. *Studies in Second Language Acquisition*, 14, 357–385.

Schneider, W. and Schiffrin, R. (1977). Controlled and automatic human information processing: Detection, search, and attention. *Psychological Review*, 84, 1–66.

Schumann, J. (1986). An acculturation model for second language acquisition. *Journal of Multilingual and Multicultural Development*, 7, 379–392.

180   References

Scrivener, J. (1994). *Learning Teaching: A Guidebook for English Language Teachers*. Oxford: Heinemann.

Seedhouse, P. (2004). *The Interactional Architecture of the Language Classroom: A Conversation Analysis Perspective*. Malden: Blackwell.

Seedhouse, P. (2013). Oral proficiency interviews as varieties of interaction. In S. Ross and G. Kasper (Eds.), *Assessing Second Language Pragmatics* (pp. 199–219). Basingstoke: Palgrave Macmillan.

Seedhouse, P. and Egbert, M. (2006). The interactional organisation of the IELTS Speaking Test. *IELTS Research Reports*, 6(6), 161–205.

Seedhouse, P. and Nakatsuhara, F. (2018). *The Discourse of the IELTS Speaking Test: Interactional Design and Practice*. Cambridge: Cambridge University Press.

Segalowitz, N. (2000). Automaticity and attentional skill in fluent performance. In H. Riggenbach (Ed.), *Perspectives on Fluency* (pp. 200–219). Ann Arbor: University of Michigan Press.

Segalowitz, N. (2003). Automaticity and second languages. In C. Doughty and M. Long (Eds.), *The Handbook of Second Language Acquisition* (pp. 382–408). Oxford: Blackwell.

Segalowitz, N. (2010). *The Cognitive Bases of Second Language Fluency*. New York: Routledge.

Segalowitz, N. (2016). Second language fluency and its underlying cognitive and social determinants. *International Review of Applied Linguistics in Language Teaching*, 54(2), 79–95.

Segalowitz, N. and Freed, B. (2004). Context, contact and cognition on oral fluency acquisition: Learning Spanish in at home and study abroad contexts. *Studies in Second Language Acquisition*, 26, 173–199.

Segalowitz, N. and Segalowitz, S. (1993). Skilled performance, practice and the differentiation of speed-up from automatisation effects: Evidence from second language word recognition. *Applied Psycholinguistics*, 14, 369–385.

Seidlhofer, B. (2001). Closing a conceptual gap: The case for a description of English as a Lingua Franca. *International Journal of Applied Linguistics*, 11(2), 133–158.

Seifoori, Z. and Vahidi, Z. (2012). The impact of fluency strategy training on Iranian EFL learners' speech under online planning conditions. *Language Awareness*, 21, 101–112.

Selinker, L. (1972). Interlanguage. *International Review of Applied Linguistics*, 10(3), 209–231.

Sheen, R. (2003). Focus on form: A myth in the making? *ELT Journal*, 57(3), 225–233.

Sheen, R. (2005). Focus on forms as a means of improving accurate oral production. In A. Housen and M. Pierrard (Eds.), *Investigations in Language Acquisition* (pp. 271–310). Berlin: Mouton de Gruyter.

Shei, C., Zikpi, M. and Chao, D.-L. (Eds.) (2019). *Routledge Handbook of Chinese Language Teaching*. New York: Routledge.

Shiri, S. (2013). Learners' attitudes toward regional dialects and destination preferences in study abroad. *Foreign Language Annals*, 46(4), 565–587.

References 181

Shively, R. (2011). L2 pragmatic development in study abroad: A longitudinal study of Spanish service encounters. *Journal of Pragmatics*, 43, 1818–1835.

Shohamy, E. (2011). Assessing multilingual competencies: Adopting construct valid assessment policies. *The Modern Language Journal*, 95(3), 418–429.

Sidnell, J. (2010). *Conversation Analysis: An Introduction*. West Sussex: Wiley-Blackwell.

Siegman, A. and Pope, B. (1966). Ambiguity and verbal fluency in the tat. *Journal of Consulting Psychology*, 30(3), 239–245.

Siyanova-Chanturia, A. and Van Lancker Sidtis, D. (2018). What on-line processing tells us about formulaic language. In A. Siyanova-Chanturia and A. Pellicer-Sanchez (Eds.), *Understanding Formulaic Language: A Second Language Acquisition Perspective*. London/New York: Routledge.

Skehan, P. (1996). A framework for the implementation of task-based instruction. *Applied Linguistics*, 17, 38–62.

Skehan, P. (1998). *A Cognitive Approach to Language Learning*. Oxford: Oxford University Press.

Skehan, P. (2001). Tasks and language performance assessment. In M. Bygate, P. Skehan and M. Swain (Eds.), *Researching Pedagogic Tasks* (pp. 167–185). London: Longman.

Skehan, P. (2003). Task based instruction. *Language Teaching*, 36, 1–14.

Skehan, P. (2009). Modelling second language performance: Integrating complexity, accuracy, fluency, and lexis. *Applied Linguistics*, 30(4), 510–532.

Skehan, P. (2014). Limited attentional capacity, second language performance, and task-based pedagogy. In P. Skehan (Ed.), *Processing Perspectives on Task Performance* (pp. 211–260). Amsterdam: John Benjamins.

Skehan, P. (2015). Limited Attention Capacity and Cognition: Two hypotheses regarding second language performance on tasks. In M. Bygate (Ed.), *Domains and Directions in the Development of TBLT* (pp. 123–156). Amsterdam: John Benjamins.

Skehan, P., Foster, P. and Shum, S. (2016). Ladders and snakes in second language fluency. *International Review of Applied Linguistics in Language Teaching*, 54(2), 97–112.

Skehan, P. and Shum, S. (2014). Structure and processing condition in video-based narrative retelling. In P. Skehan (Ed.), *Processing Perspectives on Task Performance* (pp. 187–210). Amsterdam: John Benjamins.

Slabakova, R. (2012). L2 knowledge at the mapping of syntax and discourse. *Second Language*, 11, 5–23.

Smith, S. (2011). Corpus-based tasks for learning Chinese: A data-driven approach. *The Asian Conference on Technology in the Classroom Official Conference Proceedings*, 2011, 48–59.

Spada, N. (1986). The interaction between type of contact and type of instruction: Some effects on the l2 proficiency of adult learners. *Studies in Second Language Acquisition*, 8(2), 181–199.

Stowe, L. and Sabourin, L. (2005). Imaging the processing of a second language: Effects of maturation and proficiency on the neural processes involved.

182 References

International Review of Applied Linguistics in Language Teaching, 43(4), 329–353.

Sun, Y.-C. (2012). Examining the effectiveness of extensive speaking practice via voice blogs in a foreign language learning context. *CALICO Journal*, 29(3), 494–506.

Sunderman, G. and Kroll, J. (2009). When study-abroad experience fails to deliver: The internal resources threshold effect. *Applied Psycholinguistics*, 30(1), 79–100.

Swain, M. (1995). Three functions of output in second language learning. In G. Cook and B. Seidlhofer (Eds.), *Principle and Practice in Applied Linguistics: Studies in Honour of H. G. Widdowson* (pp. 125–144). Oxford: Oxford University Press.

Taguchi, N. (2007). Development of speed and accuracy in pragmatic comprehension in English as a foreign language. *TESOL Quarterly*, 41, 313–338.

Taguchi, N. (2011). The effect of L2 proficiency and study-abroad experience on pragmatic comprehension. *Language Learning*, 61, 904–939.

Tannen, D. (1984). The pragmatics of cross-cultural communication. *Applied Linguistics*, 5(3), 189–195.

Tannen, D. (2012). Turn-taking and intercultural discourse and communication. In C. Paulston, S. Kiesling and E. Rangel (Eds.), *The Handbook of Intercultural Discourse and Communication* (pp. 135–157). London: Wiley.

Tao, H. (Ed.) (2016). *Integrating Chinese Linguistic Research and Language Teaching and Learning*. Amsterdam: Benjamins.

Tavakoli, P. (2004). Oral narrative tasks and second language performance: An investigation of task characteristics. Unpublished PhD thesis, Kings College London.

Tavakoli, P. (2009a). Investigating task difficulty: learners' and teachers' perceptions. *International Journal of Applied Linguistics*, 19(1), 1–25.

Tavakoli, P. (2009b). Assessing L2 task performance: Understanding the effects of task design. *System*, 37(3), 482–495.

Tavakoli, P. (2011). Pausing patterns: Differences between L2 learners and native speakers. *ELT Journal*, 65(1), 71–79.

Tavakoli, P. (2016). Fluency in monologic and dialogic task performance: Challenges in defining and measuring L2 fluency. *International Review of Applied Linguistics in Language Teaching*, 54(2), 133–150.

Tavakoli, P. (2018). L2 development in an intensive Study Abroad EAP context. *System*, 72(1), 62–74.

Tavakoli, P., Campbell, C. and McCormack, J. (2016). Development of speech fluency over a short period of time: Effects of pedagogic intervention. *TESOL Quarterly*, 50(2), 447–471.

Tavakoli, P. and Foster, P. (2008). Task design and second language performance: The effect of narrative type on learner output. *Language Learning*, 58(2), 439–473.

Tavakoli, P. and Hunter, A.-M. (2018). Is fluency being 'neglected' in the classroom? Teacher understanding of fluency and related classroom practices. *Language Teaching Research*, 22(3), 330–349.

Tavakoli, P., Kendon, G., Hunter, A.-M. and Slaght, J. (forthcoming). TEEP Speaking test fluency rating scales across four levels of proficiency. Internal Report, International Study and Language Institute, University of Reading.

Tavakoli, P., Nakatsuhara, F. and Hunter, A.-M. (2017). Scoring validity of the Aptis Speaking Test: Investigating fluency across tasks and levels of proficiency. ARAGs Research Reports Online. London: British Council.

Tavakoli, P., Nakatsuhara, F. and Hunter, A.-M. (2020). Aspects of oral fluency across assessed levels of proficiency: Do 'fluency profiles' for different proficiency levels exist? *Modern Language Journal*, 104(1), 169–191.

Tavakoli, P. and Skehan, P. (2005). Strategic planning, task structure, and performance testing. In R. Ellis (Ed.), *Planning and Task Performance* (pp. 239–273). Amsterdam/Philadelphia: John Benjamins.

Tavakoli, P. and Uchihara, T. (2019). To what extent are multiword sequences associated with oral fluency? *Language Learning*, 70(2), 506–547.

Taylor, L. and Galaczi, E. (2011). Scoring validity. In L. Taylor (Ed.), *Examining Speaking: Research and Practice in Assessing Second Language Speaking, Studies in Language Testing* volume 30 (pp. 171–233). Cambridge: UCLES/Cambridge University Press.

Temple, L. (1997). Memory and processing modes in language learner speech production. *Communication and Cognition*, 30(1/2), 75–90.

Tian, Y., Maruyama, T. and Ginzburg, J. (2017). Self-addressed questions and filled pauses: A cross-linguistic investigation. *Journal of Psycholinguistic Research*, 46(4), 905–922.

Towell, R. and Dewaele, J.-M. (2005). The role of psycholinguistic factors in the development of fluency amongst advanced learners of French. In J.-M. Dewaele (Ed.), *Focus on French as a Foreign Language: Multidisciplinary Approaches* (pp. 210–239). Clevedon: Multilingual Matters.

Towell, R., Hawkins, R. and Bazergui, N. (1996). The development of fluency in advanced learners of French. *Applied Linguistics*, 17, 84–119.

Trentman, E. (2013). Arabic and English during study abroad in Cairo, Egypt: Issues of access and use. *The Modern Language Journal*, 97(2), 457–473.

Truong, A. T. and Storch, N. (2007). Investigating group planning in preparation for oral presentations in an EFL class in Vietnam. *Regional Language Centre Journal*, 38(1), 104–124.

Tullock, B. and Ortega, L. (2017). Fluency and multilingualism in study abroad: Lessons from a scoping review. *System*, 71, 7–21.

Umino, T. and Benson, P. (2016). Communities of practice in study abroad: A four-year study of an Indonesian student's experience in Japan. *The Modern Language Journal*, 100(4), 757–769.

Vanderplank, R. (1993). 'Pacing' and 'spacing' as predictors of difficulty in speaking and understanding English. *ELT Journal*, 47(2), 117–125.

Verhoeven, J., de Pauw, G. and Kloots, H. (2004). Speech rate in a pluricentric language: A comparison between Dutch in Belgium and the Netherlands. *Language and Speech*, 47, 297–308.

Walsh, S. (2011). *Exploring Classroom Discourse: Language in Action*. London: Routledge.

184 References

Wang, C., Bristol, T., Mowen, J. and Chakraborty, G. (2000). Alternative models of self-construal: Dimensions of connectedness-separateness and advertising appeals to the country and gender-specific self. *Journal of Consumer Psychology*, 9, 107–115.

Wang, J., Na, A. and Wright, C. (2018). Enhancing beginner learners' oral proficiency in a flipped Chinese Foreign Language classroom. *Computer-Aided Language Learning*, 31(5–6), 490–521.

Watanabe, M., Hirose, K., Den, Y. and Minematsu, N. (2008). Filled pauses as cues to the complexity of upcoming phrases for native and non-native listeners. *Speech Communication*, 50(2), 81–94.

Weissheimer, J. and Mota, M. (2009). Individual differences in working memory capacity and the development of L2 speech production. *Issues in Applied Linguistics*, 17, 34–52.

Wennerstrom, A. (2000). The role of intonation in second language fluency. In H. Riggenbach (Ed.), *Perspectives on Fluency* (pp. 102–127). Ann Arbor: University of Michigan Press.

White, L. (2003). *Second Language Acquisition and Universal Grammar*. Cambridge: Cambridge University Press.

Widdowson, H. (1983). *Learning Purpose and Language Use*. Oxford: Oxford University Press.

Williams, M., Mercer, S. and Ryan, S. (2016). *Exploring Psychology in Language Learning and Teaching*. Oxford: Oxford University Press.

Wilson, M. and Wilson, T. (2005). An oscillator model of the timing of turn-taking. *Psychonomic Bulletin and Review*, 12, 957–968.

Winke, P. and Gass, S. (2013). The influence of second language experience and accent familiarity on oral proficiency rating: A qualitative investigation. *TESOL Quarterly*, 47(4), 762–789.

Witkins, G., Morere, D. and Geer, L. (2013). Establishment of a phenomic clustering system for American Sign Language. *Sign Language Studies*, 14(1), 1–28.

Witton-Davies, G. (2014). The study of fluency and its development in monologue and dialogue. Unpublished PhD thesis, Lancaster University.

Wolf, J. (2008). The effects of backchannels on fluency in L2 oral task production. *System*, 36, 279–294.

Wood, D. (2009). Effects of focused instruction of formulaic sequences on fluent expression in second language narratives: A case study. *Canadian Journal of Applied Linguistics*, 12(1), 39–57.

Wood, D. (2010). *Formulaic Language and Second Language Speech Fluency: Background, Evidence and Classroom Applications*. London: Bloomsbury.

Wood, D. (2016). Willingness to communicate and second language speech fluency: An idiodynamic investigation. *System*, 60, 11–28.

Wray, A. (2000). Formulaic sequences in second language teaching: Principle and practice. *Applied Linguistics*, 21, 463–489.

Wray, A. (2002). *Formulaic Language and the Lexicon*. Cambridge: Cambridge University Press.

Wray, A. (2008). *Formulaic language: Pushing the Boundaries*. Oxford: Oxford University Press.

Wray, A. and Fitzpatrick, T. (2008). Why can't you just leave it alone? Deviations from memorized language as a gauge of nativelike competence. In F. Meunier and S. Granger (Eds.), *Phraseology in Foreign Language Learning and Teaching* (pp. 123–148). Amsterdam: John Benjamins.

Wright, C. (2010). *Working Memory in SLA*. Saarbrucken: VDM Publishing.

Wright, C. (2013). An investigation of working memory effects on oral grammatical accuracy and fluency in producing questions in English. *TESOL Quarterly*, 47(2), 352–374.

Wright, C. (2018a). Effects of time and task on L2 Mandarin Chinese language development during study abroad. In C. Sanz and A. Front-Morales (Eds.), *The Routledge Handbook of Study Abroad Research and Practice* (pp. 166–180). Abingdon: Routledge.

Wright, C. (2018b). Research in memory and processing in SLA. In C. Wright, M. Young-Scholten and T. Piske (Eds.), *Mind Matters in SLA* (pp. 203–219). Bristol: Multilingual Matters.

Wright, C. (2019). Developing communicative competence in adult beginner learners of Chinese. In C. Shei, M. Zikpi and D.-L. Chao (Eds.), *Routledge Handbook of Chinese Language Teaching* (pp. 134–148). New York: Routledge.

Wright, C. (2020). Task effects on L2 Mandarin fluency development in monologic and dialogic speech. *Journal of Second Language Studies*.

Wright, C., Lin, M. and Tsakalaki, A. (forthcoming). Teaching Academic Interactional Competence: Moving beyond performative competence in EAP settings. *JRIE Journal*.

Wright, C. and Schartner, A. (2013). 'I can't … I won't?' International students at the threshold of social adaptation. *Journal of Research in International Education*, 12(2), 113–128.

Wright, C. and Tavakoli, P. (2016). New directions and developments in defining, analyzing and measuring L2 speech fluency. *International Review of Applied Linguistics in Language Teaching*, 54(2), 73–76.

Wright, C. and Zhang, C. (2014). Examining the effects of study abroad on L2 Chinese development among UK university learners. *Newcastle and Northumbria Working Papers in Linguistics*, 20, 67–83.

Xing, J. (2006). *Teaching and Learning Chinese as a Foreign Language: A Pedagogic Grammar*. Hong Kong: Hong Kong University Press.

Yang, B. (2012). How do pauses reveal linguistic plans by L2 learners of Chinese? In Q. Ma (Ed.), *Proceedings of the 6th International Conference on Speech Prosody* (pp. 390–393). Shanghai: Tongji University Press.

Young, R. (2003). Learning to talk the talk and walk the walk: Interactional competence in academic spoken English. *North Eastern Illinois University Working Papers in Linguistics*, 2, 26–44.

Young, R. (2011). Interactional competence in language learning, teaching, and testing. In E. Hinkel (Ed.), *Handbook of Research in Second Language Teaching and Learning* Vol. 2, (pp. 426–443). New York: Routledge.

186   References

Yuan, F. and Ellis, R. (2003). The effects of pre-task planning and on-line planning on fluency, complexity and accuracy in L2 monologic oral production. *Applied Linguistics*, 24(1), 1–27.

Yule, G. (2003). *The Study of Language*. Cambridge: Cambridge University Press.

Zhang, G. and Li, L. (2010). Chinese language teaching in the UK. *The Language Learning Journal*, 38, 87–97.

Zhao, Y. (2011). Review article: A tree in the wood: A review of research on L2 Chinese acquisition. *Second Language Research*, 27, 559–572.

Zhou, X. and Marslen-Wilson, W. (1994). Words, morphemes and syllables in the Chinese mental lexicon. *Language and Cognitive Processes*, 9, 393–422.

Author Index

Ahmadian, 53, 68, 96, 110

Brown, 70, 103, 111–112, 116, 119

Derwing, 11, 85–86, 92–94
Dewaele, 16, 52

Ellis, 65, 72

Foster, 14, 16, 47, 49, 64, 67, 80, 96
Freed, 47, 51, 85

Gatbonton, 94–96

Jenkins, 90
de Jong, 11, 15–16, 23–31, 43, 51, 64, 75, 88, 94, 97, 110, 116

Kormos, 11, 13, 15–16, 51, 53, 78, 97

Lennon, 3, 5–7, 43, 46–47, 85
Levelt, 4, 9–12, 68, 76, 78, 110

Michel, 60, 75, 116

Nakatsuhara, 7, 16–17, 81, 103, 111

Pawley & Syder, 6, 95
Préfontaine, 16, 51, 99, 121

Robinson, 15–16, 64, 70–71
Rossiter, 92–94, 97

Saito, 90, 112
Segalowitz, 1, 3, 8–9, 11, 41, 85, 91, 94
Skehan, 13–15, 47–48, 65–67, 73, 76, 96, 117

Towell, 13

Wood, 15, 77, 95
Wray, 15, 95

Subject Index

accuracy, 14–15, 62, 79, 88–91, 120–121
ACT Model, 24
affective factors (*see psycho-social factors*)
amount of information, 69–70
Aptis, 106–107, 114
articulation, 9–10, 12–13, 57, 78 (*see also articulation rate*)
articulation rate, 6, 11, 48, 50, 55, 112–113, 122
AS-Unit, 49, 113
attentional resources, 15, 68–69, 72, 79
automated scoring, 121–122 (*see also machine rating*)
automatic processing, 4–5, 9–15, 51, 71
automaticity, 2–7, 12, 78, 94, 99 (*see also automatic processing*)
automatisation (*see automatic processing*)
awareness raising, 98

back channelling, 58–59
base measures, 55
bilingual norms, 17 (*see also multilingual speakers*)
bilingual speech model, 11–12
breakdown fluency, 47–52, 54–55, 112, 121
breathing space, 79
broad and narrow fluency, 2, 5–8, 46

CALF Framework, 14–16, 20, 31, 150–151
CEFR, 77, 86–88, 106, 113
chunks (*see formulaic sequences*)
CLAN, 50, 53
clause structure, 48–49 (*see also complexity*)
clinical language studies, 44–45, 60
cognition hypothesis, 15
cognitive demand, 15, 67, 70–73, 83, 87, 119
cognitive fluency, 9, 89, 107, 115
cognitive processes, 2–7, 65, 78
cognitive-interactional perspective, 19, 64 (*see also multidimensional*)

College Board's English Competence Examination, 105
communicative
  ability, 6, 17, 85
  adequacy, 16
  comprehensibility, 16
  intelligibility, 7
  purpose, 4, 60, 64, 74, 76, 79–80
communicative competence, 4–6, 45, 86
complexity (*see CALF Framework*)
complexity measures, 81 (*see also syntactic complexity*)
composite measures, 48, 50
computer-mediated assessment, 114–116, 122
computer-mediated interaction, 56, 61–62
conceptualisation stage, 9–10, 13, 68, 72, 76
consciousness-raising activities, 92–93 (*see also awareness-raising*)
context of communication, 70, 74, 76, 80–81
context dependency, 70, 119, 123
Conversation Analysis, 59, 81, 116–118, 123
corpora (*see also cross-linguistic variation*)
cross-linguistic variation, 19–20, 34, 125, 129, 131–134, 144–145, 152
cultural differences, 52
curricula, 1, 84, 86–92

declarative knowledge, 13, 24–25
dialogue, 14, 16, 56–61, 75–78
digital technology, 50, 56
disconnects with research and practice, 7, 17–19
discourse analysis, 9, 17, 118, 123
discourse markers, 60, 77–78
disfluency, 44, 51, 60, 74, 83, 92
disfluency markers, 46, 82

188

Subject Index 189

elongation, 50, 56, 60
English as a lingua franca, 19
explicit knowledge, 13, 24, 90, 91

face-to-face communication, 56, 62
familiarity, 72–73
fluency
  definitions, 4–8
  descriptors, 87, 89–91, 105–111, 120
  Mandarin, 27, 30, 125, 130, 132, 134, 139–140, 144
  measures, 53–59
  in non-European languages, 18
  strategies, 89–90, 97–98
  in the wild, 24, 132–133
fluency-focused activities, 93, 100–102
fluidity, 9, 45, 108, 110
focus on form, 68, 78
Foreign Service Institute, 106
formulaic sequences, 77, 92–97
formulation stage, 9–14, 52, 69, 76–78

grammar, 90, 106, 108

human raters, 103, 119–123

IELTS, 106–107, 117
immediacy of information, 70–71
immersion effects, 14
implementation conditions, 64, 74–75
implicit knowledge, 13, 23, 31, 90
individual differences, 50
information processing, 65, 83
institutional talk, 116, 123
instructional settings, 85, 93
interactional competence, 81
interactional perspectives, 79, 87
interdisciplinary research in fluency, 17, 46, 59
interfluency, 123
interlocutors, 52, 60–61, 75–81, 87–92, 114
interruptions, 58–59, 76, 107
intonation, 90

judgement of performance, 44, 62, 104, 120–122

knowledge, 6, 12–13 (see also *linguistic knowledge*) declarative and procedural, 13, 83
  explicit and implicit, 13

L1 influence, 11–13, 17, 20, 29–31, 36–38, 41–42, 61
L1 and L2 relationship, 12, 23, 28–29, 30–31, 34, 36, 37, 41–42, 50, 78, 135, 150
language benchmarks, 77, 86–92
language teaching practice, 84–86, 98–102
language testing, 45–46, 77, 81
lemma, 10–11
length of run, 44, 47, 55
Levelt's speech production model, 9–12, 52, 69, 76, 78
lexical
  complexity, 118, 121
  fillers, 59, 97–98, 115
  retrieval, 47, 51, 78
  units, 115, 118
lie detection, 82–83
Limited Attentional Capacity Model, 15
linguistic
  demands, 71, 87
  items/components, 52, 78
linguistic insecurity, 124, 126, 152, 154
linguistic knowledge, 6, 12–14, 24, 28, 32, 40, 41, 150–151
listeners (see *interlocutors*)

machine rating, 119–123
macro-planning, 10–12
mean length of run, 48, 50, 55, 96–97, 112, 122
measuring fluency, 43–56
  objective measurement, 44–45
  subjective measurement, 44–46, 120–121, 123
micro-planning, 10–12
mixed-method approaches, 116–119, 123
modality, 75–78
mode (see *dialogue*; *modality*; *monologues*)
modern foreign languages, 84, 88–90
monitoring, 11, 13, 47, 49, 52–53, 68, 119
monologues, 56–62, 75–78
multicomponent, 8–9
multidimensional, 17, 103–104
multilingual speakers, 1, 18, 85, 125–129, 145
multi-word expressions, 15, 115 (see also *formulaic sequences*)

native speaker, 6, 17, 20, 46, 125, 147, 151, 155
native-speaker norms, 6, 17, 44, 46, 125–126, 151, 155

190 Subject Index

organisation of information, 67–69, 73
overlaps, 57–59, 61, 116

pace, 55, 91, 107–108
pauses, 46–56, 81–82, 87, 112–113 (see
  also breakdown fluency) frequency of,
  48, 51, 54–55, 117
  length of, 51, 54–55
  location of, 51, 54–55, 76, 88
  quality and character of, 52, 54–55,
  60–61, 88
Pearson Test of English (PTE), 106–107
pedagogy, 78, 84–86, 92, 100
perceived fluency, 45–47, 99, 104, 120, 122
performative competence, 142
personal style, 50–51, 53, 110, 115, 118
  (see also L1 influence)
phonation time, 51, 54–55, 62
phonetic plans, 11–13
planning time, 74–75, 78–79, 96
pragmatics, 81–83
  pragmatic appropriateness, 6
  pragmatic function, 74–75
pre-verbal plan, 10, 69
prior knowledge, 72–73
problem–solution structure, 68
procedural/proceduralisation, 13, 83
processing capacity, 76, 83
processing demands, 52, 78, 82
processing, parallel and serial, 9, 13, 78
proficiency levels, 49, 71–79, 85, 90, 97,
  111–118, 122
pronunciation, 61, 90
prosodic features/measures, 43, 49, 55, 61
pruned data, 54
psycho-social, 20, 23, 33, 39, 41, 42,
  134–135, 138
pure measures, 48–50

rapidity, 6–7, 105
raters, 103–104, 116, 119–123
rating descriptors, 104, 106–113, 116, 120
rating scales, 103–105, 116, 120
reasoning demands, 71–72
repair fluency, 47–48, 52–55, 60, 75, 87,
  112, 115, 123
  false starts, 53, 55
  hesitation, 56, 108–111
  reformulations, 53, 55
  repetition, 48, 53, 108, 117
  replacement, 53
  self-correction, 47, 55
rhythm, 61, 99, 107–108

Segalowitz's triadic model, 3, 8–9, 91 (see
  also multicomponent)
self-correction (see monitoring)
self-monitoring (see monitoring)
sequential structure, 68
silence (see pauses; breakdown fluency)
Skehan's triadic framework, 47
skill development, 4, 22, 24, 25
social dimension, 3
social factors, 20, 23, 33, 76, 81, 128, 135
sociolinguistic features/norms/challenges, 43
speaker expectations, 127, 145
speaker stance, 37
speech pathology, 44–45, 60
speech performance, 3
speech production models, 9–14
speech rate, 43–44, 47, 55, 60
speed fluency, 47–50, 53–56, 111, 114–116
strategy training, 97
stress, 91
study abroad, 20, 32, 40, 124, 132–133,
  135, 137, 139, 151, 155–156
subjective judgement (see measuring
  fluency)
syllables, 45, 55–56
syntactic complexity, 4, 8, 14, 15, 20, 31,
  34, 35, 71, 72, 79, 81, 100, 118
syntactic planning, 47

task
  design, 64–73
  performance, 57–58, 65
  repetition, 93, 96–97
  structure, 67–69
  type, 65, 114, 120
teachers' cognition and practise, 98–102
temporal features, 43
Test of English for Educational Purposes
  (TEEP), 49, 114
textbooks, 92–94
time-buying, 56, 58
TOEFL, 107
trade-off effects, 15
T-Unit, 47–48
turn-taking, 43, 57, 59–60, 76, 81, 116

utterance fluency, 9, 13–14, 43, 89, 121
  measures of, 43, 100, 121

willingness to communicate, 23, 33, 35–37,
  41, 60, 124, 127, 152
working memory, 23–26, 33–36, 41, 95,
  135–136, 161

CPSIA information can be obtained
at www.ICGtesting.com
Printed in the USA
LVHW021600270721
693842LV00004B/322